TUNNEL RATS VS THE TALIBAN

JIMMY THOMSON & SANDY MACGREGOR

TUNNEL RATS
VS
THE TALIBAN

How Aussie sappers led the way in the war on terror

ALLEN&UNWIN

SYDNEY · MELBOURNE · AUCKLAND · LONDON

The opinions of current and former members of the Australian Defence Force expressed in this book are their own and do not represent the opinions of the Australian Defence Force.

Allen & Unwin
83 Alexander Street
Crows Nest NSW 2065
Australia
Phone: (61 2) 8425 0100
Email: info@allenandunwin.com
Web: www.allenandunwin.com

Cataloguing-in-Publication details are available
from the National Library of Australia
www.trove.nla.gov.au

ISBN 978 1 76011 354 4

Maps by Map Graphics
Set in 12/17 pt Minion by Midland Typesetters, Australia
Printed and bound in Australia by Griffin Press

10 9 8 7 6 5 4 3 2 1

CONTENTS

To army engineers past, present and future
who put themselves in harm's way
so their comrades don't have to

Follow the sapper

AFGHANISTAN

Uzbekistan Tajikistan

China

Turkmenistan

Iran

• Mazar-i-Sharif

Bagram •
Kabul ✳

Jalalabad
• Peshawar

7

3

6

Pakistan

5

Kandahar •

1
2
4

1 Nimruz
2 Helmand
3 Uruzgan
4 Kandahar
5 Zabul
6 Paktika
7 Ghazni

India

Kilometres
0   100   200   300

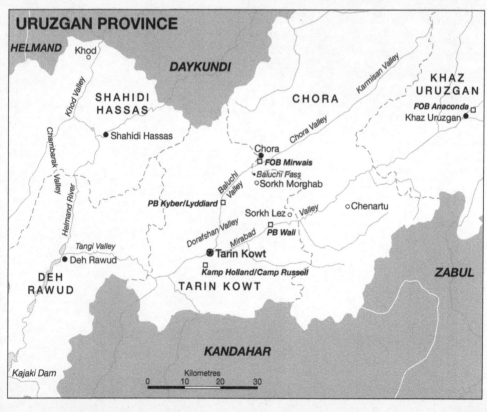

URUZGAN PROVINCE

HELMAND   Khod ○

DAYKUNDI

Khod Valley

SHAHIDI
HASSAS

CHORA

Karmisan Valley

KHAZ
URUZGAN

FOB Anaconda ☐
Khaz Uruzgan ●

Chambarak Valley

Helmand River

• Shahidi Hassas

Chora Valley

Chora ●
☐ FOB Mirwais

Baluchi Valley

• Baluchi Pass
○ Sorkh Morghab

PB Kyber/Lyddiard ☐

Sorkh Lez ○   Valley

○ Chenartu

Dorafshan Valley

Mirabad   PB Wali ☐

Tangi Valley

• Deh Rawud

✳ Tarin Kowt

DEH
RAWUD

Kamp Holland/Camp Russell

TARIN KOWT

ZABUL

KANDAHAR

Kajaki Dam

Kilometres
0   10   20   30

ABBREVIATIONS AND ACRONYMS

2IC	second in command
ANA	Afghan National Army
ANP	Afghan National Police
APC	Armoured Personnel Carrier
ASLAV	Australian Standard Light Armoured Vehicle
BIP	blow in place
CER	Combat Engineer Regiment
CFA	combat first aider
CO	commanding officer
CSM	company sergeant major
ECM	electronic countermeasures
EDD	explosives detection dog
EOD	explosive ordnance disposal
EOR	explosive ordnance reconnaissance
FOB	Forward Operating Base
IED	improvised explosive device
IRR	Incident Response Regiment
ISAF	International Security Assistance Force
JTAC	joint tactical air controller

MIA	Missing in Action
MRE	mission rehearsal exercise
MRTF	Mentoring and Reconstruction Task Force
MST	mobility survivability team
MTF	Mentoring Task Force
NATO	North Atlantic Treaty Organization
NCO	non-commissioned officer (such as a lance corporal, corporal, sergeant etc.)
OMLT	operational mentor and liaison team
OP	Observation Post
PB	Patrol Base
PMV	Protected Mobility Vehicle (Bushmaster or troop carrier)
PTSD	Post-traumatic Stress Disorder
PUC	person under capture
ROCL	Relief Out of Country Leave
RPG	rocket-propelled grenade
RSM	regimental sergeant major (the most senior NCO)
RTF	Reconstruction Task Force
SASR	Special Air Service Regiment
SOP	standard operating procedure
SOTG	Special Operations Task Group
WO	Warrant Officer

FOREWORD

Every military unit is proud of its achievements, reputation and history. That pride is an important part of the spirit that binds the unit together. It also makes it possible for commanders to call on our men and women in uniform to endure hardship, face danger and risk all.

Australian Army engineers, 'sappers' as they are known, are no exception. I have had the privilege of working with sappers on many occasions throughout my career, in peace and war. I never ceased to be impressed by their skills and amazing ability to get things done. I have also been humbled by the sappers' raw courage in protecting their mates and innocent civilians. Every sapper is rightly proud of their unique contribution to the Army team. I am honoured to contribute to a book recognising them, particularly their efforts in Afghanistan.

Our sappers have a rich history of service, stretching back to Gallipoli in 1915, when men of 1st Field Company, Royal Australian Engineers, were among the first ashore during the initial landings. In subsequent campaigns through the First and Second World Wars, sappers built on their reputation for resourcefulness and determination. During the Vietnam War, engineers added another page to their impressive history through the exploits of the 'Tunnel Rats' (first commanded by Sandy MacGregor, co-author of this book). Those sappers crawled through labyrinths of booby-trapped Vietcong tunnels, often armed with nothing more than a pistol, a torch and remarkable courage.

Most recently, in Afghanistan, the role of the sappers evolved further. They played a vital role by building schools, hospitals, bridges, roads and even mosques, to assist the deeply disadvantaged local Afghan population. Their work created a legacy that every Australian can be proud of. In the bitter and complex fight with the Taliban, sappers were at the forefront of the battle against the deadly improvised explosive devices that claimed the lives and limbs of many Australian soldiers. It was the sappers who took the lead, literally and figuratively, in the struggle to find and make safe those deadly devices.

In 2010, at one of our bases in Southern Afghanistan, I introduced the then governor general, Quentin Bryce, to a group of dusty sappers and a couple of bright-eyed explosive detection dogs. I told the governor general, 'Ma'am, we hear the term "hero" used too casually these days, to describe footballers, rock stars or TV personalities. These men are Australian Army sappers. These guys are the real deal. These are true heroes.'

Finally, I note this book has a chapter called 'Wounded Warriors', which relates the mental and emotional damage endured by some sappers, as well as the physical wounds others suffered. My own book, *Exit Wounds*, relates my struggle with psychological trauma. This is an all-too-familiar story for Australian service men and women. I hope this book shines a little more light into the dark recesses of the minds of those still fighting inner demons, long after the last shots of their war have fallen silent.

John Cantwell AO, DSC
Major General (Ret'd)
Australian National Commander
Afghanistan and the Middle East, 2010–2011

PROLOGUE
THE TUNNEL RAT LEGACY

There's a strange kind of silence. The wind is whispering gently around the crags and gullies. The bushes, such as they are, seem to crackle rather than rustle in the breeze. You are lying flat on your belly, your arms outstretched in front of you, delicately prising apart the tiny metal clips and wires of a device that was designed to kill or, at the very least, maim you.

There are easier ways to deal with this improvised explosive device (IED), the official name for a booby-trap bomb or homemade landmine. There's BIP, blow in place, or you could just mark it and leave it. Either would be acceptable to the infantrymen clustered behind you, leaning on rocks and crouched in ravines, anything that could provide cover from a 'shoot and scoot' attack from Taliban guerrillas.

They just want to move on, having already sweated it out, literally and figuratively, for a couple of hours waiting for you—an expert in dealing with these deadly devices—to come forward and do your thing. The sappers who found it, first with the help of their dog, then with their portable mine detectors, are muttering that they could have dealt with it just as easily. BIP and it's gone.

But the Brass insist on three things: IEDs have to be disarmed and dismantled so that vital intelligence can be gathered from them, they can't be left where they might be harmful to both army personnel and local civilians, and EOD (explosive ordnance disposal) techs are the only people allowed to deal with them.

And that's why you are carefully pulling this thing apart, ever conscious of the possibility that it may be fitted with an anti-tamper device intended to mete out the ultimate punishment to those who would dare to even try to render it safe.

The IED is a repository of vital information. From fingerprints on sticky tape to the materials used to put it together, through to the techniques employed in doing so, the DNA of this device will be traceable back to a bomb factory or even an individual bomb maker. Learning its secrets could save dozens, if not hundreds, of lives.

Crouching behind you, your offsider is carrying the electronic countermeasures (ECM) 'man pack'—a device that blocks mobile phone signals just in case a Taliban fighter, or even just a local kid in their pay, is about to press a button on their phone and blow you both to kingdom come.

In this war of acronyms rather than words, the man with the ECM is close enough to the EOD tech to be effective, but far enough away to survive a blast from an IED ... FYI.

The bomb itself is more than likely a used palm-oil container, filled with diesel-infused fertiliser that, even in its smallest form, will produce a strong enough blast to kill a man or disable a vehicle. And, like earlier Australian foes the Vietcong, the Taliban are not above placing a second charge nearby to take out unwary disposal techs focused on the more obvious problem.

This is war on the cheap for the enemy. It costs somewhere north of 50,000 dollars to equip a sapper for combat engineer duties, and ten times as much to train them. It costs about 50 dollars for the Taliban to plant a roadside bomb, which is more likely to be effective than a firefight and has a much lower risk to their fighters.

This is what the sappers faced in Afghanistan. This is also the legacy of the Tunnel Rats: to go above and beyond, to rewrite the standard operating procedure manual and discover, often the hard way, that regardless of technical, financial and firepower superiority, you can't always fight a war on your own terms.

Just as the original Australian Tunnel Rats realised, when they were the first Allied troops to enter the tunnels of Cu Chi in Vietnam, necessity is the mother of fiendish invention for an outgunned indigenous guerrilla force. Booby traps, tunnels, your own landmines recycled for use against you—it's hard to know where to start in combating a resourceful, industrious and ingenious enemy.

However, you can prevail. You don't have to be stronger, just smarter. This kind of war is a battle of wits. They've got ingenuity, you have sappernuity. In Vietnam, the Tunnel Rats threw out the centuries-old rule book for engineers and created an entirely new way of operating to combat the Vietcong. Unwieldy troops and platoons were broken down into splinter groups and mini-teams, more flexible and better equipped to deal with the myriad, ever-changing challenges with which they were confronted every day.

And it almost worked. There are military historians today who will argue that the Allies didn't lose the Vietnam War, they just stopped fighting. What's the difference, you may well ask, but had they won, perhaps in the interim the old ways would not have been so readily re-embraced by the army. However, the fact remains that before Australian troops entered Afghanistan, sappers were an adjunct and an afterthought once more.

But by the time the Aussies pulled out, like their Tunnel Rat antecedents against the Vietcong, they were literally front and centre in the war against the Taliban.

INTRODUCTION
SAPPERS IN AFGHANISTAN

There is a much-quoted (and misquoted) line by nineteenth-century writer and philosopher George Santayana that those who cannot remember the past are condemned to repeat it. That lesson seemed to have been lost on American, European and Australian leaders when they entered Afghanistan at the beginning of so-called Operation Enduring Freedom in 2001.

That's not to say that there was no moral, political or military justification for the invasion. The Taliban-ruled country was a safe harbour for terrorists, including al-Qaeda leader Osama bin Laden, who masterminded the 9/11 attacks on New York City. Its brutal version of already harsh sharia law was cruel and inhuman, and women in particular were treated appallingly. From Alexander the Great in ancient times, through the British in the nineteenth century, to the Russians 100 years later, invading armies had come and gone, usually having learned an expensive lesson. So, by the late twentieth century, albeit with periods of peace and progress, Afghanistan had long been a fractured country, torn between tribal loyalties and religious differences.

So it's surprising to note that, as early as the 1920s, Afghanistan was on a road to a modern and liberal society, with King Amanullah

1

Khan initiating reforms such as the abolition of the traditional Muslim veil for women and the creation of co-educational schools. But after he was forced to abdicate in 1929 there followed decades of switching allegiances, coups—bloodless and otherwise—executions and assassinations, as well as occasional bold attempts to modernise Afghan society. Following the assassination of prominent left-wing leader Mir Akbar Khyber in 1978, there was a military coup instigated by members of Khyber's Soviet-leaning People's Democratic Party of Afghanistan (PDPA). Coup leader Nur Mohammad Taraki of the PDPA declared himself president, prime minister and general secretary of the party, but in September 1979 he was overthrown and killed by Hafizullah Amin.

The PDPA government was both progressive and repressive, promoting women's rights while brutally disposing of its perceived enemies in their tens of thousands. In a push against religion, specifically Islam, men were forced to cut their beards, women could not wear the chador, mosques were closed, forced marriages were banned and women were allowed to vote. But the PDPA was far from united and some rural areas erupted in open revolt. Meanwhile about 1.5 billion dollars of Soviet aid had poured into the country and the PDPA leadership had signed an agreement with the Soviet Union for military support should it ever be required. With the country in turmoil, and Moscow increasingly worried about growing American influence, on Christmas Eve 1979 the Soviet Union's Red Army invaded Afghanistan, Amin was killed and replaced by his PDPA rival and former coup partner Babrak Karmal.

The ensuing ten-year war against the Mujaheddin—with two factions, one financed and armed by the United States, United Kingdom and Saudi Arabia, and another supported by China and Iran—became known as Russia's Vietnam. The vacuum created when the USSR pulled out in 1989 eventually led to the Taliban's rise to power in 1996.

It's probably far too soon to judge effectively whether the NATO-led invasion of Afghanistan was worth the cost in the lives of the thousands of Australian, American, British, Canadian and European soldiers and contractors who died, not to mention the Afghan civilians who perished in even greater numbers.

But when we refer to the failure to learn from history, we don't need to look at geo-politics that go back more than two millennia. Much closer to the present and, literally, to the ground, is the example of our own sappers who learned valuable lessons in Vietnam, 50 years ago, only for many of them to be largely forgotten in the ensuing 'fog of peace'. The sapper, if you are unfamiliar with the term, is a military engineer, although that term encompasses everything from soldiers who operate heavy plant and machinery to those who function as part of special forces troops, helping them to discover, avoid and, if they can't do that, deal with IEDs. In Vietnam, sappers were initially there to build infrastructure for the incoming troops but soon became responsible for dealing with booby traps, landmines, tunnels, bunkers and caves. Once the parallels between our troops' experiences in Indochina and Afghanistan became clearer, the true value of the sapper as the key to a foot patrol's survival—and not just a back-up in cases of extreme inconvenience—was appreciated and exploited. In both Vietnam and Afghanistan, we were fighting on one side of what was effectively a civil war, against a foe more likely to use booby traps—or IEDs, as they became known—than engage in a conventional firefight. Furthermore, in both wars the enemy could simply merge with the local population at will and hide arms and explosives caches in houses and villages. And even the troops that were supposed to be on our side could turn out to be treacherous, with deadly results.

There were differences too, of course. The barren, parched rocks, compacted earth and jagged mountains around the main Australian base in Tarin Kowt could scarcely have been more different from the humid rainforests and rubber plantations of southern Vietnam.

But there is one more chilling fact that links the two conflicts half a century and a world apart: in both Vietnam and Afghanistan, sappers suffered a disproportionate number of casualties. That's partly because, in both theatres, once the infantry commanders realised how vital sappers were to the men on the ground, combat engineers advanced from a supporting role at the rear to the very front. Sappers have a few pithy and highly appropriate mottoes: '*Ubique*' ('Everywhere') is on their badge and '*Facimus et frangimus*' ('We make and we break') is around just as much. But the one to come out of Afghanistan says it all in simple English: 'Follow the sapper'.

That lesson had been lost between the wars as Australian sappers found themselves sidelined by their infantry commanders who, on training exercises, would routinely tell the engineers to step aside and let them do all the running around and shooting. They'd call them forward when they were needed. But in the reality of war in one of the most belligerent countries on the planet, it soon became evident that the sappers were needed right at the front.

History had been repeated because the lessons had been forgotten. Long before those planes smashed into the World Trade Center, before bin Laden became a household name in the West, Australian Army engineers had been operating in Afghanistan. As ever, given a chance, sappers had been leading the way, in this instance dealing with the deadly remnants of another war from another time.

1

OPERATION SALAAM

Before the Soviet Union quit Afghanistan in 1989, they—like Australian and American troops who followed fifteen years later—tried to train the Afghan army to fight its own battles against rebels and insurgents. They failed. In fact, the only enduring legacy they left behind—apart from radicalised Muslim minorities and battle-hardened Mujaheddin fighters—was between ten and fifteen million landmines.

The Mujaheddin had been waging a guerrilla war of hit and run, so the Russians became highly dependent on secured minefields. Mines were laid not as booby traps, but as a deterrent to prevent enemy troops getting too close to their bases. These were mainly anti-personnel mines and the minefields were clearly marked. Unlike Vietnam's Barrier Minefield, the Russians guarded their minefields fairly effectively so there was little recycling of their mines for use against the people who had planted them.

Later, as the Mujaheddin got their own armoured transports, both sides began to lay anti-tank mines that *were* intended for use against the unwary. Add to that unexploded bombs, rockets and shells, and post-Russian Afghanistan in the 1990s was a sea of deadly devices that had killed an estimated 25,000 Afghans during the war, and threatened to continue to kill civilians in their tens of thousands if they weren't dealt with. At one point, the Red Cross estimated it would take more than 4000 years to clear all the landmines left in Afghanistan.

In response to this humanitarian crisis, in 1989 the United Nations sent a peacekeeping force to neighbouring Pakistan, which is how the first Australian troops to operate in Afghanistan came to be sappers. The United Nations Mine Clearance Training Team (UNMCTT) arrived just across the border in Peshawar, Pakistan, five months after the last Soviet forces rolled out of Afghanistan.

For the next four and a half years, the UNMCTT conducted Operation Salaam, initially to train Afghan refugees in mine clearance and bomb disposal. Then in 1991, they crossed the border to help plan and supervise mine clearance in Afghanistan itself. In all, almost one hundred Australian sappers took part in the exercise, in groups of between four and nine at a time, alongside soldiers from eight other United Nations countries.

However, just one year later, only Australian and New Zealand troops were left on the ground. Then a young captain, Major Mark Willetts, was posted to Operation Salaam as a detachment commander in 1992.

'I was operations officer for the seventh rotation of sappers there,' Mark recalls. 'The fifth had been based mainly in Pakistan but the sixth had managed to get all their members across the border into Afghanistan at least once. By the time we arrived, it was routine business to go across the border.'

There were about five million Afghan refugees in Pakistan at that time, and even more in Iran. But their refugee camps were like nothing Mark Willetts had ever seen before.

'When we first arrived in Peshawar, we were being driven out to the house and the guys were saying, "Oh, this is all refugee camp here." But I was looking out of the window at classic central Asian mud-brick construction. Just a sea of it, housing tens of thousands of people. The Afghans, and particularly the Pashtuns, wear poverty very well and they don't like living in tents. So they would start with tents but very quickly bang up walls around them, then put the roof over the top and the tent's gone.

'It was a refugee camp but they turned it into a suburb. It looked just like another suburb; another domicile suburb of Peshawar complete with its own bazaar where you could buy anything.'

Among the things the Aussie sappers bought at the Peshawar bazaar were the same clothes that the locals wore, all the better to blend in and make their hosts realise they were all on the same side. The engineers were also able to ignore the rule that soldiers must shave every day when they have access to hot water—a small fact that would have significance later when the war in Afghanistan was in full swing. 'The exciting thing was that we were allowed to wear coveralls and grow beards before we left,' says Mark. 'We got pulled up all the time by RSMs [regimental sergeant majors] and sergeants when we were in barracks. The purpose of wearing beards was so that we could integrate as much as possible with the population we were working with. We wore a Pakistani army safari suit when we were on the Pakistan side and then traditional Afghan clothes—the long baggy shirt and pants—on the other side. Partly it was to blend in better but also because the Australian Army camouflage gear was very similar to Russian camo gear and the locals were quite willing to take pot shots from a distance before they asked any questions.

'We lived in houses in a nice suburb in Peshawar in a walled compound with locals. The previous contingents, because the 1991 Gulf War had just started, weren't allowed out. They had to stay in for their protection. The sixth contingent started going out again and we just continued that.

'We could go out at night. The United States government had a consular office and an employees' club run by Australians so that was where we could go for a drink. We'd go running through the suburbs and, if I got the time, my Pakistani driver would take me to the old city in Peshawar. It was the classic *Arabian Nights* bazaar type of thing, like [the film] *The Thief of Bagdad*. I would wander through that at night and talk with the locals and have cups of tea and play cricket with the kids.'

The original United Nations mission had been to train some of the Afghan refugees in general mine awareness and to show them how to clear areas of mines and unexploded ordnance and bombs. The previous rotation had changed from training individuals to teaching trainers so that the process could be sustained after the United Nations had pulled out.

Mark's unit took that a stage further and crossed the border to make sure the trainers in Afghanistan were working effectively, that they were being managed properly and to investigate any incidents where mines or bombs had gone off. They checked the working, living and sleeping conditions of the mine clearers, right down to food and hygiene. They also checked that United Nations funds were being properly allocated and spent and observed the mine clearers working to make sure they were doing everything by the book.

'We discovered early on that they would put on a bit of a show when we turned up. At training, everybody would be lined up in neat rows, lines would be painted in the dirt and they would look very impressive. Out in the minefield they would do everything exactly as they'd been told.

'But when they thought they weren't being watched they would take short cuts, so we started hiding on hillsides with binoculars and loudhailers. We had a translator with us, we'd hand him the bullhorn and he would yell abuse across the *dasht* and then all these heads would pop up.

'The Afghans didn't like getting their hands or their clothes dirty, so they would kneel down over the mines, rather than lying flat on the ground. Think about it. When they're kneeling they're more likely to have their head right over a device. If it goes off, it takes their head. But if they're lying down, particularly working at full arm's length, they won't even scratch a fingernail if the blast goes off. They'll get a ringing in their ears but no other injuries so the injuries we got were from inappropriate technique or occasionally just fatigue mishaps.

'It's a very boring tedious job. Nine hundred and ninety-five times out of a thousand the signal on the metal detector will be from a piece of shrapnel or ammunition cartridge. It won't be a mine. This was the first humanitarian de-mining operation the United Nations had run so we learned a lot.

'I recall one investigation where the fellow had prodded, found a device, put the marker in place but as he stood up he stepped forward straight onto the mine. He had one-rupee notes in his pockets and it was a blast mine. It turned his pockets inside out so there was a lovely big ring of one-rupee notes in a circle around the place where he died. Unfortunately, he bled out.'

But while carelessness came at a high cost, what Mark Willetts saw in a town called Khost, and as other sappers would observe when the reconstruction phase of the Afghanistan war was under way, was that peace and security were soon followed by prosperity. 'I have very fond memories of Khost. When we first went in there, there was nothing. The main street and the side streets were empty. But you could tell that Khost had been a lovely provincial town—you could tell that from the castle on the hill—but there was nobody living there. We stayed in an old bombed-out schoolhouse out on the edge of town.

'But as soon as we could clear arable land—and I don't know how they knew—we had refugees coming back across the border and ploughing the land as quickly as we could clear it. We had some friction when they didn't seem to understand that they had to stay a certain distance away from where we were working for safety reasons.'

When Mark and his team came back to Khost a couple of weeks later, there were old Russian army shipping containers, three metre by three metre dark green crates, set up in the main street and operating as shops. When the team came back a couple of months after that, the bazaar was back in action, with dozens of stalls now trading. 'This was a direct consequence of us clearing the land so that people could get back onto it and farm it. And it was almost immediate. As soon as they thought it was safe, they were back farming the land.'

The landmines and unexploded missiles and shells that Mark and his team discovered came from a wide variety of sources. 'Initially we found only Soviet ordnance that was used by the Russians and their puppet government in Kabul against the Mujaheddin. But later on we found all sorts of ordnance, particularly Chinese, Czechoslovakian and Italian, that had been bought on the open market by the Mujaheddin to be used against the Russian and the Afghan army.'

Among these discoveries was that the Russians were not above targeting civilians—even children—with their deadly devices: 'The thing that affected me most were the kids. The Russians have a particular mine commonly called the butterfly mine. It's quite small and is a nice bright limey green. It's quite attractive to kids but it's a mine with a small fuse that requires a liquid to be moved from a flexible container like a little balloon or a sac through a very small hole before it will activate.

'What would happen is that the kids would find these things that had been dropped from the air and they would be in a little group looking at it. You can hold it and play with it for quite a long time if you are not applying pressure to the sac. So kids would pick them up and play with them—and then bang!

'I used to visit the hospitals in Kabul and you'd get half a dozen kids brought into the hospital all with blast injuries to their faces and then the one little boy or girl would have their fingers missing. They were the ones that were holding it when it went off.'

Mark had already discovered on his initial mission that locals were content to put their lives on the line if it meant they could scrape a little more out of their subsistence living. 'Back in 1991 we would see kids along the Afghanistan–Pakistan border sitting there pulling apart ordnance. There were just huge piles of scrap. People had collected it, sold it to merchants from Pakistan and it would go somewhere to be recycled. But we are talking unexploded 2000-pound bombs with fuses in. All sorts of shit. But their attitude was, "If it went off, it went off". That's *inshallah*, "God willing". But they'd get it on the truck and they'd get it across to a merchant and sell it.

'Anything that could have value was stolen. We couldn't mark minefields with anything other than painted rocks. Because, if you used wood, that was cooking fuel so that was nicked. Wire, or metal stakes, that's metal that's sold for scrap. So a little clumsy mine— which is just a wooden stake [with] a pineapple-like grenade on top and then a hole where the fuse went in and the trip wires would run out from it—was a goldmine. I've got one in my office. The wooden stake was used as firewood. The metal in the fragmentation case was sold as scrap. The fuse, if you could get it out, was sold to the Mujaheddin. It was kids who were sent into the minefields to go and scavenge all this stuff and anything that could be sold as scrap would be.'

One of the major differences between this mission and those that would follow, was that the Australian sappers were welcomed into the country.

'We were most definitely the good guys,' recalls Mark. 'Part of the problem we had was that they were treating us too well. They treated us like royalty everywhere we went. But we had to refuse their gifts. They were very poor but part of their culture would be to try and get us things even when they and their families couldn't afford it. We should have been giving stuff to them.'

Fortunately, the Australians were recognised for doing good work for the community at the very highest levels, including by the local Mujaheddin warlord, Gulbuddin Hekmatyar, despite his well-known, virulently anti-West views.

'Hekmatyar was a very, very brutal man. You crossed him, you died very slowly and very painfully,' recalls Mark. 'Fortunately for us we had been identified as being on a jihad because we were going into the minefields for the Afghans. That was seen as a great thing.

'Operation Salaam originally had thirteen nations involved but after the Iraq war in 1991, only Australia and New Zealand remained. Because we had stayed after the other eleven nations left, and then we started going in the minefields and working with the Afghans, that was a really big tick in the good box and the word was put out that the Australian and New Zealand de-miners were under Gulbuddin's protection.

'So the message was, fuck with the Aussies and the Kiwis, and you were fucking with him and he was sending his boys around to collect you so he could have a very brutal play with you and your family. If a petty criminal or somebody wanted to mess with us then they didn't have to fear the police, they had to fear Hekmatyar. We were very well looked after, even during the 1991 Gulf War.'

Each rotation, or tour of duty, in the mine clearance training mission was six months, but at the end of his, Mark was seconded from the Australian contingent and sent to finish setting up a regional de-mining office in Kabul. 'Previously the United Nations had been excluded from government-controlled areas but we were able to set up now. I became the acting regional manager until the Northern Alliance invaded Kabul later in 1992.'

The invasion of Kabul by the Northern Alliance—a loose coalition of Mujaheddin tribal forces that had previously formed the resistance to the Russians and their puppet government—marked the beginning of the Afghan civil war and a sequence of events that would lead to the al-Qaeda attacks on New York and, ultimately, the Allies' invasion of Afghanistan.

In the ever-shifting political and military landscape of Afghanistan, former foes would become allies and former friends would turn their guns on the very people who armed them. The push to replace a corrupt government installed by the USSR was hijacked by extreme forces, some of whom, though not all, wanted Afghanistan to be an Islamic state.

The extremists would prevail for a while and before they were ousted, the world would be set on a path to war into which Australian forces would inexorably be drawn.

2

THE RISE OF THE TALIBAN

To understand what happened next in Afghanistan, you have to go back to the Russian invasion. As the country swung from tentative attempts at social reform to often brutal repression, there was a clear divide between the city dwellers who tended to be progressive and the country people who were anything but. However, there was a balance of sorts, even if political leaders were despatching each other with the gusto of a *Game of Thrones* episode. But when Russia invaded in 1979 they not only crushed Afghanistan's traditions, they created a common enemy against whom the Afghanis could do something that simply wasn't in their nature—unite.

'Within weeks, independently and separately, seven separate Mujaheddin groups organised themselves and started fighting locally,' explains Mark Willetts, who has had three tours of duty in Afghanistan and is a keen student of its politics and social change. 'They were loosely affiliated and occasionally at war with each other, but all with a common enemy: the Russian puppet central government and the Soviet troops.

'The Russians replaced the normal social structures that kept the country alive and thriving and just destroyed everything else that existed. Then in 1989 they pissed off and left a vacuum. Their puppet government was not strong enough to maintain what was left.

'After the Soviets withdrew, from 1989 to 1992 the central government tried to hang on against the growing strength of the Mujaheddin. As well as their own army, they had a number of militia forces led by pro-government warlords. There was an entire mechanised brigade that belonged to one militia commander up north, so there were some big forces at play in Afghanistan.'

However, Afghanistan had never had a central government that was fully in control of the country. Loyalties were determined more by family and tribe and, with Mujaheddin forces fighting each other as often as they fought the government, it wasn't unusual for allegiances to be transferred mid-battle. 'You've got several racial cultures there, including the Hazara, the Pashtun and so on, but the main structure in Afghan society is based on blood and family. Family, tribe and race, or whatever the hierarchy is, all originates with the honour and the prestige of the larger family group and then its implementation at the local level. If it causes frictions with other families then things can erupt. But that's the way their society is structured and it works for them when people don't fuck around with it.

'Gulbuddin Hekmatyar was the main Mujaheddin leader who controlled Peshawar and the Pashtun areas of Afghanistan to the south-east. We never saw any evidence of the Taliban in 1991 and 1992 but I understand there was training being done in the religious schools in Pakistan. I haven't really gone into the whys and wherefores but they were just another player in this great game being played in Afghanistan.

'Pakistani military intelligence had their finger in the pie as well and I certainly heard stories about them supporting one Mujaheddin faction right up to the point of engagement in combat with another Mujaheddin faction and then pulling all the support out.'

In 1992, Burhanuddin Rabbani officially became president of the Islamic State of Afghanistan, but had to battle other warlords for control of Kabul. These battles for control of the capital left the former 'Paris of the South' in the ruins we know today.

In the midst of this anti-communist, pro-Islamic, anti-Western, tribal, warlord-led soup, there was Ahmad Shah Massoud, an engineering student turned Afghan military leader, and a leading light in the fight against the Russians and the government they left behind. He sided with Rabbani and became his minister of defence. 'Massoud didn't control a large area. He had the Panjshir Valley, which was just north of where I was deployed last time in Bagram,' explains Mark. 'He was known as The Lion of Panjshir, and had direct and immediate access to the Salang Tunnel, which was the choke point on the Russian supply line coming directly into Kabul. So he was in a very significant location and was wise enough not to get involved in general engagements.'

In late 1994, Massoud defeated Hekmatyar in Kabul, ending the continuous bombardment of the capital. Devoutly Muslim, Massoud also had progressive views and, in the Panjshir Valley women and girls did not have to wear the burqa and were allowed to work and go to school.

'Instead of just being a fighting force he provided public education and health. He provided everything a society needed rather than operating just as a fighting force and he only engaged the Russians or the Afghan government as and when necessary,' says Mark.

But Massoud was straddling two cultures—the democratic structures of the West and the traditional patterns of Afghan society. On the one hand, he set up committees to help govern his area, but might also intervene autocratically on behalf of individuals who had pleaded their case to him. He tried to nudge his countrymen towards a national political consensus and free elections but individually they had too much to lose. On the principle that you can't get turkeys to vote for Christmas, influential warlords Mohammad Ismail Khan and Abdul Rashid Dostum clung grimly to their power and influence.

In 1994, Mullah Mohammed Omar Mujahid, better known just as Mullah Omar, a Pashtun Mujaheddin, returned to Kandahar from Pakistan, where he had run Islamic schools, or *madrassas*, and founded the Taliban with his religious students. Omar recognised something that previous Afghan leaders had missed: religion could unite the country in a way that political doctrine never could. He believed strict imposition of Islamic law would see the end of the warlords. By the end of 1994, the Taliban had captured all of Kandahar province. They marched on Kabul the following year.

When the Taliban suffered a series of costly defeats, neighbouring Pakistan offered them support. The Taliban started shelling Kabul in early 1995, and although they were initially driven back by Massoud, on 27 September 1996, assisted by Pakistan and Saudi Arabia, the Taliban took Kabul and founded the Islamic Emirate of Afghanistan.

There immediately followed a campaign of brutal oppression, especially of women who were forbidden from working outside their homes, attending school, or leaving their homes without a male relative. Confronted by this massively regressive step, once bitter enemies Massoud and Dostum joined forces to create the Northern Alliance, a united front against the Taliban, comprising Tajiks, Uzbeks, Hazara and Pashtun forces, all with the blessing of the exiled Afghan King Zahir Shah. In a geo-political shift reminiscent of George Orwell's novel *1984*, former enemies were now collaborating. Russia, Iran, Tajikistan and India backed the Northern Alliance while Saudi Arabia and Pakistan supported the Taliban.

The ensuing conflict was brutal, with multiple atrocities on both sides. United Nations observers estimated that there were fifteen massacres between 1996 and 2001. For instance, in retaliation for the execution of 3000 Taliban prisoners in 1997, the Taliban killed about 4000 civilians in Mazar-i-Sharif in 1998, driving Dostum into exile in the process.

By 2001, the Taliban controlled most of Afghanistan, assisted by about 30,000 Pakistani troops and, significantly, 2000 al-Qaeda militants. Osama bin Laden had founded al-Qaeda in the late 1980s to support the Mujaheddin against the Soviets, but became disillusioned by the constant infighting among the warlords. However he returned to Afghanistan from Sudan in 1996, teamed up with Mullah Omar and moved al-Qaeda's operations to eastern Afghanistan. There, al-Qaeda was able to train fighters, import weapons and plan terrorist attacks.

Long before the horrors of 9/11, America had identified bin Laden and al-Qaeda as a major league terrorist and a potential target. The bombings in 1998 of United States embassies in Nairobi and Dar es Salaam led to President Bill Clinton ordering missile strikes on suspected al-Qaeda training camps in Afghanistan. America demanded that the Taliban surrender bin Laden and, when they refused, sanctions were imposed on Afghanistan, to no avail.

Meanwhile CIA special operations teams were operating under cover in Afghanistan, awaiting orders to kill or capture bin Laden. Those orders never came but the connections they made with anti-Taliban forces would prove invaluable in the 2001 invasion.

In early 2001, Massoud addressed the European Parliament in Brussels, asking for humanitarian aid for the people of Afghanistan. He complained that the Taliban and al-Qaeda were giving the West a distorted view of Islam. He also warned that he had information that al-Qaeda was planning a large-scale attack on American soil.

At first, Western powers had pressured Massoud into surrendering to the Taliban, to bring some vestige of peace to the country. However, in August 2001, United States President George W. Bush agreed to start supporting Massoud if the Taliban refused, again, to hand over bin Laden. And if this covert support for anti-Taliban forces failed, the United States would set out to overthrow the Taliban regime through more direct action.

A few weeks later, on 9 September, two days before the attack on the World Trade Center, Massoud was fatally wounded in a suicide bomb attack by two Arabs, probably al-Qaeda agents posing as journalists. His funeral was attended by hundreds of thousands of mourners.

Thus, just 48 hours before the attacks on New York and Washington, the strongest voice of reason and moderation in Afghanistan was silenced. When al-Qaeda planes sliced into the twin towers in New York 'direct action' was inevitable.

3

HUNTING BIN LADEN

In the immediate aftermath of the attacks on New York and Washington, shock was followed by outrage and then accusations, denials, claims, counterclaims and, from the Taliban, obfuscation. In brief, the United States accused Osama bin Laden and demanded that the Taliban hand him over and, while they're at it, that they close all terrorist training camps in Afghanistan. The Taliban leadership demanded proof that bin Laden had been involved before they would do anything of the sort. Bin Laden himself denied the accusation (although he recanted in 2004, admitting that he had planned the whole operation). Afghan President Omar rejected a proposal by Pakistani religious leaders that bin Laden be placed under house arrest in Peshawar and then tried there under sharia law.

Patience was growing thin in the United States. On 18 September, President Bush had signed legislation authorising the use of armed force against the perpetrators of the 9/11 attacks. Then days later, less than three weeks after the attacks, Bush issued a statement, effectively drawing a line in the sand: 'First, there is no negotiations with the Taliban. They heard what I said. And now they can act. And it's not just Mr bin Laden that we expect to see and brought to justice; it's everybody associated with his organisation that's in Afghanistan. And not only those directly associated with Mr bin Laden, any terrorist that is housed and fed in Afghanistan needs to be handed over. And finally, we expect there to be complete destruction of terrorist camps. That's what I told them; that's what I mean. And we expect them—we expect them to not only hear what I say but to do something about it.'

The same day, Mahmud Ahmed, director of Pakistan's Inter-Services Intelligence—or ISI, the country's main intelligence organisation—led a delegation to persuade Omar to accept having religious leaders from Islamic countries examine the evidence and decide bin Laden's fate. Omar refused. Coincidentally, Mahmud had actually been in Washington discussing regional security in general and Osama bin Laden in particular, when the attacks occurred. As a result he became a key figure in negotiations between the Taliban (whom he supported in principle), Pakistan and the United States.

Three days later Omar agreed to a proposal by a Pakistani politician to have bin Laden taken to Pakistan where he would be held under house arrest and tried by an international tribunal under sharia law. But Pakistani president Pervez Musharraf blocked the plan, claiming he couldn't guarantee bin Laden's safety.

Increasingly, demands for evidence and the various plans for tribunals were seen as stalling tactics. The United States felt the Taliban already had a responsibility to hand over bin Laden for his part in the United States' embassy bombings in East Africa. They presented evidence of his part in 9/11 to senior Pakistani politicians and they agreed there was clearly a case to answer.

America's allies were also growing impatient with the Taliban. British Prime Minister Tony Blair called on the Taliban to 'surrender the terrorists or surrender power'. Australian Prime Minister John Howard had, only the day before the attacks, been celebrating a renewed commitment by both America and Australia to the ANZUS military cooperation treaty. Later, Howard would address the Australian Defence Association with a clear statement of support for the United States and condemnation of al-Qaeda and the Taliban.

'September 11 was a defining event,' he said. 'It demonstrated the appalling means that terrorists now have at their disposal to inflict unimaginable casualties with evil precision. The attack was designed not only to shatter our faith in the ability to live our lives in a free and open manner, it was designed to shake the world's economic foundations. It had the twin goals of crippling fear and economic chaos.

'The sheer scale of the carnage inflicted has taken terrorism to a new level unprecedented in the history of mankind. The world, including Australia, must respond.'

On 5 October, the Taliban offered to try bin Laden in an Afghan court, so long as the United States provided what it called 'solid evidence' of his guilt. The United States government dismissed this as delaying tactics and two days later United States warplanes and missiles began bombing Afghan military installations and terrorist training camps, including the airport in Kabul, in Omar's home town of Kandahar, and in Jalalabad. The same day, the US State Department asked the Pakistani government to pass on one last message to the Taliban: they must hand over all al-Qaeda leaders—not just bin Laden—or 'every pillar of the Taliban regime' would be destroyed.

Meanwhile, teams from the CIA's Special Activities Division landed in Afghanistan, followed by United States soldiers from the 5th Special Forces Group and other units from United States Special Operations Command. Relationships created by the CIA in earlier hunts for bin Laden proved fruitful as a coalition of invading forces and existing local opposition was quickly formed.

In October 2001, the first contingent of the Australian Special Forces Task Group left Perth, headed for Afghanistan where they would join troops from the United States, the United Kingdom and

Canada while other allies provided bases and allowed overflight by American and British warplanes, as well as four F/A-18 Hornets from the Royal Australian Air Force.

It is worth pointing out that the Australian contribution on the ground in this initial invasion of Afghanistan was predominantly special forces missions and air strikes, with little or no regular infantry or large-scale sapper involvement. American troops and special forces from its allies, including Australia, combined with Northern Alliance Mujaheddin to fight the Taliban in the north.

Initially the American air assault, backed by cruise missiles fired from warships in the Arabian Sea, focused on training camps and communication and command posts, with air defences very quickly wiped out. But the Northern Alliance wasn't making any headway on the ground so, two weeks into the campaign, they requested air support for their troops on the front lines.

The results were immediate. By the first week in November, Taliban front-line positions in the north were all but destroyed and the capture of Kabul seemed eminently possible. With that in mind, the Northern Alliance launched an attack on Mazar-i-Sharif, Afghanistan's fourth-largest city, the capture of which would cut off Taliban supply lines and open up the airport, a critical strategic asset.

On 9 November 2001, Northern Alliance forces, under the command of Abdul Rashid Dostum and Ustad Atta Mohammed Noor, took the city's main military base and airport. The city itself, held by the Taliban since 1998, fell after only 90 minutes of ferocious fighting. The Taliban retreat confounded Allied planners' speculation that it would take months of slow progress to conquer the enemy.

With more than 1000 troops airlifted into the city to rebuff any attempt to retake it, the Allies had their first locked-down position from which Kabul and Kandahar could be easily reached, and an airport that would allow them to fly more attack and resupply missions, as well as provide humanitarian aid. This allowed shipments of food and medicine to up to six million Afghans facing starvation on the northern plain.

The ease with which Mazar-i-Sharif fell was even more exaggerated in Kabul. When Northern Alliance forces arrived there on the morning of 13 November, they were confronted by a token resistance of no more than twenty Taliban fighters. The main force had fled the night before under cover of darkness, most into the Tora Bora Mountains on the Pakistan border to the east of the capital. There it was believed that the Taliban and al-Qaeda had dug into networks of caves and underground bunkers.

The Taliban grip on Afghanistan was crumbling. Within a day or two of the fall of Kabul, all the provinces along the Iranian border had surrendered and local warlords had taken over throughout north-eastern Afghanistan, including Jalalabad, cutting off the main route to Pakistan from the Tora Bora mountains, 50 kilometres south-west of the city. By 13 November, about 2000 al-Qaeda and Taliban forces, probably including bin Laden, were in Tora Bora. On 16 November the United States began bombing Tora Bora and about the same time, CIA and special forces operatives were enlisting local warlords and planning a ground attack.

Further to the north, another 10,000 or so Taliban fighters, mainly Pakistani volunteers, had fallen back to the city of Kunduz, where, after a nine-day siege, they surrendered to Northern Alliance forces. However, shortly before the surrender on 25 November, Pakistani aircraft arrived to evacuate up to five thousand Pakistani intelligence and military personnel as well as Taliban and al-Qaeda troops.

By the end of November, apart from Tora Bora's caves and tunnels, the heartland around Kandahar in south-eastern Afghanistan was the Taliban's last stronghold, but it was coming under increasing pressure. Nearly 3000 tribal fighters, led by future president Hamid Karzai and

Gul Agha Sherzai, the governor of Kandahar before the Taliban seized power, squeezed Taliban forces from the east and cut off northern supply lines to Kandahar, where Mullah Omar remained, while the Northern Alliance was advancing from the north and east.

After calling on his troops to fight to the death, on 7 December Omar crept out of Kandahar with a group of loyalists and escaped into the Uruzgan mountains. Other Taliban leaders fled to Pakistan through the remote passes of areas to the south-east of Kabul. As Afghan forces under Gul Agha seized Kandahar, and United States marines took control of the airport and established a base there, the border town of Spin Buldak to the south surrendered, effectively ending Taliban control in Afghanistan.

Meanwhile al-Qaeda fighters fought on at Tora Bora, desperately resisting the advance of tribal militia backed by coalition special forces as well as air strikes. Eventually, the al-Qaeda fighters agreed on a truce on the pretext of letting them surrender their weapons but it was merely a trick to allow bin Laden and others to escape into Pakistan.

Fighting erupted on 12 December, again probably to cover bin Laden's escape, but by 17 December, the last cave complex had been taken. Coalition forces continued searching into January, but bin Laden and his commanders had gone.

On 20 December 2001, the United Nations authorised the creation of an International Security Assistance Force (ISAF), tasked with helping the Afghans maintain security in Kabul and surrounding areas. Eighteen countries would contribute to the force in February 2002.

The Taliban were defeated but they were far from destroyed. Al-Qaeda forces regrouped in the Shah-i-Kot Valley area, Paktika province, in early 2002, while Mullah Saifur Rehman began rebuilding his Taliban militia forces to a total of more than 1000 fighters by the beginning of spring. The plan was to copy the tactics used against the Soviet Union more than a decade before, including guerrilla attacks and possibly a major offensive. Mullah Omar, meanwhile, had disappeared and has never been photographed since (although, he has been 'seen' more often and in more bizarre places than Elvis Presley). The general consensus is that he is either dead or severely incapacitated. Either way, he played no obvious part in the Taliban revival.

In any case, the build-up was detected and the Australians were involved in their first concentrated ground offensive, called Operation Anaconda, along with special forces from Canada, Germany, New Zealand, Norway and the United Kingdom, as well as the United States. However, the Americans had seriously underestimated the numbers who would 'shoot and scoot' from the caves and bunkers to be fewer than 200. Instead the guerrillas were between one and five thousand-strong and by 6 March, eight American, seven Afghan Allied, and up to 400 al-Qaeda fighters had been killed. Special forces from Australia would be involved in other similar operations throughout 2002 and 2003.

The Taliban had not gone—they had just gone to ground. They set up bases just across the Pakistan border, from which they operated hit-and-run raids, while others simply melted into the local populations of areas such as the four southern provinces of Kandahar, Zabul, Helmand and Uruzgan.

As time went on, and feeling disappointed that, although they had largely driven the Taliban out of Afghanistan they had failed to capture bin Laden, American, British and Australian politicians were distracted by the impending war in Iraq which would divert their attention and resources fully in March 2003 when the 'coalition of the willing' invaded the country on the pretext of finding and destroying Saddam Hussein's weapons of mass destruction (which turned out never to have existed).

Inevitably, Taliban and al-Qaeda influence grew as the coalition forces melted away like the spring snow on the Afghan mountains.

This should have come as no surprise. In her book *An Unwinnable War*, SBS political correspondent Karen Middleton claims John Howard was 'adamant he didn't want to be embroiled in longer-term fighting, reconstruction or any messy "nation-building". He wanted a surgical operation with a finite duration.'

Howard said: 'I was conscious given the potential for difficulties in our own part of the world, that the right combination was to provide sharp-edged forces for a limited period of time during the hot part but not get bogged down in a long drawn out peacekeeping operation.'

By April 2003, Australia had only one soldier in Afghanistan, assigned to the United Nations Assistance Mission in Afghanistan (UNAMA). Then shadow foreign minister Kevin Rudd referred to the officer as 'John Howard's one-man war on terror'. It would be more than two years before Australian special operations troops were again deployed in Afghanistan to respond to the Taliban's growing resurgence, and even longer before the peace-keeping and nation-building that both Howard and Bush wished to avoid would be in full swing.

But the defeat of the Taliban had created unwanted side effects that could and should have been foreseen. If the Taliban government had one redeeming feature—and it wasn't nearly enough to expunge their many terrible failings—it was that they had suppressed the warlords. Now the former Mujaheddin were back in business, rearmed and re-energised, and often revisiting some of the unresolved feuds from their past.

Corruption was soon at epidemic levels, as you would expect from a country that is one of the world's biggest producers of opium, the basic ingredient of heroin. Today Afghanistan routinely features in the top five in lists of the most corrupt countries in the world. As a CIA report puts it, 'Criminality, insecurity, weak governance, lack of infrastructure, and the Afghan government's difficulty in extending rule of law to all parts of the country pose challenges to future economic growth.'

But the full consequences of the coalition's own version of 'hit and run' were yet to be seen. The Australian military commitment to Afghanistan was somewhere south of token. However, in November 2003, another soldier was deployed there, assigned to the Mine Action Co-ordination Centre.

Naturally, he was a sapper.

4

FOLLOW THE SAPPER

The role of the sapper changed during the course of the Vietnam War. From being expected to always operate as a large group, so as to maximise their effectiveness and efficiency, sappers had to respond to a new kind of threat in the form of guerrilla attacks and booby traps.

As we described in *Tunnel Rats* and *A Sappers' War*, confronted with these challenges, their traditional standard operating procedures, or SOPs, had to be dispensed with and new ways of doing their jobs developed. What evolved in Vietnam were splinter teams of two sappers, assigned to either ride on armour, to spot and deal with anti-tank mines, or mini-teams of two or three sappers who would patrol with infantry to deal with booby traps, tunnels, bunkers and landmines.

Then there were the combat engineer teams who could be dropped in on any situation that was too big or hazardous for the splinter teams or mini-teams to deal with. It was a typical sapper response to changing conditions: assess the problem, find a solution and worry about protocols, paperwork and SOPs when the job is done.

These skills were never lost to sappers—they're ingrained in their DNA—but the vital part sappers can and should play in a modern conflict was forgotten in the 30 years between the end of the Vietnam War and the start of the conflict in Afghanistan.

As Major General John Cantwell observed in the foreword to this book, the men and women of every regiment in every army think that their unit is special. It's a feeling that's encouraged as part of the team building that allows soldiers to face terrible dangers and apparently insurmountable challenges and overcome them.

In the elite forces, like the SASR (Special Air Service Regiment) and the commandos, the level of training required probably justifies their perceived arrogance. With cavalry and artillery, their sense of who they are has as much to do with their history as the qualities required for the job that they do. The average infantryman, meanwhile, takes justifiable pride in being at the pointy end when the shit hits the fan and the bullets start flying.

But what about the sapper?

Traditionally, the sapper hasn't been held in the highest regard by their comrades in arms. Sappers are by definition hands-on people, and that means they are more likely to be dirty, sweaty and scruffy than parading around in neatly pressed uniforms. They also claim they have a sixth sense—sappernuity—the ability and desire to get things done and treat problems as challenges rather than obstacles. Other soldiers think sappers are different; sappers *know* they're different.

And they have, literally and figuratively, moved their way from the back of the battle group to the very front. As they did in Vietnam, sappers in Afghanistan found themselves patrolling in front of the forward scouts, dealing with a new kind of enemy in a new kind of war. Sappers again evolved and in so doing created not just a whole new role for themselves but a whole new regiment.

There were basically three kinds of sappers who went into Afghanistan. The first was fundamentally a construction engineer and that included plant operators, builders, joiners and plumbers—anyone that you might find on a building site anywhere . . . only in armoured vehicles painted in camouflage colours and carrying guns.

Then there were combat engineers, one of whose jobs was often euphemistically called 'mobility assistance', which actually meant finding roadside bombs so that other troops weren't going to get blown up travelling from A to B.

They could also be dog handlers and EOD techs, more highly trained combat engineers whose job it was to either dismantle or destroy the IEDs that the other guys found.

On top of this, any sapper was expected to play exactly the same role as an infantryman at any time.

In May 2002, a new unit called the Incident Response Regiment (IRR), was formed from a variety of units, including the Joint Incident Response Unit and the Chemical, Biological and Radiological Response Squadron, which had been set up variously to deal with chemical and biological threats and Sydney Olympic Games anti-terrorist measures. It also included an Emergency Response Squadron and a detachment of military and civilian personnel forming the Scientific and Technical Support Organisation. And, of course, the IRR included sappers.

When, after an absence of three years, Australian combat troops were reintroduced into Afghanistan in Operation Slipper in 2005, IRR soldiers went in with the SAS and commandos, and continued to do so throughout the war. Even before it was established that infantry really needed to 'follow the sapper' in areas where there might be IEDs, it was apparent that special operations forces, like the SAS and the commandos, needed that level of protection too. And so combat engineers and EOD techs who could match the special ops guys in fitness and endurance were selected for attachment to those units.

The IRR troops had a broad range of skills, including combat engineers, electrical and mechanical engineers, intelligence and signals specialists. But no longer were they expected to wait until an emergency occurred. They were trained to a higher level of physical ability and were deployed with the special ops troops, ostensibly to deal with problems before they arose.

As well as being the first boots on the ground, special ops were also deployed on different rotations from the main force so that even when the main task forces arrived and were operating on roughly a six-to-eight-month cycle, the special operations task groups were operating independently on shorter rotations, partly due to the higher intensity of the work they were doing.

Warrant Officer Reuben Thomas was an EOD sapper with special ops. He wasn't in the first deployment, but his experience was typical. Already having a raft of skills, stepping up to special ops meant acquiring a lot more. For a start, it wasn't just bullets and bombs that might provide a threat: 'I was an EOD and I was in the unit to do some of the more technical searches. There was more equipment that was not available to other army [personnel] and a lot more training in nuclear, biological, and chemical stuff so we had to do "live agent" training in Canada. They had more technical equipment to search with, especially in a decontamination space.

'I stepped up to EOR [explosive ordnance reconnaissance] and then again they had some more tools available there so you do another course at that level to get you up to speed with them. And as EOD, again they have more tools and processes available and you do a course to catch up there.'

On top of learning new skills, special ops sappers had to learn to use different kinds of weapons from standard infantry issue, and had to raise their physical fitness to roughly the same levels as their comrades in the commandos and SAS.

'You weren't expected to do exactly what they did but you couldn't be a burden to them either,' says one sapper. 'You had your job to do but you had to keep up. And if things went pear-shaped, you were expected to use your weapon and help them fight their way out.'

The regular combat engineer's job was generally to identify and deal with IEDs and weapons caches. But the special ops sapper's role was different. It was his job to find routes that avoided IEDs so they wouldn't have to deal with them.

'My role was to get the team to where they needed to be and back safely, as quickly as possible,' says Reuben. 'If that meant avoiding areas where we thought IEDs would be, that's the way we'd go.'

While both the SAS and commandos are elite fighting units and their roles in Afghanistan overlapped to some extent, generally speaking the SAS operated as smaller groups and would be sent on missions that had very specific outcomes planned, including targeting Taliban leadership. Often their missions were time sensitive. Their target would be expected to be in a specific place for a limited amount of time and they had to get to the place, complete the task, and get back out in the most efficient way.

Commandos, while having a similar skill set to the SAS, would go into areas in a larger group with a more general mission to, say, disrupt Taliban activity, or flush enemy fighters out or clear the area in preparation for the arrival of conventional troops. But still this demanded a higher level of military skill and physical ability than conventional troops possessed and the sappers had to match that.

In 2012, the realities of the sapper's role in special operations were recognised when the IRR was disbanded and the Special Operations Engineer Regiment was created.

But long before that, a change of seismic proportions had rattled the Australian Army. Going back into Afghanistan in 2006, with a brief to both quell the resurgent Taliban and rebuild the infrastructure of this fractured society, the army commanders did something that had never been done before: they put an engineer in charge of the entire operation.

5

LIVE . . . MOVE . . . FIGHT

Brigadier Wayne Budd could see it coming. As head of the Royal Australian Engineers corps, Brigadier Budd was in Iraq in 2003 as a senior Australian staff officer in the coalition Joint Task Force that was running the war there. While the rest of the army focused on clearing Saddam Hussein out of Iraq, Australia's military commitment to Afghanistan had been reduced to one man liaising with the NATO-led security forces. But once Brigadier Budd was back in Australia, he picked up the signals that Australian troops might be going back to Afghanistan to help finish the job that had been started after 9/11.

For almost two years from 2001, when the Taliban had been driven from government (but not from Afghanistan), the NATO-led, United Nations-sponsored ISAF had been ordered not to go outside of Kabul, with military leaders warning that any expansion into the country would require another 10,000 troops on the ground. Neither the Australian nor the American governments of that time wanted to be involved in long-term nation rebuilding. The idea had been all along that as soon as the Taliban were defeated, national security would be handed over to the Afghan National Army (ANA). The problem was that a secure Kabul did not mean a secure Afghanistan, which had

34

rarely if ever been under the effective control of central government and that wasn't likely to have been changed by driving the Taliban into hiding in rural areas. The Afghan army was neither equipped nor prepared to quell a resurgence of the Taliban.

Therefore, on 13 October 2003, the United Nations Security Council voted unanimously to expand the ISAF mission beyond Kabul, prompting a serious reconsideration of the whole mission by its major participants. Canada, who provided more than half the troops to the ISAF, bluntly refused to deploy forces outside of the capital, although they relented in 2005, after the Afghan elections, and sent troops to Kandahar. But that was all part of a significant deployment of larger numbers of troops from several countries. Back in Australia, Brigadier Budd had a strong feeling that things were changing. Australia's 'one-man war on terror' was about to be reinforced several hundred times over.

'I'll always remember, when the Secretary General of NATO visited Australia—I think it was some time in the middle of 2004—turning to my staffer and saying, "Hmmm, it looks like we might have a role in Afghanistan again in the future." NATO was courting Australia to come back as they were expanding their forces in Afghanistan. I sent an infantry lieutenant colonel to Afghanistan to look at what was going on and what NATO was doing, and from his reconnaissance report we wrote a submission that was sent up to the strategic levels of government to say, "Hey look, here's what's going on in Afghanistan and here are the sorts of things that we might get involved in if anyone was considering doing anything there."

'Senator Robert Hill was the defence minister at the time and I recall his guidance, which was if we're going to get involved in something, let's base planning for a role in Afghanistan around a commitment that does something for the people of Afghanistan. That was the political intent from the defence minister at the time. So subsequently, throughout 2005, I was involved as the lead operational planner in a series of coalition meetings around the globe.'

At this point, despite their earlier reservations, Canada had already chosen Kandahar in the south, the Taliban heartland, as their base and were trying to get others to join them to expand the operations.

'So in 2005 we started to plan for what role Australia might play given our political guidance that we needed to do something that was focused on the people of Afghanistan,' says Brigadier Budd. 'NATO, of course, had its own agenda and wanted forces to, symbolically, at least, look after the provinces of Uruzgan, Kandahar, Zabul and Nimruz. Up till this point they only had American special forces operating outside of Kabul.

'This was about putting a proper force in there to rebuild Afghanistan governance and security and everything else,' recalls Brigadier Budd. 'And it became very interesting because by then Uruzgan had become the opium production heartland of Afghanistan where all the opium poppies were grown. The heroin that was subsequently trafficked into Europe started there.'

A series of meetings were held with Australia's NATO allies— Australia isn't part of NATO, but often works closely with its members. 'The country was divided into four regional command areas. The Americans helped set up a task force in Zabul province—although they were everywhere, basically—the British took Helmand province, in the far west. Nimruz was just local security really. And the Dutch took Uruzgan.

'It came down to what we were offering NATO and what fitted best was for us to go and work with the Dutch in Uruzgan province. It came back to the original instructions—we are going to do something that benefited the people in Afghanistan. So the Dutch performed the traditional security roles, while we designed and developed the Reconstruction Task Force, or RTF. In 2006, a special operations task group went back into Uruzgan to shape the environment. Then we followed by going in with the Dutch.'

The Australian Army's role would change dramatically over their time in Afghanistan but the original plan was based on experience gained much closer to home. For more than ten years the Army's Aboriginal Community Assistance Program (AACAP) had been going into remote Aboriginal communities to build houses and set up much needed infrastructure and facilities.

'The core of this idea was based on our AACAP experience—the army have Aboriginal community systems programs which were being run across the country very successfully for years. We go in and help build infrastructure but a key part of it is to deliver skills to locals so that they can help themselves.

'Every time we went to an Aboriginal community we'd teach them skills and get them involved in the activities and we'd train them to help themselves. The United Nations wanted us to help people and this is how you help people—it's what we do in Australia all the time. But if you don't transfer skills, nothing is sustainable. It was vital that they could sustain, maintain and develop and rebuild their community.'

However, while all this planning was going on, Australian soldiers, including sappers, were already on the ground in Afghanistan with special ops forces who had a very different mission—to target the insurgents.

When Brigadier, then Lieutenant Colonel, Mick Ryan learned that the Australian Army was sending a task force back into Afghanistan in 2006 with a mission to help rebuild the country, he put together a plan. His proposal had many complex levels within it, not least how they would coordinate with their Dutch hosts, but there was one significant issue that he knew would cause ructions in the military hierarchy—he believed the best people to run the show were engineers.

'You start with a mission and you build the organisation around it,' says Brigadier Ryan. 'The mission was very clear and in our brigade it was also very clear what unit had to lead it: a combat engineer regiment. I sat down over Christmas and did about twelve different versions of a mission analysis or what I thought might come along, which was only speculation, and I briefed my brigade commander, and I said, "Sir, I reckon this is coming along. I reckon this is the analysis of the mission. And, I reckon 1 CER [Combat Engineer Regiment] is the right organisation to do it."

'And he goes, "Your analysis is sound. I agree with you. Go brief the divisional commander." I went and gave the brief to the divisional commander and he said, "Well, you're the man for the job." We became the go-to guys because we'd thought about it. We'd anticipated, we planned for it. It was just logical to go, "Why wouldn't we give it to you?"'

And so, having given the army the detailed blueprint for its re-engagement as part of NATO forces in Afghanistan, Mick Ryan then had to make it work.

'I commanded the first Reconstruction Task Force [RTF 1] between 2006 and 2007. So we built it, we trained it and we built the concept of operations and all the SOPs and the planning process. We put together a whole new kind of unit and we deployed it and conducted operations for eight months.

'There were multiple levels. One was to form a partnership with the Dutch and the next level down was to devise both construction and training tasks for the local community whilst being able to protect ourselves, so the first part of the operation was heavy in construction and light in training [of the Afghans].

'After several months we just switched that around to focus every bit as much on training the Afghan army combat engineers, through the training school. Our task force did everything else too. So we had our own infantry, I had my own combat engineers and construction guys. I had intelligence. I had everything in my task force.'

But there was still the question of who should run the show on the ground. Logic pointed to the task force being commanded by a sapper, but this had never happened before in the entire history of the Australian Army.

'My time in the joint planning had taught me that selling a plan was easy, deciding the command structure was always hard,' recalls Brigadier Budd. 'It was a big breakthrough for sappers. But we designed it to be a Reconstruction Task Force, and therefore engineer-centric and most appropriately commanded by a sapper.'

Brigadier Budd had by this time been posted to run Headquarters Joint Operations Command: 'I was able to get that force accepted by government at a strategic level—that needed to be our focus. We'd agreed the plan that we were going to work with the Dutch in Uruzgan province and that this force needed to be of sufficient size that when you added security, added intelligence, added supply, it still needed to have sappers to deliver effect. It ended up being bigger than initial thoughts but eventually we designed a force of around 400 that was agreed by every government.

'When Mick Ryan took it across, it was of sufficient size and weight to integrate with the Dutch, protect itself on ops but deliver the effect that we had intended in the initial planning, because if you get away from what the government intent was—well, that means that we've strayed.'

But while having a sapper in charge of what was essentially a sapper operation made perfect sense to the senior defence force commanders, it did not sit well with infantry whose mindset had reverted to pre-Vietnam thinking that sappers were a force that you held in reserve until they were needed for a specific task. The very idea of them commanding the whole operation was almost heretical.

'The infantry hated that there was an engineer in charge of the task force,' says Brigadier Ryan. 'It drove some senior officers just crazy that we would have an engineer commanding infantry companies. But I was quite comfortable in my ability to do that. In 1st Brigade we did it all the time so it was just business as usual in our brigade; it wasn't in places like 3rd Brigade. 1st Brigade has had a very strong battle grouping culture. 3rd Brigade has a strong battalion group culture and they are worlds apart. A battle group starts with a mission and you build an organisation around it. So the mission is key. The battalion group starts with a unit and the unit is key.'

Even with a sapper in charge of the whole show, the importance of engineers to individual missions on the ground was lost on some infantry officers. 'Yes, there were some infantry-engineer issues,' says Brigadier Ryan, 'but they got to understand that both had a role to play and that the sappers were the experts in "defile" drills and route clearance, IED response, all those kinds of things. The infantry just can't do any of that.'

Defile drills are the procedures that have to be gone through when a patrol enters a narrow pass or gorge, one of the most vulnerable situations for troops who may be exposed to roadside bombs or ambush, or both. Sappers are trained in identifying choke points where the threat is greatest and finding the safest way through and around the threat, often by discovering and dealing with IEDs.

'There were certain individuals who never got it,' says Brigadier Ryan, 'but there were a lot who did. There were individuals, though, that were backward. I think the biggest problems were in elements that didn't come from my brigade. There is a profound cultural difference between our brigade and others. For example, in 3rd Brigade, the alpha units—the alpha dogs—are the infantry battalions, and then there is everyone else. In 1st Brigade it's never been like that. There are seven co-equal units, any of which can lead a task group.

'I think it is partially because we had mechanised formation [comprising armoured vehicles as well as infantry]. So we've all had that common approach. I think that it's built even further since we've all been in the one place in the brigade. I think the fact that we are the only element in the army that has 1st Brigade officer's mess and 1st Brigade sergeant's mess. We socialise, we eat together. We know each other outside of just the plain unit environment, whereas in the other brigades just engineers would eat together. The culture was very different.'

One sapper, a troop commander who preferred not to be named, said the problem mostly existed at junior officer level and above: 'I think at the lowest level the sappers were instinctively looked after by the infantry—the guys who are out on patrol—and that bond was made even stronger once they saw what the sappers actually did.

'So it was there from the start. Their NCOs [non-commissioned officers] would tell them, "You need to listen to the sapper, you need to watch what he does." And then once they started seeing people get injured, started seeing several IEDs in a row, started seeing what these things could do, that appreciation of what we did for them became much stronger at that low level and we were always looked after.

'That view wasn't always shared at the higher levels, at infantry headquarters, but that was a very individual thing. For some senior officers there was very much a culture of "my way or the highway". But I know the lieutenant tried to get the sapper point of view across to the infantry: simple things like, how about we use the info we've got out of all these IEDs to target specific individuals or specific areas? How about we put an engineer in here that's going to look for stuff—and you protect that engineer looking for stuff, things like that?

'How about we create a target for our patrol, we don't have to do it that often, but we can do that once a month, twice every second month. We can build enough info to target specific areas to get a better effect other than walking the ground randomly every day, which is what I felt we did. In saying that, we made sure the insurgency couldn't get involved but I don't feel we targeted much and there was a lot of unused potential especially on the engineering side.'

The way the war was being fought would evolve and change, partly in response to the Taliban's increasing use of IEDs as time went on. Once again, sappers were changing the way the army thought as well as fought.

'What's the role of the engineers?' asks Wayne Budd, quoting Lieutenant General Frank Hickling. 'To help the army live, move and fight. So any deployed force, first and foremost, they start to look to their engineers for the "live" and then the "move" and then they think about the "fight" . . . in that order. Live, move, fight. And that's kind of what happened. Engineers helped set up [the infrastructure for living] and then it became important to be able to move as we subsequently learned in Afghanistan with the IEDs. To move became the engineer war.'

But even at the training stage, and especially on full-scale exercises, the importance of that role was routinely forgotten. 'The problem for the sapper—and this is the way things operated in Afghanistan—you might only have to go 20 kilometres but that might take you all day. Because the engineer search teams were clearing the five vital points along that route that prevented you driving that 20 kilometres in 30 minutes, because of the IEDs—the asymmetric threat. And we know from previous training activities that the infantry commanders would say, we won't play the minefield because that will just slow down the exercise as all the infantry and everyone else will be sitting on their arses back here while you sappers do your business and who's getting any training activity out of that?'

'But,' says Brigadier Budd, 'sappers are doing their job and the infantry supporting a bridging operation gets to understand what needs to happen. And so when you get these big exercises there will be some involvement but at other times there won't be.

'I remember when the big exercises started again as we began to try and focus back on our foundation war fighting skills. Putting in the sapper tank ditch [a ditch shaped so that tanks get stuck in it] held up a whole exercise to the point where they just said, "Okay, stuff it, let's breach the minefield, let's breach it from the other side because we need to get on with things."'

Former Warrant Officer Jeff Newman, a member of 3 Troop—the legendary Tunnel Rats—experienced the same frustration, if at a much lower level: 'A lot of the other corps went through a phase there where they didn't know how to use the engineers, so we would get pushed off to the flank and let them do their manoeuvring, especially when it came to live fire activities. They'd go, "You engineers can go and sit off at the side, we are going to do our live fire shoots."

'But now, over the years, because we are getting the guys on the courses and that and all working together in these little combat teams as part of the brigade, the engineers are getting more and more involved with the live shoots and probably being more accepted into the combat teams.'

Brigadier David Wainwright, former commanding officer of RTF 3 in Afghanistan in 2007 and 2008, was also frustrated by the difficulty in training sappers and infantry grunts about the realities of working together. 'I've always organised assets from the sapper regiment in a splinter team mentality using a combined arms team framework. So that you've got sappers, gunners, cavalry and infantry all forming the elements. But the true role of sappers when working in complex terrain was never really incorporated properly into a collective training exercise . . . it was just too hard, in that it sort of took away from the other elements, particularly infantry, armour and, to a degree, artillery, and their training and objectives and their skills sets.'

One example he describes was a large formation exercise at Shoalwater Bay, south of Sydney, where it had been agreed it would be conducted under full battlefield procedure. In other words, it would be as close to reality as possible without actually shooting each other. 'It became too hard. Halfway through, sappers doing proper battlefield procedural clearance took too long. It disrupted the activities for the remainder of the elements. Until the lives of other units are at threat they won't understand the necessity for sappers to take time to do their bit.

'We were never able to be incorporated properly into combined arms exercises. It fully confirmed for me that officers in the army did not really understand how to deploy engineers in the battle space, particularly not searching for and firing IEDs or just dealing with ordnance on the battle space. Nor things like clearing choke points, or clearing roads for a road move, or coming upon small protective-like obstacles that had to be cleared before actually getting to our objective.'

So it's no surprise that sappers were initially relegated to supporting roles. That's all the other troops had ever trained for. 'For all these engineer-type tasks, the other elements [were supposed to protect] the sappers so that they could get on with their job. It was important that all elements understood the dangers associated with engineer tasks on manoeuvres and clearing obstacles.'

But on the few occasions the infantry and cavalry had to train with sappers under realistic conditions, their commanders would cut to the chase and ask the sappers to step aside so they could get on with the war games. 'We never got above combat team level and sometimes splinter team level in a lot of our lead-up training,' laments Brigadier Wainwright.

Looking at the bigger picture in Afghanistan, the roles of sappers varied greatly, even though all of them started with the same skill set. There were the special ops sappers attached to commando and SAS units. There were combat engineers who mostly went on patrol with infantry or who allowed infantry to get from point A to point B as safely as possible. And then there were those primarily involved in the construction (and occasionally destruction) of buildings, bridges and infrastructure. All those roles overlapped to some extent but it was the latter, helping to rebuild a fractured country, that was Mick Ryan's prime concern.

6

BACKYARD BLITZ

In late 2005 the NATO-led ISAF in Afghanistan was doubled to 20,000 troops, with a mission to prepare the country for a return to democracy and prepare its security forces to be able to maintain that when soldiers from the (mostly) Western nations went home. At its peak, more than 50 countries would provide troops to ISAF, from one soldier from tiny Luxembourg to more than 6000 from the United States.

It had been decided that Australian forces would be placed with the Dutch in Kamp Holland at Tarin Kowt, a small market town in south-central Uruzgan province, itself in the middle of Afghanistan. Tarin Kowt sits in the middle of a dry, dusty, flat plain—or *dasht*—surrounded by mountains that rear up spectacularly in the middle distance and form gorges and valleys that spread like fingers, offering both a threat and a challenge to anyone who thought they could tame this wild country and its people.

Snow on the mountains from Afghanistan's bitter winters would melt in the spring, filling the rivers and streams and creating ribbons of vegetation, known colloquially as the green zone. Kamp Holland, built around a military airfield on the outskirts of the town, contained some 1200 to 1400 Dutch troops, comprising a battle group of infantry with armoured vehicles and artillery, supported by F-16 fighter-bomber jets, six Apache and five Eurocopter helicopters of the Royal Netherlands Air Force. Also stationed in Kamp Holland were elements of the Afghan army and, surprisingly, the Afghan police. The Australian forces were under instructions to work with Afghan security forces, and that included the police as well as the army.

Into this came the Australian task force of an engineer squadron, an expanded infantry company with another platoon of infantry mobility vehicles from 6 RAR (6th Battalion, Royal Australian Regiment), an expanded cavalry troop of about half a squadron plus a lot of intelligence officers and logistics support, adding up to about four hundred pairs of boots on the ground. It was always complicated, sometimes confused and often confronting, especially for then Lieutenant Colonel, now Brigadier, Mick Ryan when he first stepped off the plane in the northern summer of 2006.

'Brown, everything is brown,' recalls Brigadier Ryan. 'The hillsides are brown. The dirt is brown. The bull dust is brown. The dust in the air is brown. It's all brown. I remember that very clearly. It's a very bleak and austere physical environment. No trees except some in the green zones, but none on the mountains, none in the *dasht* . . . I looked around and there were a few timber buildings and a lot of bull dust and I thought, *Well, we've got a lot of work ahead of us.*'

The camp itself was even less inviting: 'It was pretty grim. The base itself was yet to be built. There were a few old timber B huts. There was an American special forces detachment and there were a few Dutch hanging around to start building. There was an old dirt airfield but that was it. The town itself was pretty run down, really. I think it was a reasonably large provincial town and it had a radio station but there was no TV or anything like that.

'The biggest challenge to start off with was, how do you work this new organisation because there wasn't such a thing as a Reconstruction Task Force. There was no doctrine. There were no procedures, so we had to come up with them ourselves. We had to come up with all our own SOPs and then train the organisation before we left.'

Brigadier Ryan says the most important element of how they worked was to put the population in the forefront of their thinking. 'We were not focused on the enemy,' he says. 'My job was to make the Taliban irrelevant. So if I could build physical and human capacity in the people of Uruzgan province, they would be less susceptible to what the Taliban was offering. We had no problem if the Taliban attacked our side: we were the biggest, toughest bunch around, really, so they were of peripheral concern.

'The main challenge there was understanding what the local priorities were. First of all, I was not going to repeat what some others had done where they'd come in and told the local people, "This is what you need." I was very close to the mayor of Tarin Kowt and with the minister for construction and redevelopment and we sat down and agreed on what the priorities were that I was going to work towards. And then just all the normal issues like getting the materials in and those sort of things. For that we had a contract with a company in Dubai that had an aircraft fly in every week.'

As with AACAP, the idea wasn't just to build infrastructure for locals, it was to teach them how to build and repair things themselves. The same applied to passing on skills to Afghan army personnel, but there were very basic obstacles in the way before that could even be attempted.

'The biggest challenge on the trade training, was having somewhere to train people. So we got there in the August and we started building a school straightaway but it wasn't going to be open until February and I said, "Well, I'm not waiting." We put up a tent and we'd train them in that. We completed the first trade training course in the October and we trained them out of the back of the tent for several months and then a couple of guys we had trained we employed as trainers. The whole aim was to build a sustainable trade training school where the Afghans were the trainers and administrators as well as the trainees. That's what we were always working towards.

'The Afghan National Army turned up one day with two American embedded trainers with them. One of them asked if we could help them out and I said I reckoned I could. So we put together a program. It was a monthly battle rhythm where we would do one week of formal training for the Afghan army engineers with our combat engineers, and then for two weeks we would deploy them on all our missions. They would come out on every single mission and then one week when they would go back to Kandahar on leave. We ran that battle rhythm for the whole time. They were fantastic.

'They were different, but these young Afghan army engineers that were there, they were keen to be part of the task force. Two American army guys used to wear our patches. One of the Americans asked if he could wear our big RTF patch. He said, "Sir, can I wear your patch because I feel like I'm part of your team?" And I thought, *Well, it's working.*'

Life in Tarin Kowt was tough for the Aussies, especially in the early days. Unlike in Vietnam, there was no social life beyond the wires and the camp was effectively 'dry' for a variety of reasons, not least of which was sensitivity to both the local population and their Afghan army comrades who were predominantly Muslim and therefore teetotal. 'Two beers, per man, per day, perhaps . . .' was as remote from Tarin Kowt as the girly bars of Vung Tau.

'Was it tough keeping the guys interested and stopping them getting bored? Absolutely. We had a battle rhythm where for one night a week we had professional training for soldiers and another one for corporals . . . Every Saturday night I put on a big Aussie barbecue so we had at least one decent feed a week. We had the normal TVs and internet cafe. The camp was all quite austere, though, not what it is now. So it was tough for the guys to entertain themselves but we kept them busy either preparing for missions or rehearsing for missions, conducting missions or the after-action reviews that we did after every single mission. We had entertainers come around, I think once. Everyone got their leave back home as well. But these are difficult places that we send people to and we train our soldiers hopefully to be resilient enough to deal with that.'

Also unlike in Vietnam, all the Australian soldiers in Afghanistan were full-time professionals, rather than conscripts. But did any of the troops reckon that they'd joined the army for different reasons other than being sent to a foreign country to be shot at by the locals?

'I got the opposite. I think when you don't send the guys on these things they get upset. As soon as you say tell someone they're going to Afghanistan, there's no scowls there. They're more likely to say "Awesome!" That's the first reaction from ninety-nine per cent of soldiers, including myself. When you say, "Sorry, you're not going," that's when they get upset. Australian soldiers have a bias towards wanting to do the job and the job is on operations. No one wants to sit on the bench; they want to be on the paddock. They want to run on with the team.

'Now, that doesn't mean that at some point during the deployment everyone doesn't get pissed off. Everyone has that day or days where you go, "I've had a gutful of this place." But it's how you and their friends manage them. Sometimes I would tell them to go and sit with the dogs for a while [combat engineer teams had explosives detection dogs]. If you play with the animals for a while you can't help but cheer up.'

Outside the wire, boredom was far from the biggest threat. In many regards, the Afghans were a conundrum of tradition and technology.

'You'd see one guy working a field by hand or with a donkey pulling a plough,' one sapper says. 'Then he'd stop and pull out a mobile phone and make a call.' That call could be as innocent as asking his wife what was for dinner, or telling his Taliban connections that an army patrol was on its way. Or he could be detonating a bomb by remote control.

Away from the camp, the Aussies had to be on high alert, permanently. 'We were very robust at the very beginning about not setting patterns,' explains Brigadier Ryan. 'This was a very big thing. We had a very good intelligence approach; we used intelligence in our planning. But we also made sure we were doing things that we felt the community wanted and when we were doing something the local people wanted you were less likely to get attacked.

'There had been a special operations task group before us but they were a very light force, and went out in light vehicles, so they were a bit more of an attractive target. But it's different when you turn up with ASLAVs [Australian Standard Light Armoured Vehicles] and PMVs [Protected Mobility Vehicles, or Bushmasters] and you're a large force and you say to them, "Listen, I'm here to help but if you attack my soldiers I'm going to smash you. I will destroy you."

'And when they tried it once or twice that's exactly what we did. So I think we generated a bit of shock just by the size and capability of our soldiers and so the locals had to sit back and think, *How are we going to attack all these guys? They're different. They're not like the Dutch.* So I think for very many months there the Taliban kind of re-cocked and re-calibrated how they were going to get us. They already had IEDs when we were there but you had to use roads to hit IEDs and we didn't use roads. Everything was cross-country because that way you're not setting patterns. The only time we'd use roads was when I had to move plant on heavy vehicles and then we had very robust clearance and detection systems to take care of that.'

Moving large and heavy pieces of equipment on even larger trucks was a logistical challenge. The slow-moving convoy was an easy target for IEDs and RPGs [rocket-propelled grenades], and moved even slower when sappers at the front needed to search for the former. Where possible, cavalry and infantry would occupy the high ground on either side of this giant metal snake, leap-frogging the main convoy to guard against opportunist insurgents.

One way that the Australian troops were not like the Dutch, according to Mick Ryan, was in their generally more aggressive attitude. 'If we go to a bit of ground, we want to own it. It doesn't matter what corps you're in, whether it was the special forces, combat engineers or infantry, if we're somewhere, we like to own the ground. I don't know that the Dutch army had that kind of culture. They had a bit different attitude to battle discipline.'

There's a story told by sappers that the only soldier ever killed in a Bushmaster troop carrier was a Dutch infantryman who'd decided to lie on the floor rather than be strapped into his seat. When an IED went off under the vehicle, he was fatally injured just by being bounced around inside. Even if this is apocryphal, it does reflect the very slight disdain the Aussies felt for their Dutch hosts.

'There is one standard of discipline for Australian soldiers whereas the Dutch have military unions and they can wear facial hair and earrings and all this kind of thing,' says Mick Ryan. 'They have a different type of discipline to what we had. We have very good institutional discipline if it comes to mission preparation for executing missions, for reviewing missions and rolling back in what we had learned. The Dutch army has a different culture; they'd only just transitioned out of being a conscript army. We hadn't had nashos for many, many years. Every Australian there is a volunteer. Everyone wants to be there.'

Sometimes the strict discipline of the Australian Army was a source of frustration for sappers, especially when combat engineers had discovered an IED but had to wait for an EOD tech to come forward and deal with it. The average sapper would have been happy to BIP the bomb, as would the infantry patrol he was leading through the danger zone.

'Honestly, what's the rush?' asks Brigadier Ryan. 'Okay, so you've got to wait around for two hours. You go into defence posture and you wait for the tech. If you get to the town and you're two hours late, is there an issue?

'Even if you waited for a day, we're there for eight months. Honestly, what's the rush here? So I found that the expectations of instant gratification when it came to these kinds of things was poorly calibrated in some of our people. They expected . . . an EOD tech should be there straightaway. Well, maybe, but maybe not, and if it's not, you wait.'

And what about sappers who reckoned they were capable of dealing with the IEDs themselves? 'I'm sure there are lots of instances where people had confidence that they could deal with it but not having the evidence to back that up,' Mick Ryan smiles. 'Remember, it's not just dealing with the IED itself. There's collection of evidence and all those kinds of things and if you can render it safe, you can collect forensic evidence. If you just blow it up the amount of evidence that you can collect is much less. We are not dealing with a high tempo, really high threat environment here. We are dealing with a quasi-military police kind of operation where collection of evidence against the limited number of insurgents who are out there is every bit as important as everything else that we were doing there.

'You collect intelligence on every operation for the after-action reviews. That's why they were so important. As soon as you came in from a mission you did a hot wash up and then you did a detailed after-action review the next day. All that went into the pool of knowledge for planning the next operation. That was just one example. But I think in some respects EOD became a great industry and I must admit I grew uncomfortable with guys in suits approaching IEDs when robots can do it. My view is that if an explosive is found these days, let a robot do the dirty work. You don't have to write letters home to robots' mums when they get blown up.'

Dealing with IEDs was something the members of RTF 1 did as a sideline, so to speak. If they encountered them on a patrol, on their way to a job or a meeting, they dealt with them. But they weren't searching for them. There weren't as many in the early days of the first RTF, for a start, but they had other priorities, including their mission to build and train, for which they borrowed the name of a television show. 'We had this operation [which] we called Backyard Blitz,' recalls Mick Ryan. 'Very early on, we were out doing recon missions and the locals are going, "Oh, great to meet you. When are we going to see you again?" And I said, "What do you mean? We're going to come back and do this." And they said, "No. That's what everyone says but they never come back." And I thought, *We've got a problem here.*'

So Brigadier Ryan told his men that the next time they went out, he wanted armoured trucks piled with building materials. His troops asked him what he wanted to build with the materials and he replied that he didn't know until he got to where they were going and asked the locals. 'I felt if we didn't build credibility in the first months of our tour we'd never build it. So really what I was after was to get some stuff moving here while some of the bigger projects like the hospital got going. So we'd turn up, we'd have a talk to the village leaders and say, "What do you want?" I think the first request was to do some renovations to a mosque and we spent about four or six hours replacing the roof and the floor and the windows and all these kinds of things because the mosque was also the local schoolhouse. It was also difficult for the Taliban to attack.'

The sappers refined the process even further when a young corporal carpenter suggested to Brigadier Ryan that he could put together all the materials needed to do a four-hour renovation on a local mosque. 'We called it the Mosque Kit. We'd have a quick *shura* [the Afghan word for a meeting of elders], secure the place, and—boom!—renovate the mosque. Boom! And we were doing all this short term to gain credibility for the Red Rat, which is what the locals called the red kangaroo on our badge. But what I wanted was that every time they saw that the guys who wore it, if they said they were going to do something, they did it.

'I told them never to promise anything they couldn't deliver, so we delivered on everything we promised to those people and that was very important to me. This concept of Backyard Blitz evolved over time into a broader range of things but it was at its heart getting out there and in the very early days establishing our legitimacy and our credibility.'

In these early, innovative days in Afghanistan, sappers were starting to come into their own again. Mick Ryan only ever built one remote army post, and that was eventually abandoned by the Afghan police for whom it was constructed. But, on the one hand, he set a template for the reconstruction program that would be expanded and refined over the next eight years. They made regular patrols into the Baluchi and Mirabad valleys, gradually expanding the Australian sphere of influence from its Tarin Kowt base.

Most significantly, perhaps, he also oversaw the evolution of the role of the combat engineer and the gradual acceptance by infantry that, rather than keep the engineers at the back, they needed to follow the sapper. 'It was a re-birth,' says Mick Ryan. 'I think in the Vietnam era they understood very well what sappers did. We'd also led Namibia, I think very, very well. But we went through the long peace, didn't we. People forgot what we were supporting. They forgot what a lot of the different elements of army did.'

7

MOVING ON

Through the winter of 2006–07, Mick Ryan's RTF 1 got on with the job of rebuilding the infrastructure of Uruzgan province. As RTF 1's tour of duty came to an end in April 2007, Brigadier Ryan's only regret was having built a forward patrol base at Kulmar. 'That would have been the first one but then the Afghan police pulled out of it and it got stripped and burnt to the ground,' he recalls. 'So, after that you can understand my suspicion of building these things if there weren't the people to occupy them. During my tour, there was roughly a platoon strength of Afghan National Army in Tarin Kowt, [and another platoon] in Deh Rawud. There was no one there that could occupy these things. That came much, much later.'

Apart from that, it was mission accomplished, as far as Brigadier Ryan was concerned: 'I think we achieved everything. We had a limited mission. We went beyond that in a lot of things. The Afghan army engineers were not part of it. We did more reconstruction missions than we anticipated and we trained more people in the trade training school. We trained people in a broader range of skills than we anticipated, so I came back very satisfied.'

But there was one other noteworthy achievement, marked as much by a sense of relief as satisfaction. He didn't lose any troops: 'Not losing any of my soldiers was obviously fantastic. It's hard to describe the feeling of satisfaction to be the last person to walk off the plane and know that every single one of your soldiers walked off in front of you.'

Mick Ryan knows as well as anyone that there's an element of luck as well as good planning, training and management in that. Winter is normally a time of low insurgent activity in Afghanistan for a variety of reasons, from snow in the valleys making travel impossible to the ground being too hard to dig in and conceal IEDs. As RTF 1 rolled out, RTF 2 moved in, under another engineer, Lieutenant Colonel Harry Jarvie, with fresh troops to replace the weary warriors of the first rotation. Fortunately for us, RTF 2 created their own collective memoir—a kind of yearbook, if you like—that provides an insight into the kinds of challenges they faced and how they responded to them.

Under Mick Ryan, RTF 1 had established a trade training school which was intended to pass on basic trade skills to Afghan locals so that they could not only contribute to building, repairing and maintaining the physical infrastructure of their communities, but could earn a living doing so. There was some tactical thinking behind this too: young men who have a purpose in life and a means of supporting their families are less likely to be wooed by the temptations of guerrilla warfare against a superior military force.

At least, that was the theory.

'RTF 1 had engaged seven local nationals that were to be trained and would one day run a trade training school such as this one in the township of Tarin Kowt,' says the report. 'They are all characters with different backgrounds and life stories and have learned trade skills well from the RTF 1 boys.

'The first course after taking over from RTF 1 looked positive and started with twelve students. The first week went well with the students receiving their first pay packet of US$3.50 per day. Come Monday morning the boys rocked up to the front gate to pick up the students and there were only four. The interpreter informed us that it was poppy picking time and "poppies pay more than trade training school". So we finished the course with four well-trained students.'

The sappers of RTF 2 then tried to marry their ability to teach various skills with the locals' ability to learn them. So they split the existing Basic Building Construction Worker Course up into two: one that focused solely on hand tools, the other, an intermediate course, introduced power tools.

The Basic Generator and Small Engine course had an electrical component that involved wiring up light fittings and power points. But, as the report observes, a little knowledge can be dangerous, especially when electricity is involved, so they altered the course, purchased local generators and had a sergeant from Workshops teach generator maintenance and safety.

A more advanced course on building construction was developed, which included water storage and distribution, an aspect that was taught by two plumbers, Sappers Reid and Beatson, borrowed from the support troop. The final course on the design board was the Allied Trade course, which involved teaching concreting, tiling and painting. The locals had these skills but their finishing wasn't that good, so the course was designed around producing a quality product.

'Between courses we have made some improvements to the trade training school facility so it will be quite comfortable for RTF 3 when they arrive,' says the report, which notes that, despite the alarming dropout rate when poppy season arrived, a substantial number of students passed through their courses, including 45 from the Generator and Small Engine course, 35 from the Basic Building Construction

Worker course, and twelve from the intermediate and six from the advanced versions of this course, ten from the Allied Trade course and six from the Basic Plumbing course. Just as importantly, they created a training culture that should continue long after foreign troops are withdrawn. 'We have also worked on the skills of the local nationals who are learning to be instructors. They successfully ran the last two Basic Building Construction Worker courses with a small amount of overview from the Australian instructors.'

Many of those graduates from the trade training school were able to put their newly acquired skills to good use when they went to work on a school in the village of Talani. As reported by then Captain Haydn Barlow in the *Army News*, Australian sappers worked closely with soldiers from the Afghan National Army (ANA) to completely renovate the school for 400 local children. 'The project was a result of ongoing liaison between the RTF and key members within the village of Talani, specifically the school principal and the village *malik*,' writes Captain Barlow. 'One of the main concerns raised by the principal was the poor state of the windows, most of which were broken and had shards protruding from the frames. It was also identified that the students . . . had no chairs or desks at which to work in their class rooms.'

The renovation was completed at rocket speed in less than ten hours and the result were described as 'magical' by the school principal. 'It included the removal of over 50 broken windows and the installation of Perspex inserts—which are stronger and provide protection from rain and extreme dust storms that frequent the summer.'

The engineers didn't limit their work to the school building. They also fixed up the playground which had been neglected for many years. 'One of the simplest tasks conducted, but by far the most popular given the children's expressions when let loose on them, was the installation of play equipment in the schoolyards. A swing set, seesaw, monkey bars and outdoor table setting; all designed, built and installed by the Australian and Afghan engineers, now provide the children with a safe area to play outside.'

The engineers also installed a 4000-litre water tank with plumbing to multiple taps, providing a reliable source of clean drinking water as well as a place where the schoolkids could wash their hands.

But it was in the response to the school's dire furniture shortage that a combination of the mentoring and training schemes ticked every box in the mission's aims. Desks, chairs and bookshelves produced by local students of the trade training school were installed.

'In a move highly symbolic of the overall effort in Afghanistan, the furniture was emphasising self-sufficiency within the community,' writes Captain Barlow. 'Engineer Troop Commander Lieutenant Kieran Jackel said it was extremely rewarding work and noted how small things can make big differences in this part of the world: "The project was an example of how some simple reconstruction work can provide a lasting impact on the community. Ideally it will encourage more students to attend school now there is a safe and enjoyable environment to learn in."'

The other vital educational role being undertaken by Australian troops was the mentoring of ANA engineers. Putting it bluntly, if the ANA isn't up to scratch, the Taliban will move on Kabul the moment the last ISAF soldier leaves Afghanistan, if not before. Australian sappers with RTF 2 developed a training program to boost the ANA engineers' combat capabilities. This was the only military engineering training provided to the ANA in all of Afghanistan.

'This training was conducted over five days to a section size group at a time and usually concluded with the ANA supporting RTF missions outside the wire,' writes Warrant Officer Glen Donaldson. 'Some of the basic combat lessons taught were first aid, navigation, patrolling, weapon handling and marksmanship.'

Many ANA soldiers already possessed these skills but the RTF course enabled them to boost their individual abilities. 'The highlight of the month is the range day with the ANA demonstrating their shooting ability. After a little bit of coaching, however, we soon had them hitting their targets.' One sardonic comment in the report noted that aiming may have been something of a novelty to some ANA soldiers. 'Our own soldiers also had the opportunity to fire foreign weapons such as the AK-47, RPG and MP4,' noted Donaldson.

'The combat engineering period proved to be the real test. The ANA soldiers, even though nominally engineers, had never conducted any formalised engineer-specific training. During the seven days of training, the engineers covered such topics as mine incident and awareness, IED awareness, route check, vehicle search, personnel search and vehicle checkpoint operations. This training proved to be very successful, with the ANA conducting a test of objectives at the end, which they passed with flying colours.

'The construction week allowed the ANA to test their skills in construction methods. We taught them skills that would allow us to employ them during quick impact projects. Construction methods included building outdoor settings, tank stands, window and door frames and combat engineer tool boxes.'

In a highly practical as well as symbolic development, while these courses were going on, an area of land was fenced off to become the ANA training compound. Buildings were erected and other examples of combat engineering capabilities went on display and the yard was officially opened at the graduation of the first course. An ABC TV *Four Corners* documentary team turned up to record this highly auspicious day. However, the process wasn't without its challenges, which were many and considerable.

'Even though we had an interpreter, the students sometimes found it hard to understand the lessons,' writes Captain Barlow. 'We used a lot of demonstrations to assist with the learning process and help overcome the language barrier. Another difficulty we found was getting them used to the concept of structured learning. Some of them had had very little schooling in their life, so the process of theory–practice validation was foreign and would frustrate them sometimes. They were more used to trial and error.'

A number of missions were planned for the completion of the training, which allowed the ANA soldiers to be assessed in the field. 'The engineers working alongside our own forces have completed missions in the Gulkana, Talani and Sharqi areas, each with exceptional results,' says Captain Barlow. 'The training that we have conducted has both been rewarding and beneficial to the Australian and Afghan forces. One day the ANA will be able to conduct their own security operations, and our efforts will have helped them get there.'

While all this was going on, of course, sappers were involved in very real and tactically important projects, such as the construction of a police checkpoint to the east of Tarin Kowt. The worksite was on top of a ridiculously steep hill in the middle of a cemetery, recalled one sapper, who added that the task was completed in record time due in no small part to a firefight between Taliban and an infantry platoon less than a kilometre away.

They also improved facilities at the Afghan Health Development Services centre where local nurses, medics and first aiders from the local community were trained. The sappers installed a septic tank and new sewerage services and toilet, repaired a well and installed a new water distribution system.

In the heroic pragmatism and sappernuity of the various RTFs' 'hearts and minds' civil affairs projects, the spirit of the Tunnel Rats lived on. Many young sappers are still inspired—and perhaps overawed—by the exploits of their forerunners in 3 Field Troop, half a century ago. But, just as exploring Vietcong tunnels wasn't all fun and games, sappers put themselves very much in the line of fire in Afghanistan.

In September 2006, the Special Forces Task Group had returned to Australia, and there were effectively no Australian special forces in Afghanistan. In April 2007, coinciding with the arrival of RTF 2, the Special Operations Task Group landed at Tarin Kowt. It comprised members of the SAS Regiment and commandos supported by the Incident Response Regiment, which included highly trained combat engineers.

The special forces' mission, to target the insurgents, put sappers right on the cutting edge of the conflict in Afghanistan.

8

SPECIAL OPS AND LOCAL COPS

As he treads carefully through the rock-strewn gulleys of Uruzgan's treacherous valleys, and even more tentatively through dangerous defiles after dark, his night vision goggles turning the world to green and black, there is nothing that distinguishes the special ops sapper from his SAS or commando companions. He may not have quite the same levels of physical endurance as them, or their finely honed fighting abilities, but then he has a broader range of skills—sometimes to a ridiculous extent. One sapper's tour with special ops spanned the seriously life-threatening to the frankly comical, including how he came to destroy an Afghan police car, then lose another, only to find it again somewhere completely different.

'On arriving in Afghanistan in 2007, I spent the first month doing barracks sentries and maintenance,' says Corporal Shane Potter. 'But I was also on the first patrol since Vietnam in which sappers had deployed with the SAS.'

The patrol was searching buildings, trying to uncover arms and explosive caches, with Shane often man-packing—carrying the heavy electronic countermeasures device that jams signals that might be used to trigger IED explosions on patrols.

Although individual sappers had worked on and off with special forces from the start of the Afghan war, 2007 was the first time a large engineer force worked with commandos and SAS. Special operations work in very small teams and, due to this, sappers found it hard to get a seat in the vehicles as the commandos and SAS took priority.

'Because of this, I had to work more as an infantry man than a sapper,' he says. 'When my time came to support the commandos, I was primarily an engineer "high risk" searcher working in a special liaison role between the Afghan security forces and our task force.

'It was also the first time we, as Australian troops, worked with the Afghan partnering forces. The Afghan police were very poorly trained and the Afghan army was very battle-hardened. Both were very tribally divided. The Afghan police, mostly of Pashtun ethnicity, were often recruited locally and had corruption ties to the local communities.

'The Afghan army were normally trained in Kabul, outside of the province, then were sent to the south to fight in the conflict areas. The benefit of this was they weren't as corrupt, but the downside was they were not welcomed by the locals as they were seen as outsiders to the provincial Afghans. It also created internal conflict within their ranks.'

With the potential for confusion and conflict so great, Australian soldiers and officers were needed for special liaison roles with the Afghans. Shane found himself in just such a position, purely by chance. 'Out on a patrol with the SAS we came under heavy fire in the Chora Valley region. The commando alpha company had a mortar and the SAS needed it to get out of a sticky situation. I was taken out of the Bushmaster quickly so they could get the mortar team in and allocated to a new role in the conflict: driver for the Afghan police vehicle.'

His role then evolved into the liaison between the Australian task group and their Afghan partnering force. For a variety of political and

tactical reasons, it was decided by ISAF that all the coalition forces
should partner with local security forces, most commonly Army
units but also the police. The story goes that Australian special forces
thought that if they didn't ask for a specific partner, the partners would
all be allocated to other units and special forces would be allowed to
operate without one. Instead, they drew the short straw and ended up
being teamed with Afghan police. Until then, the Australian troops
had worked independently from the Afghan partnering forces, often
conducting their own war by fighting missions without the Afghan
security force, or, taking very limited Afghan security forces personnel
on patrols.

'The Afghans were often seen as dirty, corrupt, untrusting and
random. The professional approach of our soldiers meant they had a
lot of difficulty working with the Afghans. I had a very important role
on this mission, it was like getting kids ready for school each day, but
also it was a lot of hard work to understand all things Afghan from
cultural differences, religion, tribal laws, food requirements and the
language barrier. I had to learn from the Afghans, to educate myself
in their customs, and then I educated our own forces, who were often
reluctant to learn.'

Every day, Shane had to liaise with the platoon commanders who
were trying to use the Afghan troops in Australian patrols. He had
to first work out what training and abilities the individual Afghans
had, then suggest how the commandos could use them on patrols,
without them being a burden to the mission. So his job became
understanding how the Afghans worked, then training them in the
field, so they could be more effective on patrols.

'During my first deployment, on one specific mission, we were
rushed for time to get to Forward Operating Base (FOB) Anaconda,
a desolate outpost manned by the United States special forces Green
Berets about 130 kilometres north-east of Tarin Kowt. We had been

driving under night vision in an Afghan police vehicle with very poor, dusty visibility and the road in front of me suddenly vanished and the vehicle rolled. After it stopped rolling over, I made sure everyone was okay, and then we tried to recover it. After a valiant effort but with no luck, it was ordered to be destroyed by an air strike and the use of an M-203 grenade launcher [to prevent it falling into enemy hands].

'The soldiers on this patrol said it looked "real impressive" and blowing up the damaged police vehicle was one of the best things they'd done!

'Losing the rolled vehicle meant for the next few days I was homeless as far as transport was concerned. I had to learn how to survive between the different vehicles and, at the same time, needed to look after four Afghan soldiers by learning their language, culture, food requirements, and, at the same time, be constantly ready for any foot patrols the commander wanted the Afghan security force to be involved in.

'I really had to learn a lot of resilience, have a good calm temperament, and have the ability to quickly be organised with both the Afghans and the task force. As the mission patrol would constantly change with the evolving battle space, requirements frequently changed.'

Reaching FOB Anaconda, the realities of their mission were brought home to Shane when a large explosion erupted in the distance; a United States special forces patrol had found an IED and just disposed of it without any warning.

'As we drove into the compound the stacked wreckage of police cars was incredible and the cars were riddled with bullets. It was then that we sappers realised the IED threat, which had been minimal, was now increasing. I was also aware that my chances of surviving an IED strike or a shooting in a "soft vehicle" like an Afghan police car were very grim. As we parked our vehicles, we could see the base was protected by a large 120-millimetre mortar tube and a *kandak* of Afghan commandos. The condition of the forward operating base was very poor.'

Shane introduced himself to the senior Afghan commander in charge of the Afghan commandos and got his four Afghans settled into the base. The group spent the next few days resupplying their vehicles and planning for the next patrols. 'I had been working with police a few weeks earlier and I had built up a friendship with them, but after that mission I didn't see them again. Unbeknownst to me, they had been reposted from Tarin Kowt district to Khas Uruzgan, the village closest to FOB Anaconda, and were stationed as the local police detachment there. As I was leaving the Afghan army building, a police vehicle arrived on the FOB and, to my surprise, in it were the police I worked with before.'

Shane was now able to solve the mystery of the other Afghan police car he'd 'lost'—except in that instance, it had simply disappeared. 'I asked them what had happened to the police vehicle we had on the previous mission. It turned out at the end of that mission, it had been taken back to their police station, unannounced and without the Australian Army's knowledge, by the Afghans. Amazingly, they said it was in Tarin Kowt police headquarters and if I needed a police car I could use their car . . . although it did have a damaged windscreen. They told me the security situation in this area was dangerous and one day, while they were driving, a bullet went straight through the windscreen between the driver and passenger and then went straight through the back window without shattering the window. So, after a short discussion, I had seconded another police car for the next few missions. My fellow sappers, soldiers and task force commander were impressed that I had acquired another vehicle. Thankfully, I wasn't the homeless sapper anymore and the other police vehicle in Tarin Kowt was finally found too.'

Shane had to modify the new vehicle by taking out the light fuses for sirens and lights so he could use the vehicle tactically without the risk of the Afghans flipping any switches in the cars. 'There's nothing like flashing lights and noisy sirens going off to alert the Taliban that there's a mission in the middle of night or early morning raid, so I had to assure the commander of the patrol this would not happen. I was then re-tasked to conduct vehicle checkpoints and building searches with the Afghan security forces, and use my Minelab skills to oversee the Afghan search techniques and to ensure they were thorough. I also had to make sure they didn't steal from the local people, but, more importantly, we had to investigate any suspicious items that could pose a danger to our forces by clearing the item first and making it safe.'

As Shane's missions increased, his role as the Afghan army and police liaison increased. As he learned more of the language and the Afghan people's cultural traits, he would be increasingly used to help with medical *shuras*—meetings where locals received treatment from medics in the field.

'It was a way for us to show we were here to help the Afghans and not oppress them. It also was a good opportunity for team commanders to engage with local tribal leaders so we could find out if the Taliban were a threatening presence in their lives and assure the Afghans that we were readily available to help them if they required assistance.'

The Afghans were often reluctant to work alongside the ANA forces in Afghanistan, as they had been heavily involved with the Russians and many other invading armies in the past. On the other hand, it couldn't be assumed that they were particularly keen on the Taliban, either. Most Afghans just wanted to be left in peace to grow their crops and ply their trade. But they were caught between the Afghan army, who they mistrusted, and the Taliban, who they feared.

'We had to first earn the trust of the people in Afghanistan before we could help them. As sappers embedded with special ops teams, we learned vital information by being out in unexplored areas first. We were able to pass on vital firsthand knowledge to conventional army engineers on how they could get reconstruction resources to these outposts so they could build patrol bases and provide reconstruction and development assistance to the locals.

'The first few years of the campaign we would deploy to unknown areas then leave, having no soldiers or Afghan security forces to police the area. As a result the Taliban would simply take control and the threats to coalition forces and Afghan security forces increased and along with that, so did the sappers' workload and role.'

Eventually, patrol bases were gradually built up along the various valleys around the Uruzgan province. This not only provided better security, it was also safer, as helicopters could resupply troops in the field from the patrol bases and limit the sappers' exposure to the dangers of IEDs as they were clearing the roads ahead of transports. But dangers were everywhere.

During one SAS patrol, an Afghan interpreter was blown up by an IED and the Afghan army shot a young Taliban. It was also on this deployment that the explosives detection dog (EDD), Razz, was blown up and her handler, Lance Corporal Craig Turnbull, injured. Years later, when Razz was posthumously awarded the Australian Defence Force Trackers and War Dogs Association medal, Craig Turnbull said that Razz was part of his family. 'She was a wonderful dog. A top EDD that was very intelligent. She was a family member to me and I'll never forget her.

'When the patrol returned to base the SAS were very humble and gave great credit to the respected engineer dog handler who had lost his loyal companion, having made the ultimate great sacrifice that saved the patrol from harm's way,' says Shane. 'They were very professional and grateful, despite saddened for what happened, then refocused and got on with the mission.'

The sappers in Afghanistan, originally deployed as a Reconstruction Task Force, were now finding their job a lot more difficult due to the increasing IED threats. At the end of his first rotation in 2007, Shane made a full report to the senior commanders on how to work with the Afghans for future mission planning. On return to Australia he received his unit's first commendation from 4 RAR Commando (now 2 Commando Regiment) for his work as the Afghan army and police liaison.

Shane would return for two more rotations in Afghanistan, but he had already established new processes for working with Afghan troops that would form a template for sappers in the difficult years to come.

9

ON PATROL WITH SPECIAL FORCES

When Jeff Newman arrived in Tarin Kowt in 2007 to begin his attachment with a commando platoon, he had been training for months in preparation. In his mind's eye, he was flying into a hell-hole of heat and dust, random IEDs hidden in the shimmering sands and bullets flying from behind sun-baked rocks. He was in for a shock.

'I was pretty excited but it was cold,' he recalls. 'I got there in March with my team. Another two teams had already gone over in November and December to support 1st Commando Regiment, then my team went over to support the company from 2nd Commando Regiment. So by the time I got there one team had been there for a few months and the other team had been there a bit longer so they had already settled into their routine.

'You know that feeling you get when you go somewhere new and you're learning all the ins and outs and the do's and don'ts on the base. It was exciting. For our guys [special ops] it was positive because we were a compound inside a compound. I know a lot of the guys that supported the conventional forces were tired and over it and not really enjoying their tour, but for us, well, we were being treated like adults—with the special forces community you are always treated like an adult.

'It's hard to describe going from a conventional sapper background to working with the special forces. It was good; it was exactly how you wanted to be treated as an engineer. Because the special forces guys had been working with sappers for so long, they always took on board what you had to say.

'Yes, they knew we weren't special forces but all the commando guys that I worked with treated me and my guys as part of the team—it was really good.'

The 2nd Commando company that Jeff's team was there to support hadn't arrived yet, and still had another two weeks before they hit the ground. But there were still elements of 1st Commando there as well as some troops from the SAS who were mentoring the Afghan police partnering force. Unexpectedly, Jeff got a chance to have a practice run before getting down to the real thing.

'One of the other team leaders said, "Jeff, we are going out on patrol for a couple of days—do you want to come with us?" I said, yes, of course. It was a chance to get out on the ground to see what it's like; they get to know what was expected of me, just to get a feel of how things would go. So I jumped in a helicopter, left my team behind and went with the other team leader and his team. They had some SAS guys and a few from the partnering force, about ten or fifteen Afghan police officers, myself and the other team leader with the headquarters element, four or five guys, an interpreter, etc. I remember flying in the helicopters, I think it was about a 15- or 20-minute flight. But in the Black Hawk everybody is piled in and by the time we got there my legs were numb and I fell out the door. I didn't exactly hit the ground but it was hard to start running.

'It took about five minutes to get the circulation through, although the adrenalin helps. As we are running up a hill the helicopters make a lot of noise and you can't hear much so if you're taking fire you don't realise it, really. You're a bit disorientated too, with dust kicking up, as to where the shots might be coming from. Sometimes depending on what helicopter you are using, that noise can be drowned out so, when you hit the ground you always run out to find an area of cover while the helicopter takes off. The good thing is, the rotor wash just picks you up and forces you to run faster. So, if you're running 100 metres in 10 seconds, with the rotor wash it's more like 8 seconds. If you've got a backpack on it can actually pick you up and throw you.'

However, there was no enemy fire that day and falling out of the chopper was the only drama. This was just a patrol to let the locals know the Aussies were still around and for them to get a sense of what was going on.

'They didn't want to stop and search compounds; it was just a presence patrol but some of the locals would run away and hide anyway. There had been a few Australian patrols in that area over the previous years. It was probably a 5 to 8 kilometre-long valley—we had a dog and handler as well—and we just moved up there, having a look at the compounds. The police in the partnering force would gauge whether there were hostile people in the area. Then we finished the patrol and made our exit up a massive mountain and waited for the helicopters to come in.'

It had been a long road that brought Jeff Newman to Afghanistan, starting before he even went to school. But he was always going to end up in the army and, once he had chosen the sappers—and the Tunnel Rats of 3 Troop, no less—the top of that mountain was waiting for him. (To put this in context, 3 Troop was the direct historical descendant of 3 Field Troop, co-author Sandy MacGregor's boys who became the original Tunnel Rats back in 1965 in the Cu Chi tunnels of Vietnam. The word 'Field' is only attached to a military unit's name when their regiment is not there, in theatre. However, years later, 3 Troop ceased to exist but that meant no active engineer unit shared the US citation that 1 Battalion Group, as part of the 173rd Airborne Brigade, received for their contribution in Vietnam in 1965–66. Eventually, 3 Troop was re-raised, the citation restored and sappers like Jeff Newman could proudly wear the Tunnel Rats badge again.)

'My mum remarried, to a soldier, when I was about five so I became an army brat. But even before that I always had a keen interest in the army and that sort of stuff. I was sort of leaning towards infantry but one next-door neighbour was an ex-infantry sniper and physical training instructor, and on the other side was an intelligence corps officer who was an ex-engineer. I spoke to both of them and the ex-engineer said, "Look, if you want to get some qualifications, something that you can use in civilian life, then engineers would be the way to go." He mentioned all the variety and all the different jobs and roles that they do, so I decided to go for engineers.'

Jeff arrived at the School of Military Engineering for training in September 1989, having just turned eighteen. By March the following year, he had completed his initial training and had been taught how to build bridges and use demolitions 'and all that stuff that engineers do'. He was posted to the school of engineering as a corporal instructor in the mine warfare cell when he found out that 3 Troop were going over to East Timor in 2000 and they were short of crew commanders.

'I put my hand up and because I had the skills needed and the qualifications, so I got a posting up to 1 CER in Darwin, and then on to Timor. There we were doing one week on water point duties. The second week we would rotate through either construction of new checkpoints or building accommodation for the other battalion group or do road maintenance, rebuilding culverts and things like that— a variety of different little jobs with no real threat.

'It was exciting. You always want to deploy overseas and do your job in a hostile environment but it was good just getting back to the basics of field engineering. We didn't have a lot of the fancy stuff with us. We were doing pothole repairs and working at the water point but a lot of those jobs are disappearing and those sort of skills are being lost these days.

'After Timor, we just went back into normal training for conventional war. Then as part of 3 Troop we were deployed to Malaysia with a rifle company for three months. You go over there and you do your training for survival in the tropical jungles, and then do a combined training activity with the Malaysian defence force. It was good to take 3 Troop over there and be in another part of the world and do some really good training.

'Gradually, we were all working together in these little combat teams as part of the brigade, the engineers were getting more and more involved with the live shoots and probably being more accepted into the combat teams and all that sort of stuff.'

Despite all this, sappers were still being sidelined in major exercises when infantry and cavalry wouldn't wait for the engineers to do their jobs in real time. 'Sometimes it was frustrating. As engineers, we knew we could do the job probably to a better standard than what they're doing. Sometimes it came down to qualifications—we weren't allowed to have this qualification because of our employment category number—but we still got to do a lot of exciting things.'

Jeff had been promoted to troop sergeant, and after Malaysia he was sent on a disaster relief mission to Banda Aceh in Indonesia, in the wake of the Boxing Day tsunami of 2004. Apart from anything else, an insurrection had been brewing there for years and it was probably the least stable province of our northern neighbours. 'I was only there probably for two months. There were local rebels up in that area and we had a few occasions where people would come up and shake our hands, and say, "You are going to help us overthrow the government," and we would say, "No, we are not, we are here just to help out."

'Once or twice the Indonesian military were asking our guys to give them money. They don't get paid a lot and they don't get looked after like the Australian Defence Force. So things like food and extra money, they would generally just take it. But that was all sorted out— there wasn't really any time that we felt threatened from the local population. The locals knew we were there to help, so they were all pretty good when we were out working.'

Jeff had been an instructor at Duntroon Military College in Canberra for about two years, reaching the rank of warrant officer, when he learned that his RSM was about to be posted to the IRR at Holsworthy. That set him thinking.

'I'd just completed the EOD course, I was keen to use the new skills that I'd learned. I wanted to be able to test them out or use them in the way they were meant to be used. So we both got posted to the IRR and, because he was my RSM in the previous unit, we sat down for a career interview and I pretty much worked out the path I was going to follow. I always knew I was going to Afghanistan as soon as I got posted to the IRR.'

The IRR, which would eventually evolve into the Special Operations Engineer Regiment, supported special forces, like the SAS and commando units. This meant another level of training altogether.

'First of all we went through the six months reinforcement cycle, then we had to learn the special forces weapons and get qualified in them. We had to do a couple of vehicle courses, then there was a lot of shooting and getting all the right equipment issued and the fitness side of things. The first twelve months in the unit was pretty busy. I was familiar with most of the weapons. In my younger days we used the M16 [rifle] as well as the SLR [self-loading rifle], the special forces had the M4—very similar to the M16—but I never had a formal qualification in it from back in the day, so it was just going through getting that formal qualification with the M4 carbine and learning to shoot with the suppressor [silencer], different sights and systems. Then they had the Mark 19 automatic grenade launcher. That was the only weapon I hadn't used previously.

'We had our own training exercises, including fast roping from helicopters. It was a great way to spend my birthday—although I've forgotten which one—out at the airfield at Holsworthy, dangling under a helicopter and fast roping out of them. The training was pretty intense. It was good.'

When Jeff finally landed in Tarin Kowt, it was as part of an engineer troop that comprised three teams: one team to support the SAS, Jeff's team to support one platoon from 2nd Commando Regiment, and a third team to support another. There was also a team to help train the partnering force in search techniques.

Jeff's team comprised himself, as both EOD tech and team leader, his second in command (No. 2) who was an EOR tech, a No. 3 searcher, two sapper searchers and a dog handler. 'If we were doing ground assault force vehicle operations then my whole team would deploy with me. If we were doing helicopter assault force operations, the minimum we would go out with would be three: me, No. 2 or 3 and the dog handler. The group size all depended on how many seats I would be allocated in the helo.

'Towards the end of the tour, I was able to get more of my team-members out on patrol because we were starting to go to higher IED threats or larger markets to search. The troop commander was a captain, we had our own storeman and there was an admin corporal who ran the lab for fingerprinting and other forensics.'

The use of fingerprinting and how it was done will come as a surprise to many casual observers of the war. Virtually from day one, ISAF started building a database of fingerprints of suspected Taliban, as well as latent prints found on and, even better, inside decommissioned IEDs. In the field, each troop carried a portable unit that could not only take a fingerprint off a suspect but also check it against those that it already had on its database. If there was no immediate result, the troop commander always had the option of sending it back wirelessly to base, where it could be checked against a much larger database, although that took more time. However, the information gathered was vital in showing where bombs were coming from, how they were spreading and where they might be going next. They would also, if they got lucky, identify the bomb maker.

'Our lab tech would try to get fingerprints off certain items. If not, [the item] would then be sent to another facility in Kandahar. What we did was all about gathering evidence and gathering the data so you could actually work out their techniques, tactics and procedures. You could follow them on the map how they'd start off at a certain point in Afghanistan and then move up and then into Uruzgan province where Australians were. When people are captured they got fingerprinted and put on a database so if you found a weapon or some ID components and got a fingerprint . . . you could run that through the database. I know people have been captured that way—it was a very effective process.'

On missions with the special forces, however, evidence gathering wasn't the main game. The team had a specific job to do and the sappers' primary job was to get everyone in and out as safely and quickly as possible. 'The beauty of working with the special forces, you are never restricted to a track unless you're in vehicles and that was the only track you could go down. But on foot, we went everywhere. We all knew the choke points or likely locations that IEDs would be positioned. I'd always have an engineer up the front that would pick the path for the guys to travel. A lot of the commandos that I worked with had been on multiple trips so they had a very good understanding of where to walk, things to look out for.

'If we came across an IED, if we could bypass it we would. If we couldn't bypass it, that was where I would deal with it. If you're making your way into a hostile area and you didn't want to warn the people that you were coming and you couldn't bypass the IED we would defuse it. But the first thing you look at is, am I safe? Is my team safe? So fingerprinting and gathering evidence wasn't always the priority— the priority was to make sure it was done safely so nobody was killed. If you could do it in a way that you could get data or evidence from it, then you would, but most of the time you just find the main charge of the IED and you would attack that and just make it disappear.' In other words: BIP, or blow in place.

Soon after Jeff got back to Tarin Kowt the company he was supporting arrived: 'I'd worked with the platoon the previous year in all the lead-up training. All my guys knew the platoon, and the platoon knew me and my guys pretty well, so that was good. The idea was that we'd form something like a ready reaction force. If a high-value target popped up, on all the listening gear that we had over there, the intelligence agencies would alert us and we would quickly deploy with our vehicles out to that area to try to track him down and capture him. There were a couple of jobs like that around Tarin Kowt but they didn't really eventuate into anything.'

Often the team was deployed by helicopter and that was a trial in itself. They had to weigh themselves before loading onto the helicopters, so they could work out the fuel load and altitude depending on the prevailing weather conditions, and carrying lots of food and other provisions would significantly add to the weight. 'If we were out for several days the company that we were supporting would organise a ration drop. You would find a compound that was secure at night-time, and then they'd have a helicopter would come in and unload rations for you, or drop your backpacks off. The first mission out of town properly, we went up north and caught Chinooks in. There was talk on the radio as we were flying in that there were guys with RPGs seen running in the area. As we hit the ground one of the guys yells out "RPG!" and all the guys start running off in all directions to take cover, but it turned out to be a false report.'

After that, thankfully false, alarm Jeff and his patrol moved into the nearby villages, where their first priority was to search the bazaars or market streets, which could be 100 metres long.

'We would go through with the partnering force and interpreters, we would clear the shops and look for any hidden explosives, weapons or ammunition. We were also looking for components that they could use to make IEDs. Later on in our trip we would also be looking for opium—but that's another story. We'd also do data capture—people's names, fingerprints, all that sort of stuff—for the database.

'A lot of people would clear out. A few of the older ones would hang around, but a lot of the younger people would be gone. When they heard the helicopters coming in they would generally lock up their shop and leave. If we were suspicious about a place we'd get the interpreter to see if we could get keys to the ones that were padlocked. If not, we had the Afghan police partnering force and we would get the police to cut the padlock off, and then they would help us do a search of the area.

'One job up north, we searched the whole outer compounds and the main compound through the town, took down some details of the people, and then we rested up in one of them. We'd always go out with some cash and we paid these people so we could stay in their place for the night. The interpreter went down and bought lots of naan bread, and we spent the night there, and the next day we continued searching the whole area for any bits and pieces.

'That particular job, we searched a big graveyard and got a signal from our detector, and found a couple of components for making radio-controlled IEDs. We also found a couple of RPGs that had been hidden in the bushes next to a track so the Taliban could run down, get them out of the bush, fire them, and then use the track to disappear off somewhere else. And we came across rice-cooker containers that were full of homemade explosives; they had a bit of detonator cord coming out of them so they could tie that into an IED. All of that was just in one day.

'When we went through and we were searching compounds I would always start on a certain area, like the feed troughs. Every compound would have somewhere they would house animals and they would hide stuff in the trough and cover it over with mud to make it look natural. Where they stored their hay for the horses or their timber piles for the house was another good area to start.'

Searching for explosives, checking fertiliser, locating the components of IEDs—it was all about preventing the problem before it happened. Because, when it did happen—when an IED was detonated—as Jeff saw with his own eyes, the results could be devastating.

10

UNDER FIRE

In a war zone, sooner or later, someone is going to start shooting at you. And even as the Taliban's preferred tactics switched from fire-fights to carefully positioned IEDs, there was always the possibility—in fact, likelihood—that someone, whether it was a hardened mercenary who wasn't even Afghan, or a testosterone-bubbling teenager with a lust for glory, would have their gun sights on you at some point. In fact, a favoured variation of the Taliban's 'shoot and scoot' tactic was to plant IEDs, then start shooting to draw unwary troops into the blast zone.

Although the patrols never knew exactly what might happen on any given day, this didn't mean they would just wander out into hostile country to see what they might encounter. Far from it. In fact, recalls Jeff Newman, the planning for operations would be meticulous. 'We would be told that we are going to this area and we are going to target the bazaar in that area and that would generally be a couple of days out. So I would go to the IED database, I would look at the threat history of that area—so any IEDs or finds, if other Australian patrols had been there—and then I would put that component together and I would write the IED threat briefing as part of the orders.

'The platoon commander would do all the other bits and pieces of his orders, like how we were going to get there. The four team leaders, the platoon sergeant and the platoon commander would all sit in one room and we would write the orders package. Everybody would have a piece to put in. One of the team-leader sergeants would look after the manning of the helicopters. In the middle of the room there would be the big map of the area where we would be going. The platoon commander would first make out his plan and then we would write the orders to that plan and then I would go away and look again at the database and the IED threat for that particular area.

'When we started going into Helmand province, I studied what their tactics and procedures were for IEDs. For instance, in Helmand the enemy would often engage from a building that had IEDs buried around the compound that they were in, to try to draw you in. Once you were in the compound, that's where the IEDs would be used. Meanwhile they would have escape holes in the compound to allow them to get away.'

Once the detailed planning had been done, the whole platoon would come in and there would be a presentation of the orders using maps with military symbols showing where they were going to land and manoeuvre, and where the support elements would be. The intelligence corps would get up and give a report on what was known about the area and then Jeff would mainly focus on the IED threats. 'When we got into the field, if it was a low threat, myself my dog handler and my No. 2 would stay with platoon headquarters. If there was a higher IED threat we would push out or start with the lead fighting team that would be closer to the threat.'

But regardless of how much planning and preparation you do, nothing prepares you for the very first time bullets start coming in your direction. 'We'd been warned that the Taliban would pop off a few rounds then run away when we returned fire. It started off pretty light when we first got there because it was the back end of the winter so there wasn't a real lot of Taliban around, and they didn't want to stay and fight. But towards the end of May we were starting to get into the fighting season and it was then that we started to do more trips out of Uruzgan.

'Once, we were on a vehicle patrol just after Anzac Day in Kandahar province down near Shah Wali Kot. There was one road into the area we wanted to patrol. It was the only road in and out, so we knew it may have been targeted with IEDs. We sat and waited until a civilian vehicle came along. If there are civilian vehicles driving along the road then it's usually all good. So we tucked in behind this car, he was 200 metres or so in front of us and that's when I heard some pops.

'I didn't know if I was being shot at or what was going on—I was always in the cupola of the lead vehicle to identify areas to stop and search and I heard these three pops and I wondered what was going on. Then all of a sudden the vehicle in front exploded. It had run over an IED. That's when I realised we had just been targeted.

'The Taliban ran away and we just followed our drill. I sent Sapper Rowan "Robbo" Robinson and the platoon sergeant and medic, Sergeant Brett Wood, off to the flank to clear a way in for the medics to get into the vehicle, then I organised my other guys to go up and search an area for a helicopter to land.'

One of the hardest things for anyone—military or civilian—observing a scene like that is to resist the temptation to rush in and see if they can help. 'If they place an IED they may put other IEDs around to get the people coming to clear the site. So you're just clearing the way in for any secondary devices. The sapper has a mine detector and he's looking for telltale signs as well, so it's just a quick sweep, shoulder width to the vehicle and we generally use spray paint to mark the safe route in. It probably took him a couple of minutes because there's a lot of metal around the area from the car that's just been ripped to pieces. He's sweeping, but he's also looking for indicators that there may be something there, picking the safest route in for the medic.

'The vehicle had nine people in it, three males in the front and six women and children in the back seat. The three men, one woman and two kids died instantly but there was a young lady, an old lady and a three-year-old girl whose vital signs were still there and we got them onto the helicopter. I think they went back to Kandahar; the women died in the hospital but the three-year-old survived.

'I saw a lot of death and destruction, but this incident? I really thought to myself, *This is now, it's now real.* I felt that I was personally targeted, being the lead vehicle. And you think to yourself, *Could I have done anything to prevent this? Was there any more we could have done to help these people out?* But obviously there was nothing you could have done—they drove over the IED.

'Then you think back to the three pops that I heard and you realise that maybe that was the Taliban shooting at the civilian car to get them to stop. If they had stopped we would have driven around and hit the IED. But I remember when I heard those three shots the civilian car sped up—they didn't want to hang around.

'I worked it out to be roughly 20 kilograms of homemade explosives. The car was bent back on itself and the engine block was thrown 300 metres down the road. There was a battery pack under a rock in the bush, so I reckon they already had the IED planted in the road with the pressure plate and a cable running out to the battery pack. When they saw an army vehicle coming they can run down connect up the battery pack and quickly cover it over and run back and hide.' Unfortunately for the civilians, but luckily for Jeff and his crew, he laid up at the head of the convoy, waiting for a civilian car that they could follow. When it came, the Taliban couldn't run out and disconnect the IED or they would have been spotted.

The medic who initially treated the civilians came from the commando platoon headquarters team.

'Sometimes I couldn't always get my whole team out on operations with the commandos because of the limited number of helicopter seats so a lot of the time there was just three of us, then I'd rotate my guys around. One time in the Tangi Valley region of Deh Rawud, south-west of Tarin Kowt, it was just me and Robbo. He was as crook as a dog as soon as we got there. He had to duck behind a rock he was that sick, but he came good during the day.

'We were getting ready to head to the helicopter extraction point when we got contacted. We had Chinooks coming in to pick us up and there was a massive amount of fire that we were putting down. There were Taliban spotters in the mountain that were all shooting at the helos as well, everybody was shooting, the helicopters were coming in shooting, we had the attack helicopters flying above us and they were shooting and firing rockets.

'Amazingly, we had no casualties from that one and it was the first time a lot of us had been in a contact, so it was electrifying. You pretty much lived on adrenalin for the whole six-month rotation because every time you went outside the wire on patrol you always had that adrenalin pumping through you, trying to anticipate something or waiting for something to happen. It's hard to describe the feeling of when you come back from being in a gunfight. There'd be a sense of elation. The guys were walking around on an adrenalin high. They've just survived some combat. It's hard to describe how you feel!'

So what did they do to unwind when they got back to camp? Some would revert to sapper basics and help out with camp building and repairs. They didn't have to but it was good therapy after a stressful patrol. Others preferred to counter grim reality with vivid fantasy.

'A lot of guys would watch movies or fire up their laptops and play *Call of Duty* together,' recalls Jeff. 'It's just like the real thing, except when you are killed, you can hit the restart button.'

11

HOLDING GROUND

When Brigadier, then Lieutenant Colonel, David Wainwright, was told that he would be the third engineer in a row to command a task force in Afghanistan, he got himself on a plane to see for himself what the challenges were and plan how to deal with them. He immediately saw something was amiss.

'One of the challenges that RTF 2 had was that they were always organising combat teams on the job, which was difficult for guys in that you're working with different people all the time. It became clear to me that again the splinter team mentality [first employed by the Tunnel Rats in Vietnam] and the combined arms team approach was something I needed to have.'

Ironically, perhaps, the special forces teams had already sussed this out and operated as tight units where the sapper teams and the SAS and commandos even trained together, back in Australia. But there was an even more basic problem in RTF 2.

'I also saw sappers being changed around from a Bushmaster to the back of a Light Armoured Vehicle and then moving their gear back into a Bushmaster. It was messy and frustrating that the engineer combat teams didn't have their own vehicle. Each time they went out that would have added extra fatigue. I needed to be able to tweak my force to meet mission requirements.'

Those thoughts were doubtless reinforced when he received reports about the battle of Chora, that June, when a large Taliban force, estimated at over 800, surrounded and attacked the town of 3000 civilians at the head of the valley that bears its name. Dutch forces counterattacked with a massive artillery and aerial bombardment that lasted three days. Well over 100 Taliban and dozens of civilians died before the insurgents retreated to the mountains. During the fighting three police outposts were overrun by Taliban, who committed hideous atrocities against locals to force the survivors to fight with them against the coalition.

To give an idea of the political and tactical complexity of this battle (or any in Afghanistan), there are some reports that Rozi Khan, a local tribal militia leader, offered about two hundred of his fighters to help defend Chora in exchange for guns. The offer was accepted but only reluctantly as Khan was notoriously fickle with his allegiances and both the Dutch and local leaders knew there was a chance that sometime in the future he might turn the weapons on them. Australian troops, meanwhile, deployed in Baluchi valley to secure the key road there. The Baluchi Pass was the Taliban's equivalent of the Ho Chi Minh trail (in Uruzgan province, at least): a narrow, winding track that provided a supply line to the larger valley that connects Tarin Kowt to Chora. Despite winning the battle, there were obvious flaws in the Dutch task force's 'ink spot' policy of defending only large population centres, as, gradually, the Taliban moved back into the valley and re-established a foothold close to Chora.

Back in Australia, David Wainwright knew that he would be marching RTF 3 into Afghanistan later that year. His first thoughts harked back to the way sappers worked in Vietnam. 'We started doing the battle procedure and planning in understanding the problems we were going to face. In all the planning was the importance of combined arms training. I shaped the thinking, both through the engineer squadron commander and as the CO [commanding officer] of 3 CER in Townsville, using the premise of a splinter team commanded by a senior sapper or, where applicable, a lance corporal. In all the training exercises, particularly supporting the 1st Battalion and the 2nd Battalion, Royal Australian Regiment, I've always organised assets from the sapper regiment in a splinter team mentality using a combined arms team framework, so that you've got sappers, gunners, cavalry and infantry all forming the elements of a combined arms team to meet the demands of the battle space.'

As reported earlier, sappers were rarely if ever allowed to train in their true role even in the most realistic exercises, as that would have involved other troops waiting until they had cleared a route or removed a potential threat. 'It became too hard. Sappers doing proper battlefield procedural clearance took too long. It disrupted the activities for the remainder of the elements.'

In readiness for Afghanistan, Brigadier Wainwright devised four preparatory exercises. 'We called them Dingo exercises which we did at High Range with the complete force. I developed a baseline, which became two combat teams which I called Spear and Hammer.'

As its name suggests, Spear was predominantly a fighting force, heavy on infantry and cavalry with a combat engineer troop to provide mobility support as well as deal with IEDs encountered during manoeuvres. Bearing in mind that this was a Reconstruction Task Force, the idea behind a fighting force was to gain control of an area so that construction could be carried out reasonably safely.

'Spear's main purpose was to set the conditions to do construction,' he explains. 'Its main other purpose was to direct it to targeted population centres. And it also had intelligence aspects and where applicable, engineers who worked in construction. It was commanded by the infantry company commander from 2nd Battalion and the engineer troop commander out of the combat engineer squadron.

'Hammer was about building and meeting the demands of local people. We were looking at the needs or requirements in those targeted population areas to make a difference. This force was engineer heavy, had an infantry platoon for its protection and had its own cavalry. The combat teams needed to have their own organic fixed vehicle.'

With a combination of independent transport and cavalry-provided vehicles, appropriately qualified and experienced combat or splinter teams were able to move between Spear and Hammer to where they were most needed.

'There may be a break-in to an area required that we hadn't worked before. We would put a very heavy engineer element that would work with Spear to get the force to an objective. Once that objective was secured we would only need a lighter engineer footprint. What we did was to have the combat team on a short notice to move or move it to a task. We could move it to Hammer and sometimes the sappers could actually be doing building work. But, of course, we had the section or splinter teams ready to move at a few minutes' notice because they had their own vehicle.

'We wanted to break out of the Tarin Kowt bowl and really start looking to some key areas of importance, particularly in the Chora Valley. It was an area that from a political perspective was important to control. Previous RTFs had not been able to get into this area. There were movement restrictions and also from a combat power perspective, we had the ability to clear that area and then be able to conduct force operations there.'

There was an emotional as well as a tactical reason for wanting to take control of the Chora Valley: coalition forces were sick of being targeted by Taliban IEDs that were being used in ever-increasing numbers.

According to the website longwarjournal.org, Operation Spin Ghar (White Mountain) was the largest security operation launched in Uruzgan at that time, with an estimated 1500 soldiers drawn from Australian troops, the Afghan National Army, the Dutch task force special forces and the British-led Gurkha rifles.

The idea was to clear the Taliban out of the notorious Baluchi Pass in Chora Valley before winter set in.

'In the lead-up to Operation Spin Ghar we did a recon into the Mirabad Valley and Trooper David "Poppy" Pearce was killed by an IED that struck his ASLAV [troop carrier]—this was in an area we refer to as IED Alley. In the operation itself some weeks later Sergeant Michael Lyddiard, while trying to gather some information from what seemed like a relatively simple IED, was severely injured and as a result he lost one eye, the sight in the other eye was reduced, and he lost an arm and a couple of fingers in his left hand.

'In RTF 3 those two things were significant changes in the battle space. Poppy Pearce was the first fatality since 2002, when Sergeant Russell from the SAS was killed, and Sergeant Lyddiard was the most seriously wounded that we had had in some years, and certainly the first to survive whilst neutralising an IED. The combat team structure needed to respond to those challenges.'

Lessons had been learned from the battle of Chora, its build-up and its aftermath. Operation Spin Ghar was more than just striking back against the Taliban—it was about reclaiming ground and holding on to it.

'There is always a limit with combat power and I was conscious of examples in the past, in particular Special Operations Task Group [SOTG] Operation Perth in the Baluchi Valley towards Chora in 2006 was an activity that cleared the Taliban but because no ground was held by the force the Taliban very quickly regained the area after the Australian force had left. So our task was to hold and operate out of Chora, which at this time was pretty well Taliban dominated.

'I made the assessment—and I suppose it was more of a hypothesis than a plan—that I was going to always live in the field. This required that I needed to be ahead of the threat. I only allowed my forces to operate with overwatch, particularly with mobility threats. I had to use procedures that would not set a pattern that then would allow the Taliban an opportunity to adapt, allowing them to maintain overwatch. I had to maintain those areas that we held and as much as I could, live in the field. With Operation Spin Ghar we came up with a decent plan to actually take over Chora as it was essentially a tactical area of responsibility.'

Reinforcing the philosophy that this was very much a sapper show, Brigadier Wainwright gave that tactical area of responsibility to the OC of combat team Hammer, Major John Daunt, the engineer squadron commander.

'It shouldn't be lost [on us] that combat engineers or engineer commanders, be they lance corporals, troop commanders or squadron commanders, are combined arms officers and NCOs. This traditionally was an infantry task and there was some slight hesitation that there was going to be a sapper in command of this pretty challenging area, and you're going to live there. But the commander had a lot of support—he had infantry to patrol and protect, he had mortars, he had intelligence staff, he had his electronic warfare people, he had an ability to target and engage. So he had all those assets that a lot of our sappers don't have the opportunity to have under command. Having all these assets allowed him to do his job and he did it bloody well.

'I'm not too sure if there's been any follow-on examples of having sapper combat teams command forces of this size. I had a colleague from special forces who said that not many people would have taken the risk of having an engineer commander. My view is that it is not a risk—all engineers are trained in combined arms training.'

It was decided to take advantage of the win over the Taliban and the seasonal reduction in their activity to build a new forward operating base at Chora that the Afghan army could use when the summer fighting season rolled around again. Using about 100 local tradesmen and braving winter temperatures that dropped from minus 5 to minus 15 degrees Celsius, the FOB was ready for the spring. And, as one sapper noted, the injection of funds into the local community probably did as much for security as the tactical advantages the FOB offered.

'It is quite interesting in the way that all the planning for Spin Ghar at Chora was done by sappers and this FOB operated for the next eight years with the Australian forces mentoring the Afghan forces in Chora. It was held without any further interruption from the Taliban and is still held today.

'We handed over this FOB in March 2008 to a battalion size force of the ANA. The base was built to Afghan standards and built by the Afghan people. We named the base FOB Locke after Sergeant Matthew Locke, MG, SOTG, who was killed on 25 October 2007, during Operation Spin Ghar, approximately 2 kilometres from Chora, providing overwatch and clearance for the RTF as our forces went into that area.'

There is a bureaucratic aspect of military command that doesn't garner the same kind of headlines as derring-do in battle or brilliant tactical decisions—but it can lead to just as many grey hairs and sleepless nights. 'There was a private commercial company that was contracted to supply all our construction materials,' says Brigadier Wainwright. 'The problem was when they delivered they were always about four or five weeks late and at ten times the price of what the rural guys could get it for. So we got the supplies from the rural guys.'

Another aspect of this was that while the company could deliver into Tarin Kowt, there remained the logistical challenge of getting the supplies up to Chora. 'The rural guys delivered to the site, ten times cheaper and on time. In addition, if you can get things local, from local people, this actually helps your border protection. The contractor does have a role but not in this forward area. For good operational reasons, I decided to not use the contracted company. Having lost a lucrative source of income, the company sued the Commonwealth and so I was investigated because I had breached the agreement.'

The Commonwealth and the company were not too happy but the logic was impeccable. All subsequent rotations bought locally.

'In November we also went up near the Baluchi Pass and built another patrol base which was occupied by the Dutch mentoring the Afghan soldiers. And as we did the handover I looked up and saw a big sign that said: Patrol Base Lyddiard. I didn't know we were going to call it that but again, a bit of sappernuity there—they took it on their own account to sort of put a bit of a peg mark in the ground for their mate.'

Sergeant Michael Lyddiard was a sapper who survived a blast from an IED that he was attempting to dismantle (see Chapter 12). At that stage, he had been through treatment centres in Germany and had been repatriated back to Australia. That level of mateship within the Australian troops made the loss of one of their own even harder to take. This was particularly so with the death of David 'Poppy' Pearce.

'Losing Poppy was a significant setback for my team,' recalls Brigadier Wainwright. 'It is something you can't fully realise. Trooper Pearce was 40 years old—he was a bit of a mentor and a father to some of the blokes—so his nickname was Poppy. Nothing in our training had prepared us to lose a guy.

'Back in Tarin Kowt we got ready for a "wake". We didn't have the facilities so couldn't really do a full and proper wake for a fallen man.

Unbeknown to me two sappers spent the whole night making signs, "Poppy", for the front and back of the vehicle, which they dressed up for use as a hearse as a sign of respect. The "hearse" had to travel through Tarin Kowt base and then to the airfield.

'We put Poppy on a plane and sent him on his way to his family and then went back to our recreation area. This was inadequate; it was made from hardened shipping containers and had no spirit at all. It was un-Australian. The guys formed a little committee and said, we're going to turn our little rec area into something that will honour Poppy and be Australian.'

Over the next three weeks, working after hours, the blokes— using their almost magical ability to acquire resources and materials where none even seemed to exist—turned the rec area from shipping containers into an outback Australian pub.

'It had corrugated iron, timber that was sort of green, rubbed back and stained, and a nice beautiful hardwood bar—mind you, it was a pub with no beer. There was definitely a great bar there. A nice big photo there of Poppy, magazine racks, big TV, coffee machines, furniture, a small area to phone home, computers so people could get on the internet. It was like a home—it now had spirit. We opened it and christened it. The "Poppy" signs that the two sappers made for the hearse were installed at the two entrances to that rec area and from that time on it became known as Poppy's.

'Poppy's became the home away from home for sappers at Tarin Kowt from that day on. Christmas lunches were had, VIPs (including the prime minister) would talk to the troops there. We made sure that everyone understood that it was not just about Poppy, it was about all our fallen comrades—sadly, the photos of them grew and were put all around the walls.'

And the spirit of Poppy's in Afghanistan spread all the way back to Canberra. On 24 July 2014, the prosaically titled Tourist Café at the

Australian War Memorial Museum was renamed Poppy's in honour of Trooper Pearce and all Australian fallen in Afghanistan. 'Poppy's family were all part of the renaming ceremony together with the prime minister and others,' recalls Brigadier Wainwright. 'That restaurant certainly now has spirit.'

12

TAKING ON A TECH KILLER

There aren't many people on this planet who have arm-wrestled a booby-trapped bomb and survived. But then, Sergeant Michael Lyddiard is no ordinary soldier.

Michael joined the Australian Army on 23 May 1995. With a father who had spent two decades in uniform, specifically in the Royal Australian Electrical and Mechanical Engineers, he was obviously going to try to join a technical branch of the army.

'It was funny, when I joined I got told I probably wouldn't get into engineers but I remember seeing a poster of an Australian Digger searching a creek with a Minelab or something and to me that was the pinnacle of being an engineer, clearing the routes and things like that. I remember my father and his friends speaking very highly about the army and the meaning of mateship and ANZAC because they were veterans.'

But Michael did get accepted and thrived as a sapper. Six years later, he was sent to America where he was one of the first corporals to complete the American EOD course. When he returned to Australia he did a couple more years at 3 CER and then transferred to the School

Military Engineering for a few more courses before being posted to the IRR.

'I just kept specialising in that area and then I went to Timor in 2006 where I led EOD operations.'

Michael had risen to the rank of sergeant by the time he was sent over to Afghanistan to be part of the handover from RTF 2 to RTF 3 in September 2007. His sojourn in Afghanistan would be a lot shorter than he had imagined. 'We left early September and met up with RTF 2 so we did a lot of route reconnaissance. I tied in with the EOD cell there as well, and helped them out on a few tasks. My primary role was to be the combat engineer sergeant—an EOD light, as they referred to it at the time—predominantly helping with research and reconstruction and then if needed I'd do all the less demanding tasks if EOD was too busy or preoccupied.

'On the north side of Tura we had just finished building a strong point and we had two engineer sections with us. We flew in a third engineer section and the movement commander decided it was best if the ASLAVs and Bushmasters moved via the road around to the south of Tura while a company of infantry with a section of engineers and myself marched to the south, clearing villages and just sweeping through. The EOD heavy went with the manoeuvre command from the road. As EOD light I went with the ground force and we swept through the Tura Valley.'

The task was to search houses and compounds for weapons and explosives and then destroy them, usually by blowing them up. 'While we were dealing with our second cache, we had a report of an IED on the road to the south which was apparently near our strong point—that was the second IED that we were going to deal with. I got permission to go through and check it out and to render it safe. When that happened I called my No. 2, and two others: Adam Powell, a medic, and a guy called Tim Key as a handler.'

Michael's No. 2, then a corporal, now a warrant officer (whom we can only call WO2 W for security reasons) and his team met the platoon commander at the incident site. A couple of infantry grunts had spotted a battery pack and some wires coming from behind some rocks. Michael decided he was going to deal with the device himself and WO2 W advised him to send the others to look for combat indicators. Combat indicators are tell-tale signs of where an IED is likely to be, such as piles of rocks, walls, disturbed earth—anything that would suggest that there might be an IED.

'Adam said, "Yep, there's a marker here and a marker there." I identified a safe area to the No. 2, probably about 40 or 50 metres away in a building and then when we had our three and four come back we told them to go forward, search or isolate the area to make sure there were no command wires going in and to clear a safe lane to the IED.

'I didn't have any robotic equipment and I had no bomb suit. It's not realistic—I was on foot so I couldn't carry the friggin' thing. So that was pretty much about it. So everyone had cleared the area and I just gave orders and I went up to position my No. 2. I walked around from the west to the south and when I got to the south my intention was to walk down, stepping on the rocks, searching as I went, so I could get back to that battery pack. I found the battery pack, put a detonator on the wires and then pulled an M60 igniter, went back to WO2 W and did a controlled detonation on the battery pack and the wires. We assumed that had separated the battery pack from what was the main charge.

'I went back down the ravine to make sure the controlled detonation was successful, which it was, and then instead of walking back I said, "I'll just keep going along the same path, and try to search for the main charge." So I was crawling on my guts at this time. Obviously prodding, brushing and blowing through this hard ground and as you could imagine it was pretty fucken hard. Finally, I traced the wires to the main charge and I recognised it to be a TC/6 anti-tank mine.

'Then I started "quartering" the mine. It's a procedure that we do . . . I'll just leave it at that. So, I did the first quarter. There was nothing. I was very cautious, so it was prod, blow, brush and . . . it was so repetitive trying to blow and brush and just to make sure there was no anti-handling devices or secondary batteries.

'The second quarter, nothing. I was wearing my body armour, flak jacket, my neck guard, shoulder guards and my helmet. But it was so hot I had to take my helmet off. My goggles were attached to the helmet so now I had no helmet or goggles on.

'I got onto the third quarter, found nothing there, and when I got onto the fourth quarter, I noticed that there was a void next to the mine, because I was digging the ground out. I lifted a bit of dirt up, and it seemed like there was a rock or something in the way. I blew and brushed, and it exposed this void, and then, what I thought was, *I'll just gently stick this prodder in here and flick the rock out.* But as soon as I stuck my prodder in there it detonated. It all happened at once, I heard this massive explosion. It blew me probably about a metre back, and everything was black.'

WO2 W, who was Michael Lyddiard's No. 2, takes up the story: 'It was 2 November 2007—I know that date very well. So I know what we did that entire day, but it's sort of the latter half of the day that I can visually see, very clearly in my mind, and it's something that I go through a lot and think about every day.

'The mission was that we would move into this particular area and sweep through—obviously there's building clearance that needs to happen. It's not like us kicking in the doors and shooting people— it's a soft knock . . . and we would have a local soldier with us who would be the face that the locals would see when we come into their buildings. The buildings were probably 50 per cent occupied,

50 per cent unoccupied. The area had been through a number of battles in the past so I guess some locals were either killed, or they'd just had enough and packed up and left.

'We left from 1 Patrol Base up in Chora. Patrolled during the wee hours of the morning, went across the river and then began our ordnance search operations. Running my own section, we were focusing on searching these buildings for any caches of weapons or explosives. So we're doing all that—Lydds was off somewhere else and we were calling him when we found a cache and he would do his job as an EOD tech [blowing up the arms caches].

'And then he got the call in that one of the infantry platoons had found a possible IED and he had requested that I go with him and then I suggested we take a couple of sappers with us. So the four of us were escorted along to this other infantry platoon and we were married up with them and they gave us a run-down of what they had found.

'One of the guys that I didn't bring with me but in hindsight, I wish I had, was young Robbo Robinson. He was my combat first aider [CFA] and that guy had a very heavy first aid kit. He has drugs and he has all of that. Robbo, unfortunately he was killed on a later operation with SOTG—that's a different story . . . but in hindsight I wanted to bring him, because it turns out that although the infantry platoon should have had a combat first aider, or at least a combat first aid kit, they didn't.

'So we got down there on-site. Lydds and I had a bit of a discussion about how we'd approach this task. What we had was a couple of buildings with a sort of track that ran through the two, that sort of ran north–south. And then we had this little stone wall that ran east–west. I tasked the sappers with us to conduct what we call an isolation of that area. We'd received all the information that we could off the infantry that there was a battery pack there. But prior to Lydds going in to do his bit, I wanted to make sure that there were no foreign cables leading into it.

'And that's what I tasked the guys with—to do that isolation and then create what we call a safe lane—it's just a path for us to walk on, so we know it's been searched and it's unlikely that there will be any devices there. So, they did all that—that was Tim Key and Adam Powell. Powelly was one of my other medics and he did some good work with Lydds, post the incident. They've gone in, they've searched or they isolated that target and then searched out . . . and then it was time for Lydds to go in. So he followed the path that they had made for him. His plan was to get in there and confirm that it was in fact an IED and then take the appropriate steps.

'The time we spent down range was probably a couple of hours, which is a couple of hours too long. In hindsight what we should have done is confirm that it was an IED and blown it in place. But anyway, Lydds was in command and he did what he thought was appropriate and we agreed that the steps he took were fine, it just so happens that the IED that was in place there had an anti-handling switch on it. And when Lydds performed a particular function, then the thing went up in his face.

'I don't think it was the first time one was ever used in Afghanistan, but certainly for the region we were operating in it was. It was a TC/6 anti-tank mine and next to the anti-tank mine was a PPMISR, which is a Russian bounding mine, so you have a charge that shoots it up into the air and then another charge that detonates it, so it pretty much sends out a frag and belts a frag at about waist high.' This is similar to the American M16 jumping jack mine that killed so many Australian and American troops when they were recycled by the Vietcong from the Barrier Minefield in Vietnam.

'We found out later that it hadn't fully functioned and it had sort of been partially detonated. And the anti-handling switch was somewhere incorporated into the anti-tank mine, so in fact you had an anti-tank mine with an anti-personnel mine right next to it and the anti-handling device—that was the IED. We were all happy-go-lucky guys at that stage. But as soon as I saw that blast and I saw Michael flip onto his back, things sort of changed for me and I was straight in there. I was concerned about him. I ran in and thankfully he was talking so I knew he was alive . . . I can't understand how he is still alive because he's just received an anti-tank mine to the face pretty much.

'But he still did his drills right—he had his arms outstretched. That's how we train the diggers and that's one of the things that saved his life—he employed those correct rules. So I give him a pat on the back for that when I speak to him about it. He was flipped onto his back like you see on the movies. I'm pretty sure I shouted out "Medic!" A couple of guys came running in—one of those guys was Powelly.

'Although Lydds thinks I have pictures of that time, I don't have any pictures and I don't need pictures, I know exactly what he looked like. Starting from the top down, he was split from his scalp right the way down one side of his face on the right-hand side. And that's obviously taken out his eye and I could see his skull. There wasn't a lot of blood, cos I guess the heat and the dirt was holding all of that in. But his whole face was split like a melon, straight down the front.

'Yeah, so he was lifting his right arm and I said to Powelly, "Let's get a tourniquet on that." And Powelly was doing that. I was tending to his face and I was sort of half cradling him. We were talking to him and he was like typical stubborn Michael. He was like, "Ohaaargh, I fucked up." He was more concerned about doing the job wrong. He wasn't concerned about his own welfare at that point.'

From the moment his prodder triggered the anti-tamper switch, Michael was fighting for his life, even if he didn't know it. 'I could hear my No. 2 calling out for me. I could taste dirt and blood and all of this crap and I thought, *Okay, yeah, fair enough. I'm alive. It can't be too bad.*

And I was trying to sit up but I couldn't really do anything. My No. 2 was still calling out to me and he says, "Don't worry, everything is just coming." And I was just talking to him and as he was talking to me I was trying to tell him what happened because I thought obviously the worst and telling him what was going on.'

In fact, Michael was trying to tell WO2 W about the anti-tamper switch and kept drifting in and out of consciousness, each time repeating his warning about the device. 'When my No. 2 got to me I just kept telling him what happened. I got to my fourth quarter, stuck the prodder in, there was some form of detonation. I must have hit a trap and it blew up. And he goes, "Yeah." I didn't realise at the time that my head had been split open and the severity of it. But the medics were trying to maintain my composure; they were talking to me about it. I was telling my No. 2 but I just kept going over the same thing, I'm going, "Yeah, mate, that's what happened." I said, "Mate, I'm starting to feel the pain, I can't talk anymore." And he goes, "That's fine, talk through your foot . . . if there's too much pain you indicate one tap, if no, two taps." And I went, "All right. Two taps, no."

'So my No. 2 started talking about fishing and getting home and seeing the boys and as soon as he got on to fish, I told him I fucken hated fishing. Much later I remember blacking in and out but still talking to the guys about fishing and about the boys or my children. I also remember trying to tell them once again that this is what happened. I was just ensuring, saying, "Look, you need to double check." I told him the whole incident again.'

WO2 W recalls vividly that Michael was desperate to make sure other sappers were warned about the anti-tampering device. 'He said that and we spoke about it and I just said, "You've done nothing wrong." I don't know why I said that to him but I guess I was thinking to keep his mindset positive and don't let him go into shock and stuff like that. He wanted to let us know.

'Other guys were running in and I said, "Look, you know, we don't know what's over there—don't go over there." We had guys come in that were standing there like bloody infantry sentries. They just stood there a bit like stunned mullets. I didn't say anything. Powelly was putting a tourniquet on, we were getting some bandages around his face, one of the other infantry guys that came in, he was dealing with his left hand—that was all mashed up as well and just talking to him. And then I asked the infantry sergeant, "Where's your CFA?" He said, "We don't have a CFA." I don't know what I said to him, but I wasn't impressed.

'By the time there was a CFA on site and Michael received any drugs, it was probably about 40 minutes, so the poor bugger was in so much pain. I can't imagine being in his shoes—it would have been serious pain—but he stayed focused. We spoke about family and stuff, so that was that.

'Afterwards though we got him wrapped up, we got him on the stretcher and then the helicopter finally came in. It was like a running race—when you get to the end of it you just want to dry retch. That's what I wanted to do. Once I got him on the chopper it was just like I'd been through a marathon with him and I can't compare it to how it was for Michael, but it was certainly a shock to my system having to do that. I remember standing over him wanting to throw up, not because I wanted to be sick, but . . . I don't know what it was.'

By rights, Michael Lyddiard should not have been alive but he was hanging on. 'I eventually got some morphine and I remember being strapped down because I'd been blacking in and out due to the blood loss. I remember being strapped down to a door or something and then all I could feel was the downwind pressure of the chopper and being slid into it and then, you know, them saying, "See you, mate. See you at the other end." And then I pretty much blacked out in the chopper by the time I got back to Tarin Kowt. I remember being slid into a vehicle and a guy saying, "At least you're back here. Everything's good." And then I just went out. The pressure was off. And that's all I remember.'

While Michael drifted off into the blissful arms of morphine-induced sleep, WO2 W was dealing with the psychological trauma of what he had just witnessed. 'That has been the low point in my life and for the weeks following that I would cry of an evening, you know, when I was back at camp, not understanding why things had happened that way or, you know, what could I have done so that it didn't, and, I think, kicking myself in the arse. I wanted to blow it up so that it was just out of the picture. I could have pushed Michael more to do that but he wanted to find out what this thing was so we could put it in the intelligence chain. And I continually kick myself, but that was part of my job as a No. 2 for the EOD tech. I've got to motivate them, I've got to reassure them that what they're doing is the right thing.'

By the time WO2 W had a chance to reflect on what might have happened, Michael Lyddiard was already on a long journey home. 'By the time I got to Tarin Kowt [TK], I had all the morphine given to me and I was all blacked out,' recalls Michael. 'I was told, "You know, you've got back to TK, the only thing that saved your life was that you are fit." I got flown to Bagram [the largest United States' base in Afghanistan] after twenty-four hours, and they had to stabilise me. In Bagram they amputated my arm and hand. I then went to Germany for a week and my wife and parents got flown over by the defence force.'

Nobody had ever survived an IED blast like this before, so every day Michael lived was a bonus. For his part, he may have lost an arm, some fingers and an eye, but he hadn't lost his sense of humour, which was probably boosted by the powerful cocktail of pain-killing drugs he was being given. 'When I was in Germany the funny thing was I eventually turned around to my wife and said, "I don't know if it's working." And she goes, "What are you talking about?" I said, "I don't know if it's working. Can you have a feel or have a look?" She goes, "What are you talking about?" And I just said, "Just have a look and see if my cock's working." She was a bit embarrassed.

'The CO sent a good mate, Chris James, to Germany with me, so when he came in and he said, "G'day," and, "How's things going?" all I wanted to do was tell him again what happened at the site. It was funny—all I cared about was the guys. I wanted to make sure they knew what happened. Chris goes, "Mate, you've told this a hundred times before. We understand what's happened. You don't need to worry about it anymore." So, yeah. It was good.'

After the incident, once it was confirmed that the IED was a TC/6 anti-tank mine, which holds 6 kilograms of explosives, with a trip switch attached to a small battery to take out anyone who tried to deal with it, it was clear that but for a combination of good practice and luck, Michael would not have survived. The mine was designed to blow the tracks off tanks. Human flesh didn't even enter into the equation.

'There's a couple of things that saved my life. One is I did the drills correctly, I lay on my guts and then tried keeping as far away as possible.' Earlier in this book, Major Mark Willetts had said that by lying with your arms outstretched you'd barely scratch a fingernail if a device exploded, whereas kneeling over it, you would lose your head. He was right about losing your head but he may have been exaggerating for effect about only scratching a fingernail. The main thing is he was spot on about the prone position saving your life.

'Secondly, the ground was so hard it obviously deflected a bit of the mine away from my body. And three, the mine didn't fully explode. My understanding from what I was told was that it detonated, but not the way it was meant to detonate, and at the same time, it's very likely that some moisture got in there and instead of 6 full kilograms going off it could have been only two or something like that.'

The sappers found about six anti-personnel mines in the area around the main charge, suggesting that this was more than a simple anti-tank mine. It had been set to take out a vehicle, for sure, but it was also intended to deal, in some way or another, with anyone who tried to defuse it.

'I only just lightly put that prodder in there to get that rock out. It must have hit a pressure switch. It's like a red or black push button like you can buy from Dick Smith . . . I must have just hit that. The idea of that switch was to kill a tech. Any booby trap or any process that's built into a mine or any booby trap it had attached, is a tech killer. It's there to harm or to kill the first responder or the technician trying to dispose of it.

'The IED would have had a pressure plate or something attached to it. Which is why I disconnected the battery source. Unless it had a second one somewhere, it shouldn't have functioned so then I just had to find the main charge and find the pressure plate. The next thing I came across was the main charge [the mine] where there was a possible booby trap or secondary source, which is why I was still being so careful.

'There's a lot of people asking why I didn't just blow it up. Why didn't I put it in a controlled detonation and just blow it? But we were there to identify mines or identify the threat—identify what type of IEDs they had. So to me, we had all the time in the world. It was only just afternoon when we started. This was an opportunity to get intel. Unfortunately the intel that I got handed me my arse, but good things came from it.

'I'm not blaming anyone, and I haven't asked any questions since but RTF 3 were never given any intel or any reports of there being booby traps on any mines, any switches or anything. The only threats we had been given were about pressure plates, and a bit about low metallic content IEDs and anti-personnel mines. We were never told about a switch.

'From my understanding the weapons intelligence team within Kabul was aware that there were booby traps being used but I don't know if they knew they were being used in Tura or in Kandahar. By the time my incident finished they were definitely aware of that booby trap and how they were drilling it in and what the battery sources were, because they identified there was a 9-volt battery that was the secondary source.'

For Michael Lyddiard, lying in a military hospital in Germany, the war in Afghanistan was over but a whole new set of battles lay ahead of him (see Chapter 29). WO2 W, meanwhile, was dealing with the fall-out from having been present at two of the most devastating incidents in the whole of RTF 3's time in Tarin Kowt.

13

THE HORROR OF WAR

WO2 W, who is still serving with the Special Operation Engineer Regiment, saw a lot in his three rotations in Afghanistan—possibly a little too much. The first time, as described in the previous chapter, was as a combat engineer corporal in RTF 3, and the second and third times, in 2010 and 2012, were as an EOD tech sergeant as part of the Special Operations Task Group.

'I guess as a child of a former defence member I romanticised . . . going off to war, a lot,' he says. 'I know when I first arrived or before even getting there, we were all super excited. It wasn't my first deployment but it was certainly my first war deployment. We'd received all the briefs but nothing compares with what your eyes tell you—what's out there in front of you.

'And as we arrived there were the smells as well. That initial piece isn't too much of a shock. It's when you get out and about—out in the boonies—and you experience it for what it really is. That's where it really opens up for you I guess. I arrived in summer but I was in transition in the winter so I got to experience both extremes. The heat, the putrid smells over there, human faeces and everything else: it's not like the smells back home.'

With RTF 3, WO2 W was an engineering corporal section commander and his main job was to search for, identify and dispose of certain kinds of munitions. As engineer section commander, he was also in charge of a high-risk search team providing mobility support to all the other troops moving around the area.

'Because we're combat engineers, we also do infantry level patrolling, so we have to search all the way up to wherever we were going. Once we arrived, we searched the site and made sure there were no IEDs or leftover ordnance. Then we would either go out on patrol with the infantry platoons or alternatively we would stay in that location. Also, as part of RTF 3 we did a lot of construction. So we would assist our other engineer buddies—the tradies—by helping them build the patrol bases.

'We spent a shitload of time outside the wire. The furthest north we went was Chora, over 30 kilometres to the north. Now, it may not seem a great distance, but when you are searching all the way for bombs, it's a considerably large distance. That would take us a day, if not longer, to travel that distance. We found some IEDs as part of our rotation but I guess because it was the third rotation for conventional forces, they were not there in as prolific numbers as I experienced on other rotations later on.'

'Life was tough outside the wire, and while it was good to get back to Tarin Kowt it wasn't exactly easy street either. Camp life was okay. The thing we didn't like was when we would spend weeks on end out on patrol and then come back and we would get a rough time from the RSM. He wanted us clean-shaven and all looking smart by the next mealtime. There was no, "Welcome back, you've done a good job." So the guys didn't appreciate the lack of pats on the back that maybe could have come from the senior staff.

'Colonel Wainwright—he was at the opposite end of the scale. He would always be proud of what his guys did, so I've got a lot of time for [now] Brigadier Wainwright—he looked after his boys, he was concerned for their welfare. There were some other individuals who rubbed it in a bit. Generally, though, camp life was good. Everyone got to experience some Dutch food and working with other nations. The Dutch are really a crazy bunch of bastards.'

Outside the wire, the sappers were also building patrol bases so that, as Brigadier Wainwright explains, they could hold an area rather than just drive the Taliban out only for them to creep back in as soon as coalition forces returned to base camp.

'We did some really good work. We could see the changes, like building patrol bases. And, going down to the shops to buy the locally made naan bread, we could see that we were welcomed by some, given the stink-eye by others. But I think we were there doing a good thing.'

However mobility assistance—making sure roads were clear of IEDs—was still a huge part of their job. It was also the source of one of the most troubling events in WO2 W's entire career. 'Most people would consider a memorable moment as like a highlight. I've got some memorable moments, and one in particular that was probably a low point in my life. We had come into [the] country. We'd only been there for a couple of weeks [when] we went out on what we called our handover patrol, which involves the last rotation showing us how they did things [before] they hand over to us. We'd just moved into a position in an area known as IED Alley and I had deployed some of my search team forward of our lead vehicle to conduct a search so that we could search a path for all the vehicles to get through. A couple of cavalry vehicles thought they would push around us, unbeknownst to us. They were down in the low ground, we were on the high ground, and unfortunately they hit an IED and that resulted in the death of David Pearce (see Chapter 11).

'Poppy was driving the ASLAV and it was hit by an anti-tank mine—just a single anti-tank mine but it got right in the sweet spot, where there was a join in the vehicle. That was enough to split it and when you get a blast, it's all about the sudden expansion of hot gases, and those hot gases were pretty much what killed him as opposed to any of the frags from the mine or from the vehicle. Not a good way to die—but a painless death, one might say.

'And why I say it's a low point—yes, one of our soldiers has lost his life, but it wasn't just that. It was then I had to send more elements of my search team to go down and I sent one of the guys into the back of the APC to confirm that he was dead and he surely was. We then tasked the guys to search around the vehicle so that we could bring in the medical support to assist the other injured guys while also allowing a greater area to keep that security posture whilst we dealt with the casualties in the vehicle.

'I was there doing part of my EOR job and that's to do post-blast examination and collect what evidence we could so we can find out who's actually put this there. We got the guys out of there and we recovered the vehicle. We recovered Poppy's remains.'

There are elements of that scene that haunt him to this day, so much so that he has only spoken about them to one or two people. 'Being exposed to one of your mates spread across the battlefield is one thing, but that . . . it was a bit rough to deal with and I think about it at times. But I think I got over it.'

WO2 W and his team were nominally in combat team Spear but they occasionally hooked up with Hammer, if needed. That meant they were under an infantry company commander and then platoon commanders. 'We were to some degree attached to infantry platoons but we still had our own tasks as well. There was myself, as section commander, [and then] I had my No. 2, I had a dog handler, and then I had all my sappers, who were high-risk researchers, but I gave them my own specialist roles. So one was my combat first aider and one was my signalman and then you've got the gunners, the riflemen and so on.'

Unfortunately for WO2 W, in the early days he had a run-in with an officer who would be his platoon commander for most of his tour. 'We carried on with the operation and completed some really good tasks and went out to different areas. We did some crazy jobs, too, and there was one that we just refer to as "around the world" where we all got in a big convoy and drove all around the Tarin Kowt bowl.

'I'm not sure what the intention was but on that particular trip we got some intelligence through to say that there was an IED. So we had pulled up and I got called forward and asked where the IED was. This officer—he was a bit arrogant if you ask me—said, "Yeah, well, you see where I'm kneeling? That's the grid reference we've been given." I'm thinking, *Well, you're an idiot to start with*, although I didn't say that to his face. So we got out and we took a step back, and said, "Well, alright, we'll start searching from this point back." Because it was the lead-up to what we call a vulnerable point.

'We started searching and had been going for about 20 minutes— we hadn't even got into the vulnerable point—and this officer suddenly said, "Everyone back in the vehicle, we're driving through." When I got over my shock I got on my personal radio and said, "We're not getting back in. We are searching this route, based on the intelligence."

'Anyway, to cut it a bit short, he and I had a confrontation where he was threatening to charge me and I pretty much said to him we'd see if it stood up when we got back to base. If you receive intelligence to say that there's a device there and that the locals are avoiding the area, you put two and two together and there's the potential that there's a device there. I ended up handing over to one of my mates who was search commander and he took the task. But it was just a silly thing and I never got along with this particular infantry officer after that.'

It's worth noting that in subsequent rotations, whenever an engineer search team was out looking for IEDs, they were in charge and the whole group, whatever the rank of the others there, just had to wait until they were done. 'We are forever re-educating. It's not the sergeants and corporals who have experienced rotations, or the grunts, it's the up-and-coming gung-ho officers who think they know it all and don't take the advice of their soldiers. The infantry, they look for the shooters. We look for the bad stuff in the road . . . that's what we're out there doing. That's why people [might not] answer to us, but they should be taking all of our recommendations seriously.'

Just as sappers learn to read the signs of where an IED might be, infantry notice telltale signals that something may be afoot in the local populations. 'We got into a couple of scraps over there and there was one fairly significant contact. It was whilst a patrol base was being constructed. So, if you can imagine the patrol base in the centre and we've got an outer cordon of protected posture. We could see all the women and children were leaving the area, so we re-oriented our posture and everyone was on a more increased stand-to, if you like. It was about dusk that the first shot rang out and the whole contact lasted probably a couple of hours.

'We were on a finger—or a little rise, if you like—and we were engaged from lower ground. It was a serious contact with RPGs and small-arms fire, although we were in big armoured vehicles. We did have troops out on the ground but the insurgents were certainly brave to go up against us, although obviously they're hiding behind vehicles and buildings.

'There were certainly plenty of them that we killed . . . we could get KIA [killed-in-action] reports through the thermal imagery of some of our armoured vehicles. I was too far away to see an individual, but I could see their muzzle flashes, where they were firing from, so that's what I was firing at. And we could hear the radio chatter of the cavalry guys saying, "Yep, we're on target, 300 metres, or 200 metres, slight left," or whatever, giving their target indications to each other. Where they were shooting, we would zero in on that position and then you could see the muzzle flashes from there.

'None of our soldiers were injured during that contact, so that was good. The boys were giving each other pats on the back in the back and saying, "'Job well done." We stuck it to the enemy and they didn't harass us again for a while.'

When the sappers were back in camp, the engineering aspect of their trade came to the fore again. Kamp Holland was still under construction and there was plenty of work to be done. 'It wasn't all about just sitting around on your bum—we still had jobs to do and one of those jobs we wanted to do was build some concrete footpaths. It was snowing, so we wanted to stop mud getting all over our boots and into our lines. So we started doing these concrete paths.

'We had this one particular section that we were just trying to get right because it was frequented a lot and we didn't want any trip hazards there. So we poured the concrete and we let it sit there and I think we went off to grab a bite to eat or whatever and, being . . . cold, the concrete wasn't setting as fast as it should. We came back and somebody had come and put graffiti in the concrete. And this happened on a number of occasions and we figured it out—it was the Dutchies who were doing it. So we sort of put up a bit of a barricade there and we were having a bit of a laugh with each other. It was all friendly there: we were just trying to do a good job and they were giving us a bit of a hard time.

'I wouldn't say it petered off at any point of time, not even towards the end. We were working all the way through. I remember, it was early January we had the opportunity to go for ROCLs [leave]. It's R&R, so you could either go back home to Australia or you could go to a destination like Germany and then you pay your own way from there. I chose to go back home. At that stage I had a young son who was ten years old back then. So it was a good surprise for him, I didn't let him know that I was coming home. I grabbed him and then we both flew up and visited my parents so that was a good surprise for them. Good down time. My mother was a bit reluctant to let me go back, though.

'The rest of January and February we were flat-strap on RTF 3. We did a significant amount of work and got all of the equipment for these patrol bases out there. We searched our way in, we built these patrol bases and then we searched a way out. All the grunts had to do was sit there and look pretty and make sure no one took pot shots at us. If we compare it to other RTFs, don't get me wrong—they did a lot of work, but we certainly opened up the Tarin Kowt bowl. We'd certainly gone further than the previous two RTFs had been.'

14

CLEAR, HOLD, BUILD

By the time LTCOL S—now commanding officer of the Special Operations Engineer Regiment—arrived in Afghanistan in late 2007, the base in Tarin Kowt was really starting to take shape but it was also expanding quickly. About 1200 Dutch troops were based there, plus up to 800 or so Australians, and they all had to be housed, fed, watered, trained and, occasionally, rested. And there were more on the way. LTCOL S was there as a captain, battle adjutant, for RTF 3 under CO now Brigadier David Wainwright. But part of his job—as with any sapper—was to help build stuff, in this case, the expansion of Kamp Holland, which had been set up by the Dutch, the major partners in this local alliance.

'Kamp Holland was fairly well established at that point but I worked with Jed Egan from 19 Combat Engineering Works, getting the salvage from the special forces compound there at Camp Russell, to expand it to put a fence around the airfield and increase the security and the like.' Camp Russell was a separate but adjacent camp for special forces members, named after Sergeant Andrew Russell of the Special Air Service Regiment and a former sapper, the first Australian to be killed in Afghanistan, in 2002.

'By the time I got there, Kamp Holland was very, very comfortable, with room power, full reticulation of water and sewerage, toilets and that kind of thing. This was all created in blast-proof portable containers, which were a good little solution.' These portable containers, otherwise known as Containerised Living Units, arrive on site with electrical and plumbing connections already in place. They are based on shipping containers which, believe it or not, were actually an Australian Army invention dating back to the Second World War and quickly adopted by America, and then the rest of the world. So building an Australian military camp from adapted containers is really just completing the circle.

'There were gyms and workshops and vehicle store storage yards and all that kind of good stuff but the Afghan base was still in development. There was only about a battalion minus [less than 800] I think there on that first rotation and then when I was back a few years later they were up to a full brigade size [about 2000].'

The numbers varied over the years and later on the Australians would outnumber the Dutch as they gradually withdrew and the Aussies expanded their commitment. LTCOL S's main job, when he was a captain and 2IC of the squadron, was to liaise with the Dutch, especially if there was an incident or enemy contact, to make sure everyone was on the same page. It's a challenge in any combat environment, especially with a language barrier, but the Dutch made it as easy as possible.

'The Dutch were actually a good crew to work with. They were very similar to us in terms of European nations. The Dutch were the Australians of Europe in that they had a pretty good sense of humour. They were serious when they had to be but didn't take themselves too seriously. They were always ready to provide help where they could; for instance, the artillery was Dutch. The Dutch supported us when the guys were in contact. The aeromedical evacuations [medivac] at the rotary wing [helicopters] was mostly Dutch. When our guys were injured in IED strikes they'd provide that support. The hospital was Dutch. Essentially they were running the camp and we were guests in that part of Kamp Holland.

'We provided some engineer support to help maintain the camp, which was just sparkies and plumbers and carpenters and that kind of thing, but they essentially had ownership. In fact, they had ownership of the entire area of operations as well, so Task Force Uruzgan was commanded by a Dutch colonel. Eventually, the top job was elevated to a brigadier general and they were essentially the brigade headquarters for Tarin Kowt. There was a Dutch battle group there and they were also commanding the Provincial Reconstruction Team.

'We had an Australian engineer element in there as well, which would do the design and contract management for works that were completed by Afghan contractors in and around the town, to provide that sort of more enduring infrastructure to schools or the government. I think we built maybe one mosque but it was mainly schools, hospitals, power, bridges—key infrastructure.

'There was a team of two Afghan engineers we worked with in the provincial government—Kambir and Hashim—and they were essentially the municipal directors for Uruzgan in terms of facility roads, irrigation and that kind of thing. We worked through them to help establish what the priorities were and where we could work. Obviously we had to balance the tasks they wanted done with areas where we wanted to get some influence to help support the security side of things.'

The planning also tended to favour projects that would have a low maintenance liability and so have less chance of failing. 'If you were to build a coal-fired power plant it would fail, where something like a bridge or a road has a lower maintenance and it's easier to get it done and it's harder for the Taliban to fight a battle saying that the coalition and the government aren't providing you any support because they have provided you with a white elephant. Something like a road is enduring and when you put it in, it's there for everyone to see and you can demonstrate progress.'

However, the Afghans were understandably cautious about throwing their support 100 per cent behind anyone, least of all, foreign invaders. 'There's an anecdote that there was one family who had three sons and one joined the police, another joined the Afghan National Army and the other one was in the Taliban, so they covered all bases depending on who was in power. To be honest, in Uruzgan they weren't too concerned about broader politics in terms of what was happening in Kabul, it was all mostly local and tribal issues which then could be used by Taliban to exert their influence.

'You had two main tribes. You had the Pashtun community of the Ghilji and the Durrani. That was the main split and the Taliban were more aligned with the Ghilji. In some places you had Ghilji and Durrani living next door to Barakzai, or Durrani tribe living next door to each other. There would be feuds over water, for instance, going back generations and the Taliban would take sides and use them to gain support. Clearly, that was exacerbated by the coalition when we went there; we aligned ourselves with Durrani because the Taliban were aligned with the Ghilji. There was a period where the Durrani were nominating their tribal rivals as terrorists so the coalition forces would search for them. That then created a lot of animosity.'

The army had to be careful about where they constructed projects because it was easier to do them in pro-government areas as the security was better. But that just added fuel to the argument that one tribe was being discriminated against.

'That would then further marginalise the Ghilji because they were getting support from the government. "How come we're not getting any services and that kind of stuff from the government which is supposed to be supporting us?" So you'd go into that area but then you have to deal with the Taliban who were more prevalent there.

'That was the whole point of the RTF. It was that you could go into those areas which were a bit more hostile and start to get some security infrastructure in place which would then allow contractors to be able to work there. So the works team were providing more of a civil works structure [rather than building patrol bases] which was the broad plan of the RTFs.'

Military planners talk about the three phases of insertion into an area: clear, hold and build. 'So you want to clear the enemy influence and hold that and then start to build services of support, not just physical things but also getting the doctors and the police and all that kind of stuff to provide things that you and I would expect as a normal part of services that government provides for the population.'

The practicalities of this involved sending combat troops into an area to engage the enemy and drive them out, then build patrol bases so that a permanent force could safely be stationed there, making it harder for the enemy to come back in, then using the protection afforded by the patrol base, start building infrastructure for the locals. In short, after the 'clear' phase it was largely about building.

RTF 3 pushed up and established patrol bases in the valleys surrounding Tarin Kowt, including the Mirabad Valley, along the notorious IED Alley. 'Moving through there you'd always get in contacts and so they moved up into a patrol base there. They had Afghan forces in there which were being mentored by the Dutch and we had Australian Forces working out of there too. When I came back on the second tour they had a marketplace in there, and a police station, and you could pretty much move with a fairly high degree of assurance, apart from nuisance IED events, all the way up to Tura.

'That only worked because you've got someone in there to establish that security presence and then the population would feel more secure in engaging with you. People would see the advantage of tacitly supporting the government in that area, or at least not directly opposing them. That would then allow people to be less inclined to let those Taliban elements or insurgent elements back in.'

And that is the reality of dealing with a popular insurgency, says LTCOL S: the enemy is right there under your nose but they aren't behaving like your enemy until you give them the leeway to do so. 'The thing with an insurgency—and we would have seen it in Vietnam—[is that] an insurgent will put down his weapon and he becomes, to all intents and purposes, an old farmer, and you reckon the area is clear. So you wander off and then send other people through and that guy will pick up his rifle and shoot whoever was coming in behind to provide that support.'

A major part of LTCOL S's job was to liaise with the Dutch and he says it was mostly a myth that they rarely ventured outside the wire. 'They didn't have the broad-based engineer support that we had. They were primarily combat engineers there to provide that mobility support with IED search and clearance to allow a battle group to go around and do more of a clear. People like to throw shit at the Dutch—I guess it's just like Queensland and New South Wales rivalry—but we weren't always the best coalition partners either. If we didn't think an operation was working or we didn't think it made sense we'd call the national command and say, "No, the guys back in Baghdad and Dubai said they don't want us to do this mission. So, we're not going to do it." So our record wasn't squeaky clean.

'There was a degree of tension and it was really down to personalities and the relationship between the Australian task force commander and the Dutch task force Uruzgan commander. So we would provide some sort of local direction along the lines of, "Don't go here during these days because we're going to be here doing something." No worries. But a lot of the times the tasks we were getting from command headquarters in Baghdad and Dubai, made little sense. We should have been more aligned with the Dutch.

'My biggest challenge was just mainly managing personalities between our ops room and the Dutch as it was just important to have a good working relationship with whoever was running the whole brigade operations in the area. That meant if we needed something they would have it there on call, ready for us to use, and vice versa, looking for anything we could provide as support for them. Like I said, the Dutch sappers were there primarily for the mobility support and they would have a construction element which would come out from Holland periodically.'

As mentioned previously, many sappers felt frustrated that they were being prevented from dealing with IEDs in the most obvious, and possibly safest way, by a simple BIP. LTCOL S had a lot of sympathy for the combat engineers' point of view, but he could see both sides of the story.

'It depends on how you look at it and dealt with it. You also look in terms of what we are trying to get out of that. So, an IED is obviously enemy action and with enemy action you can get some good intelligence, so the gold solution is to get an EOD team forward to defuse it, so they can recover all the components, bring it back and they can start looking at how it's built and how we can defend ourselves against it. Then they can start talking about weapons technical intelligence. So they can look at things like how the circuit board was built, which will give an idea that this circuit board was built by the same guy who built another circuit board. And then if we find IEDs here, here, here and here with a similar circuit board, then we find another one here, and they were all built by the same person, that means that there is some sort of logistics . . . where someone is making the circuit board somewhere and they are then being distributed out.

'The weapon technical intelligence guys would look at a circuit board and how it was made and look for signatures: your handwriting has a distinctive style, so does soldering. So they would know if two circuits were soldered by the same person. They could get fingerprints off the tape on battery packs and match them. Then when our guys went back into that area and saw a bunch of fighting-aged males, they'd essentially put them through on a fingerprint detector which would take their fingerprints.' If the prints were on the database of the portable units, the sappers could get a hit immediately.

'So the last part of the action would be to destroy the device. Prior to that it is to attack the network. So if you can attack the logistics chain and find out where it's being made or how it's being transported then you can undermine the network more successfully. That's why the best solution is to get the EOD tech forward. If you can't get the EOD forward, and the mission is time sensitive, then you've got options of mark and bypass and just leave it there as long as it isn't a threat to civilians.

'With an IED, you've got to find the main charge which is obviously the key threat. You could dispose of that and then there's often a risk of secondaries and anti-tampering devices and that kind of stuff. An EOD is ideally in a special suit, which gives him a bit more protection. Or, even better, he's doing it through a robot, so if something does go wrong and something gets blown up, they're a hundred thousand dollars a pop but it's better to see a robot blown up than a sapper hurt.

'So it's down to the mission and the sapper should be able to do it to allow them to provide that mobility assurance but they require a lot of training to do it. In terms of the prevalence of IEDs, it was dependent on the area and also seasonal as well. So you'd find in the poppy season when it was being harvested, often it would be low because everyone was too busy harvesting poppies I suppose, not putting IEDs in there.'

As the seasons came and went, and the various task forces did too, the threat from the Taliban also evolved, as did the main focus of the Australian troops. The Reconstruction Task Forces now had a new word in their names—'mentoring'. The goalposts had been nudged slightly, to formally introduce the idea of passing on skills to the Afghan security forces.

But for one wing of the Australian troops, the tasks remained largely the same—find the enemy and capture or kill them or, at the very least, disrupt their activities. That was the job of the special forces and their sappers were never far from the action.

Previous page: Australian forces, including sappers, on patrol in the *dasht*.
Top: Brigadier David Wainwright handing out certificates to trade school graduates.
Below left: An Afghan student learns the basics. *Below right:* A sapper supervises an Afghan contractor to ensure his building methods are up to scratch. (All photos provided by the Department of Defence except where noted)

Top: A foot patrol leaves the Hesco-built patrol base of Camp Lyddiard.
Below: Transports, ancient and modern—ASLAVs overlook a camel train in the *dasht*.

Top: Sapper Brenton Keemik with explosive detection dog Aussie on the job in the Mirabad Valley region.
Below left: Warrant Officer Jeff Newman disarms and investigates an IED.
Below right: Sappers clear the way for a patrol.

Top: A special ops team is extracted by a Russian-built DEA helicopter.
(Photo from Jeff Newman)
Below: Weapons, explosives and opium found in a village search.

Top: A *shura* between senior officers and local leaders in the Mirabad Valley.
Below: Winter in Tarin Kowt . . . Bushmasters and an ASLAV in the snow.

Top: The presence of a 'fighting-age' male means even a donkey is worth double checking. *Below left:* A special forces platoon makes painstaking progress through Chambarak Pass to Helmand province. *Below right:* Corporal Shane Potter with his Afghan Police off-sider. (The two photos below are from Shane Potter)
Overleaf: An infantry sniper provides overwatch cover for RTF 3 patrols in the valley below.

15

ALL CHANGE

While the Reconstruction Task Forces were arriving and leaving every six months, special operations teams were rotating in and out on much shorter, more intense tours of duty. SGT T (whose name is protected for security reasons) was in Afghanistan three times—in 2007, 2009 and 2013—attached to commando troops each time. In between, he would go back to Australia for more training and return with a new skill set, ready to face a different set of challenges. But first, he joined the sappers, almost by accident, lured by one very simple attraction. 'The recruitment officers said, "Why don't you be an engineer?" I didn't even know what an engineer was but they said, "Well, you're pretty much a grunt but you just blow shit up." I was pretty happy with that so I joined.'

All joking aside, SGT T's family had a military history and he had always wanted to be in the army too: 'I had a grandfather in the First World War and three uncles in the Second World War. My dad was in Vietnam but he was a reservist who was an instructor at the time. He was part of a New Guinea volunteer office in the Australian Army and he went across just for a month or so as an observer but he had a pretty long career in the military. Originally I wanted to join infantry because I didn't know much about it . . . I was nineteen and needed to get a job.'

Following SGT T's path through three rotations illustrates the range of challenges sappers faced as the various task forces evolved and changed. Despite his fondness for blowing things up, SGT T started his deployment in Afghanistan in a role where explosions are the last thing you want. 'I was a combat engineer searcher the first time around, and for the second tour I was a 2IC for my mobility survivability team [MST]. An MST—at least, when I was in Afghanistan initially—was one EOD tech, one EOR tech, two sapper searchers and a dog handler. Later on we reinforced the MST with two additional sappers, so in total there were seven.'

The MST went out with commandos, with its members divided between assault teams. 'It all depended on whether we were conducting a road move, a ground-based move or an air move so, especially before we started to gain air assets, we were moving around by vehicle in a mounted role. The MST would be the lead vehicle in the convoy and we were tasked with providing mobility support to the platoon or company so in other words, getting them from A to B. We would be at the front searching likely vulnerable points or anywhere that the team leader would assess there was likely to be an IED. That's from a mounted role.

'In a dismounted role, once we had occupied a vehicle drop-off point and we were infiltrating into target, or we were moving via air, we split into our call signs and for every commando team there would be one engineer attached.'

All the sappers were trained searchers, able to provide mobility support. The more skilled personnel, such as EOR techs, had the ability to deal with IEDs, and the EOD tech was responsible both for planning asset management and dealing with IEDs. Sergeant T fulfilled all of those roles on his different tours. 'My first tour I was a sapper filling the No. 2 position and my second tour I was an EOR tech in a No. 2 position and in my third tour I was a team leader as an EOD tech.'

But SGT T's skill set wasn't the only thing that changed with each rotation. 'In 2007–08 I would say 100 per cent of my tour was road moves. In 2009, I was probably moving 50 per cent via road and 50 per cent by air. On my last tour apart from maybe a handful of very small missions it was completely air move.'

The reason for this could not have been simpler: they flew to missions more frequently because helicopters were increasingly made available to them. 'Where we were based in Tarin Kowt, we had the Dutch embedded with us there so we didn't have access to the same air assets as the Americans did when they eventually came down into the base. I dare say as we progressed as a task group we were getting more recognition so we were given more assets to execute our tasks.'

The sappers' job was to get the commandos safely to where they needed to be, but once that was achieved, they reverted to basically an infantry role—and that involved taking an active part in any firefights that may have broken out. 'The first time I was in deliberate contact was in my 2009 tour. We were infiltrating into the green belt when we received pretty accurate sniper fire. So we popped smoke and just bounded into the green belt. I was with the troop commander at the time and I had a sapper attached with me when an insurgent appeared around the hill. My sapper engaged that insurgent; he didn't neutralise him but suppressed him in order to allow the rest of us to move forward. It was pretty close to the troop commander, our platoon commander at that point, so it was probably a good thing.'

It was a close call but it wasn't the scariest moment of his three tours. 'I'd say the last tour I got in probably the thickest contacts I've ever been in. We lost a couple of casualties. I'd never really seen a friendly combat casualty but on my last tour I was with one of the commandos who got shot and he was in a creek bed. I was the closest to the scene so I moved to him. We established security and pulled him back out. He'd received one gunshot wound that had passed through his helmet but had missed his head and took another gunshot wound to the upper left chest, which flew out the back. I applied immediate first aid to him. Then the medic arrived and probably worked on him for about half an hour before more qualified combat first aiders arrived. He was evacuated by air.'

When it comes to what attracted SGT T to the sappers in the first place—blowing things up—he makes no apologies. Sappers routinely collected and blew up arms caches they discovered during searches as it was too hard to carry them back to base. 'It was sort of my role. The biggest cache I ever blew up included a Dushka, which is like a Russian-style 50-calibre mounted as an anti-aircraft gun with about 2000 rounds and half a dozen rockets. It made a decent bang when it went up.'

When SGT T wasn't dodging Taliban bullets and blowing up Russian machine guns, he did manage to have a laugh, even in the heat of battle. 'In that same contact where one of my sappers suppressed that enemy before he could shoot the boss, we were moving from one compound to the other and we were receiving pretty sporadic yet accurate fire between the two compounds, in the area we had to move across. We would prop and suppress and then one bloke would run across. I took my turn so I ran across and I propped and returned fire.

'My sapper came across next but an RPG was fired and impacted on the reverse side of a wall, just as he was running across. The wall absorbed all the frag but the pressure of the blast knocked him on his arse. He was a bit of a short fella and he's got a huge pack on and I just remember him being on his back, desperately wriggling his arms and legs, trying to get up. He looked just like a cockroach on its back.

I thought that was pretty funny. We laugh about it now but at the time he was shitting himself.'

Although SGT T spent all his time with commandos, he never felt he was one of them rather than a sapper. 'I felt part of them for sure but at the end of the day my skill sets are completely different to theirs. I mean, just from day to day equipment carriage, to personal drills, to my role in a combat situation, their role is to capture or kill the enemy. My role is to provide mobility so that they can do their job, although there were plenty of occasions where I also assisted in their mission set.

'I think the higher in rank you go the more you become a part of the team. I was incorporated in all their planning processes, obviously because I'm the MST expert for engineering-based discussions. I would be incorporated into anything to do with mobility and survivability, every mission. So I got the most value out of my last tour.

'I had the ability to shape their battle plan based on my recommendations or my intent as well. Intelligence gathering played a big part, especially when we could identify potential caches. In essence, they would say, "We're here. We want to get there." We would develop a plan. They were trying to remain undetected and I was trying to get the convoy safely so together we would flesh out a route and any actions required.

'The way that the sappers integrated back in Vietnam and the way that we integrate now is pretty similar, in the sense that there are slimmer teams and smaller teams now integrated with infantry. We're viewed as outsiders but we are also viewed as brothers. We've lost blokes in this unit. They've lost blokes in their unit and we always came together when that occurred. On the last tour, the tour that Cam Baird was killed, we were right in the thick of it there.'

Corporal Cameron Baird was killed on 22 June 2013 when his platoon from 2nd Commando Regiment, along with Afghan troops, flew into the Khod Valley where, it had been reported, local police checkpoints had been overrun, and police murdered. It turned out to be an ambush. Corporal Baird was posthumously awarded the Victoria Cross for his heroic actions that day. 'I remember dragging him around the corner. One of my diggers was attached to his team and, although our role in contact is to ensure that the infantry aren't moving into areas where there might be IEDs, we were in the thick of it as much as they were. They really respect us for that. We could hold our own in a gunfight and we have always done so.'

But while special ops sappers could give as good as they got, under fire, there was another group of engineers who may have been surprised to find they were in Afghanistan at all, let alone being shot at. It was a small group but it was significant . . . we mean, of course, women.

16

FRONT-LINE FEMALES

While the roles of sappers were evolving in the field, the entire Australian Army was undergoing a quiet revolution of a completely different kind. Women were not only joining the army, they were being accepted in combat roles.

Predictably, this caused much huffing and puffing in some quarters, with *The Australian*'s foreign editor Greg Sheridan writing, under the headline 'Women have no place in combat': 'A nation that sends its women into front-line combat, into close infantry, hand-to-hand fighting and killing, is a nation that either doesn't take combat seriously or doesn't take respect for women seriously. [The] wretched decision to make all combat roles in the Australian military available to women moves Australia closer to both outcomes. It will make our military less effective, and less respected, and it will make women less respected as well. It is a decision born of a postmodern fantasy, a kind of derangement of nature contrived by ideology against reason, common sense, military professionalism and all human experience. It is almost certainly a sign that the [then] Gillard government has more or less stopped taking defence seriously.'

Passing over the fact that there was very little, if any, hand-to-hand combat in Afghanistan or anywhere else, that women are just as capable of firing guns as men and that there are physical tests that all soldiers male or female must pass, Mr Sheridan was a bit behind the times. Long before he wrote his piece, women soldiers were 'in harm's way' in other non-infantry roles in Afghanistan and perfectly capable of looking after themselves if required in a fight.

At the time of researching this book, the Royal Australian Engineers had just accepted its first two women in combat engineer roles, thereby completing another link that goes all the way back to Vietnam (more on that later). One person who might have been amused by Sheridan's expostulations is Major Rachel Brennan, who is both a civil engineer and officer in command of 23 Squadron.

'I went in as a second in command [2IC] of the engineer task group. Generally 2ICs look after admin and welfare, that kind of thing, but it soon morphed into being 2IC of a combat team because the engineer task group became one. So then I was, I guess, responsible for elements of the force like snipers, mortar platoon, infantry guys, cavalry guys, which was pretty overwhelming.

'I didn't have that much knowledge on how they operated but by the end I was comfortable in the position. When my OC would go on leave, he'd leave the combat team with me to plan for the next mission. But the first couple of times I went outside the FOB on missions, I just thought, *Wow, am I meant to be doing this as a female?* Like, what did I sign up for?'

Major Brennan joined the army in 2001, went to the Australian Defence Force Academy to study civil engineering, and graduated from the Royal Military College in 2004.

'I was with 17 Construction Squadron, then in Sydney, but the contingent going was headed up by 6 CSR in Brisbane so we all flew up to Brisbane in January 2008 and we conducted about three and a half months of training based out of Wide Bay and Enoggera, including mission rehearsal exercises (MRE) mimicking what scenarios you might encounter overseas.

'The MREs are run and monitored by the combat training centre. They come in and assess how the battle group runs and make sure that we are ready to deploy. So they'll try and come up with scenarios that we'd encounter overseas and the battle group just steps through those scenarios.'

By the time Major Brennan was being prepared for Afghanistan, the habit of engineers being told to stand aside while the infantry got to complete their exercises was long gone.

'The interesting thing about RTF 4 was that it was engineer led. So the 6 Engineer Support Group Regiment, they were the head-quarters so it was a very engineer-heavy battle group and the infantry were tacked on to the engineers, so it was a bit of a role reversal. That said, I think it was hard for them to get this idea that they weren't the main effort. Engineer construction was the main effort.'

Exercises were one thing but doing real work in a hostile environment with the potential of being shot at or blown up by an IED was another story. But Major Brennan wasn't fazed, far from it. 'I was really excited by the prospect of going to Afghanistan. I was ready for something like that. I'd just done my troop command time and I'd been to Papua New Guinea for three months and an Aboriginal community for four months, if not longer. We were going to be doing a similar thing, like construction and reconstruction. Obviously the threat level was different but I felt like the two years leading up to that I'd gone through all the training and experience that was needed.'

Major Brennan joined the army in 2001, before Australia deployed in Afghanistan or Iraq (for the second time), so was she one of these people who joined the forces in peacetime but find that there's a war on and say, 'Oh, wait a minute. I didn't sign up for this. We're going to get shot at?' 'Yes, definitely, there were moments like that. Especially as a female, I never thought I'd be in some of the positions I was eventually in, in Afghanistan, like being on the main gun of a vehicle or commanding a convoy, looking after all the security arrangements.'

But the level of her involvement and responsibilities wasn't the only thing that surprised Major Brennan. There was the country itself. 'I was really amazed at how beautiful it was. I arrived at the end of winter, so there was still snow. I was just blown away about how amazing the landscape was. It was surprising. But then I remember when I first got into the camp thinking what a sort of hovel it was. Everything was so crowded and there was equipment everywhere with containers and office space all over the place. It all seemed very crowded and hectic. There wasn't much allowance made for the fact that there were women on the base. There wasn't really much of a separation. We lived with the guys, but had separate toilets. That was about the extent of it.

'I guess the security issue was more of a problem than gender issues so if you were going to go for a run around the base regardless of whether you're a male or female you had to carry a pistol. So I didn't really notice any specific gender issues.'

But, of course, this wasn't purely an Australian camp—in fact, the majority of troops in it were Dutch. 'They were quite different to Australians, was my initial impression. You'd see them around the gym or eating in the mess hall. They'd have long hair. Some of them had mohawks. They'd get around in their lycra get-up. Just different. We thought they were a bit more loose than how we ran things. They'd come around in normal vehicles and not armoured vehicles. They had a different approach to things.'

When she went out on patrol, Major Brennan wasn't as big a shock to the locals as she thought she might be. 'There was another female engineer that was getting out and about quite a lot so I think she sort of paved the way. Some of the key figures like engineers and the leadership in the town, I think they were used to it. But the little villages and local areas, it was a bit strange for them I think.'

One of the main projects that Major Brennan supervised was to build a support base. 'I think it was about 20 kilometres away from Tarin Kowt but it felt like a universe away, especially the first few times we went out. It took eight hours, I think, the first time we drove out there, being super careful with the threat of IEDs.

'The convoy was massive, a big conga line of vehicles. We had all our construction stores, so there were heaps of trucks lined up with stores on the back but security elements were broken up within that convoy. So you'd have cavalry guys in ASLAVs, generally on the side of the roads providing like a screening effect. We had Bushmasters too, heaps of those providing protection. Scattered among the security element was all your engineer vehicles, your plant equipment and the trucks with all the construction stores on them.'

They were heading for a small village called Sorkh Morghab where they built a patrol base and then another one further down the road. The Baluchi Valley was a largely untouched area at this point and the CO wanted to impose Australian Army control on that region.

'We wanted to not only build a patrol base but stay there for quite a while,' says Major Brennan. 'So we were there for about three months, built the patrol base and then lived out of it. At the same time, we started the construction of a school, a health clinic and a river crossing. We really tried to have an impact on the whole area. Not just sort of go in, build a patrol base and then bugger off.

'After about three or four weeks the Taliban realised, *Oh, these guys are staying here for quite a while*, so there would be rocket attacks every couple of days. Our construction site got targeted quite a bit as well. The first time we came under fire I was shitting myself. I was pretty nervous until I realised that their aim was crap and that it wasn't like they were going to hit us.

'The headquarters element had been a patrol base that was semi built and the walls were up, the HQ was inside and then we had two construction sites outside the patrol base—the school and the river crossing—so during the day I'd be either in the patrol base or down on the construction sites. My OC [Major Brennan was 2IC] would work out of the patrol base which was about 300 metres from town on a ridgeline.'

The school and river crossing were partly in response to local needs but the latter was also a tactical asset. 'We required the river crossing because there wasn't an existing one and it was a fairly significant river. So it was partly to help the locals but it also gave us a way to get across. I guess the patrol base was my biggest achievement in terms of construction. It was quite an advanced patrol base at that time as well. So all your accommodation and office blocks had air conditioning, running water and power whereas the previous patrol bases were just drop toilets, no power.

'Last I heard, yeah, it is still being used. I don't know what condition though. It was interesting to see how the local Afghan forces used the patrol base. They weren't used to having the type of taps that Westerners use or the type of toilets that we use so when we first opened up the toilet block that had running water and power they were using the taps as urinals, so it was quite interesting.

'There had been a girls' school there already that got used until it was burnt down by the Taliban. I can't say for certain that they wanted the school there again, but I imagine so.

'The three months out there was really tough. Some of the guys lost 20 kilograms in that time. The boys still had to shave every day. They would whinge and bitch about it, especially when we were in close proximity to the special forces guys who were unshaven, but we still maintained that discipline.

'When the boys knocked off they'd have a feed and then pretty much go to bed. We spent so long out in Baluchi that they were knackered come knock-off time. There was no access to alcohol—we had fake beers, that's about it. We had ice creams—they were great. I remember I took up smoking. There wasn't all that much to do. There was no internet. We had two 20-minute phone calls for the whole three months on an army satellite phone. I was single at the time so I gave my phone card to a friend who was going through a tough time with her boyfriend. The thing I least enjoyed about my tour in Afghanistan was coming back from my two-week break in Europe straight back out to the Baluchi Valley.

'After we got out of there the contingent then built a couple of bridges in two other provinces. I didn't go on those missions because I was planning for the subsequent mission, which was the building of a health clinic. My last couple of weeks was spent conducting reconnaissance for future patrol bases.

'That was quite different to my first couple of months where it was engineer based. The reconnaissance was led by the security group, which was an infantry company. An infantry commander led that so I was just one of a couple of engineers attached to that. I enjoyed that. I think maybe the last part, doing the recons, was the most interesting job for me.

'I think it was going into the unknown and I felt like I had quite a bit of freedom as the sole engineer as well, going out for three or four days at a time. When we were on foot, I would be part of a section or platoon. But, vehicle-based recons were generally combat teams sized, company plus.'

Looking back, Rachel Brennan thinks involvement in Afghanistan made a huge difference to the sappers as a corps. 'We've just got so much experience now, not just construction but every other aspect as well, like operating with other elements of the army, and working closely with infantry and armoured elements. The corps is better for it, for sure. And, personally as well, I learned so much on that.'

In another unexpected parallel between the conflicts in Afghanistan and Vietnam, women played a role in Vietnam as well . . . just on the other side of the aisle. The Vietcong had female fighters. But more than that, when the Vietcong started 'recycling' jumping jack landmines from the Barrier Minefield, it was women with their small delicate fingers and, perhaps, a little more patience, who were by far the most adept at digging them out and making them safe so they could be carried away to be reused against Australian and American troops.

We asked Brigadier Mick Ryan about the women who had qualified as combat engineers. He was unequivocal. 'There are more coming. It's fantastic.'

Would he put a female combat engineer out the front of an infantry patrol looking for IEDs? 'Yes, because she's a combat engineer. Not a female. Not a male. She's a combat engineer. That's all that concerns me. She can do a job—[that's] the determinant of how they get employed.'

Given the history of female Vietcong and their facility with landmines, did he think a female combat engineer has skills that are at least equal and possibly better than many of her male counterparts?

'Yeah, at least as good. Sometimes better.'

So is the future of combat engineers going to be increasingly female?

'Yes.'

17

HEAVY DUTIES

Imagine, you have been dropped by helicopter into a remote area which is basically dirt and rocks, you have to trudge for miles over ankle-twisting terrain, clamber up mountains and slide down gravelly screes. You have to do this undetected, be on the lookout for IEDs and be ready to fight for your life if you *are* spotted. Then, at the end of a day's march, you may be expected to engage Taliban guerrillas in a fight to the death.

One other thing: you have to do all this, and more, carrying 50 kilograms of kit.

Special ops Sapper Jeff Newman had worked out from being weighed prior to a helicopter mission that he was packing 30 kilograms extra for a short mission and 50 kilograms for a long one. Every Australian soldier who went out on patrol would have their standard issue camouflage gear, a combat helmet with a night-vision mount, a personal radio and headset, some water, tiered body armour, pelvic protection system, combat boots, an Austeyr rifle, an optical gunsight, an aiming device, a multiband team radio with whip antenna, combat gloves, a GPS watch and field packs of food and basic wound dressings.

On top of that, sappers would have a portable, foldaway metal detector, tools, explosives, detonator cord and detonators and an ECM 'man pack' to block radio and mobile phone signals intended to detonate IEDs. There would be a prodder, of course, and six to ten ammunition magazines.

Many would augment their basic kit with specialist equipment they had bought themselves and extra basics like spare batteries. It all adds up, especially for the special ops guys.

'You're carrying ten magazines, explosives, spare batteries, food. A lot of the food would either be a couple of packets of beef jerky, or tuna packs and some biscuits, then a sachet of salsa and you'd mix it all up in the field. We wouldn't take the standard ration packs because they are big and bulky and too heavy. So you'd just take the small stuff.

'We always had our patrol pack, in which we'd always have our night-vision goggles, some rations. I'd carry six-litre bottles of water, which I'd freeze and then put it in my pack for the flight out. In the fighting season I would have to go out with ten magazines and I'd have three on me and seven in my backpack.

'We used Eagle Marine body armour and not the tiered system the conventional forces used. We also used the M4 rifle fitted with the AN/PEQ-2 infrared laser illumination and sighting system and the ACOG scope. Some guys would purchase their own mounts for cameras and torches etc.

'Depending on the job, I would carry in my backpack five slabs of Composition B block type explosive, each of which weighs 600 grams. On my body armour I would carry one stick of PE4 or C4 equivalent. And I would carry about 500 grams of sheet explosive so I can do bits and pieces. I've had three initiation sets: two for 3 minutes and one for 5 minutes. Then my seven members, if we were all out, would have a similar amount of explosives on them.

'Everybody in the platoon has a radio all on the same net. But the radio operators had bigger radios obviously, with different frequencies so they could contact the joint control, as well as the team-members. Some guys, me included, would purchase their own pouches to accommodate specialist tools. I had a special pack made for a three-day patrol. In the end it was too small for all my equipment so I had to use the three-day assault pack.'

At the other end of the equipment scale, when they weren't travelling on foot or in helicopters, troops would be transported by either ASLAVs or Bushmasters. The ASLAV is an eight-wheel-drive, amphibious vehicle modified to deal with Australian conditions, making it ideal for Afghanistan. According to the Australian Army website, 'Modifications include the addition of air-conditioning and the widest wheels and tyres available. The ASLAV is an attractive capability due to its reliability, low maintenance costs and ability to travel quickly over long distances.'

'ASLAVs are fitted with an electric turret, enhanced drive train, improved thermal optics, and integrated laser range finder. Selected deployed vehicles are also fitted with remote weapon stations [guns that can be fired remotely from inside the vehicle]. These enhancements, together with run-flat tyres, small arms resistant armour, internal spall protection, a counter improvised explosive device suite and a fire suppression system, provide a battle-ready platform which optimises crew and passenger survivability.'

ASLAVS are generally operated by cavalry units and, according to the army, their versatility is expanded by the installation of non-permanent mission role kits. 'The kits allow the generation of several variants from a single ASLAV hull design. This is a unique Australian Defence Force capability, with much of the design and development work undertaken in Australia.' Current variations include reconnaissance, personnel carrier, command, surveillance, ambulance, fitter and recovery vehicles.

These 13.6 tonne all-terrain transports accommodate three crew and six passengers and can hit 100 kilometres per hour on land and 10 kilometres per hour on water. They have a range of 600 kilometres. Standard armaments include a smoke grenade system and 76-millimetre grenade launcher, a 25-millimetre M242 Bushmaster chain gun, and two 7.62-millimetre MAG 58 machine guns.

Despite improvements to its structure and armour, however, the ASLAV can still be vulnerable to powerful IEDs and anti-tank mines, as occurred with David 'Poppy' Pearce. For that reason, many soldiers prefer to travel in the even more advanced Bushmaster, which has a V-shaped hull to deflect any upward blast away from the vehicle and thus protect its passengers from landmines. The external storage bins add extra protection for the crew.

'The Bushmaster protected mobility vehicle is sustaining jobs in Australia and saving lives in Afghanistan,' says the army website. 'The locally produced vehicle can rapidly deploy up to ten battle ready troops in all environments and is blast resistant. Its innovative cabin design gives it the flexibility to serve many roles.

'The Bushmaster can carry ten, is fully air-conditioned and stores up to 250 litres of drinking water and a three-day supply of food. The wheels have run flat tyre inserts and a central tyre inflation system allowing them to continue running, even with punctures.

'The vehicle's welded one-piece shell is designed to protect troops against all small arms fire. Windows also carry similar ballistic protection. The Bushmaster's fuel and hydraulic tanks are positioned outside the crew's compartment to protect troops from possible fires. There is also a protected emergency fuel tank so the vehicle won't be left stranded.'

At 12.5 tonnes, with a top speed of more than 100 kilometres per hour, a range of 800 kilometres and a reputation for few, if any, fatalities despite numerous IED hits, it's little wonder that many armies around the world are looking at this vehicle as a potential troop carrier.

The construction arm of the sappers also has its own specialised equipment, although you might think at first glance the trucks, diggers, dozers, cranes and graders were just civilian gear painted in camo colours. In fact, they are armoured up as much as practicality allows—so never again should plant and equipment need to have steel plates welded on in the field, as happened in Vietnam. One unnamed female plant operator described working on a forward operating base as 'safer than working on a building site in western Sydney'.

The threat of IEDs, which steadily increased through Australia's involvement in Afghanistan, led to the creation of Project NINGAUI to provide vehicles to assist in detection, clearance and bypass of explosive hazards to make roads safer for soldiers in Uruzgan province. Almost 40 per cent of Australian troops killed in action in Afghanistan have been as a direct result of IED attacks, with many more wounded. Current route clearance relies heavily on combat engineers dismounting to search for, detect and deal with IEDs. 'While dismounted manual search offers an effective and battle proven method of route clearance, it can be time consuming and exposes personnel to significant risk of injury and loss of life.'

The idea is to combine 'mounted' mine detection systems with foot patrols to make the most of both capabilities while reducing the risk to both troops and vehicles. 'The United States, United Kingdom, Canada, Germany, France and Italy have developed mounted protected capabilities that are currently being utilised in Afghanistan,' says the army's webpage on Project NINGAUI.

One of the increasing challenges to sappers has been the development of low-metal content IEDs, making them harder to detect with usual methods such as metal detectors. And that has seen the introduction of a new kid on the block: the Husky, a vehicle with ground-penetrating radar which can detect non-metallic IEDs without the operator leaving the safety of their cab. The cab looks more like the control deck of a spaceship than a traditional army vehicle.

And in a belt-and-braces approach, the army is also deploying self-protective adaptive roller kits (SPARKs) to attach to the front of Bushmasters. These are basically rollers intended to deliberately detonate landmines and IEDs that were missed by the Huskys. Readers of *A Sappers' War* will recognise this as a modern adaptation of the rollers attached to APVs that were used to clear minefields in Vietnam.

All of this has led to the development of four fleets of anti-IED vehicles which will cost about 70 million dollars, each of which includes: two Husky Mark 3 protected route clearance vehicles with ground penetrating radar; one Husky Mark 3 with telescopic interrogator arm to check potential IEDs from a safer distance; two protected high mobility engineer excavators to repair or bypass damaged routes; and two Bushmasters fitted with SPARK mine rollers to provide a greater level of protection against explosive hazards.

When the NINGAUI systems are in play, backed by remote-controlled drones, the battlefields of the future will be more like science fiction than *The Art of War*.

Even so it will be hard for this sophisticated technology to replace the efficacy of a creature with senses one thousand times sharper than a human being, married with technology as simple as a piece of rubber covered in felt.

18

THE DOGS OF WAR

One of the most effective pieces of soldiering kit employed from the very start of Operation Slipper wasn't a hi-tech, laser-guided gizmo with all sorts of bells and whistles attached. It was a tennis ball. That was the reward dog handlers used to encourage their charges to seek out IEDs. Doggie treats are one thing but, from a dog's point of view, nothing compares with the fun and games you can have with a ball thrown by your favourite human being.

Dogs and their handlers were an essential part of sapper search teams and their importance to those missions can't be overestimated. 'Having dogs sped the job up and it made it easier when we did route search,' says former sergeant Jeff Newman. 'I would have three men clearing the road with the detectors. My dog handler would either be behind the last guy or pushed up to the flank on the higher ground. He would get the dog to sweep up and down the road. We would have commando elements that have pushed out even higher and further forward as overwatch so no one could sneak up on them.'

Probably the most famous dog in the Australian Army even had a book all to herself, *Saving Private Sarbi*, which tells the story of how she was lost in Afghanistan and found more than a year later. Before all that, Sarbi had already served one tour of duty with her handler, Warrant Officer, then Corporal, David Simpson, as part of RTF 2.

During her first tour, Sarbi got a reputation for being fiercely protective of her human friend. 'This team could be tagged as the pack leaders, Simmo being the section head and Sarbi the self-appointed top dog in the kennels (or the alpha bitch),' reports the task force's journal of their rotation. 'They have a strong bond which every person who has woken Simmo up for piquet has found out. Strangers approaching in the dark plus Sarbi equals possible dog attack.'

But fate was to separate this power team when they were deployed with the Special Operations Task Group (SOTG) in September 2008. Warrant Officer David Simpson takes up the story: 'We'd gone up to Khaz Uruzgan, up to Anaconda, to do some patrols with the Americans up there and we'd been there maybe four or five days before a major contact on 2 September. We'd gone in and been ambushed and as we were going through an RPG landed, hit the ground close by me, probably maybe only about 5 metres away, and some of the shrapnel cut the lead that I had her attached to my body armour [with].

'So . . . she was able to get free but for the majority of the remainder of the contact, which was for another three hours or so, I could see her off in the distance. She was just keeping in line pretty much with our convoy but she was staying about 50 or 60 metres away, mainly because of the heavy machine guns that were firing off the Humvees. But she didn't just run off and go and hide, she stayed with us for most of it.'

But eventually, Sarbi disappeared from sight and the convoy had to get out of there so that the wounded—including David Simpson—could be attended to. 'I just spoke to one of the Americans recently and he said that he could see her running behind the vehicles as we were finally getting out of there but she just wasn't able to keep up. She was trying to stay with us right to the end.'

Back at FOB Anaconda, everyone was dealing with the fallout from the incident—one for which Corporal Mark Donaldson of the SAS received a Victoria Cross for his actions in saving an Afghan interpreter under heavy fire.

'I was quite worried about Sarbi when we got back to camp, but also quite worried about the boys as well because . . . I think . . . nine out of the eleven or twelve of us had been shot, fragged or both and so there were a few boys there that were quite seriously wounded and they sort of took a lot of the focus. I guess at that time, as well, after going for four hours, and being fragged and shrapnelled myself, and shot in the hip with a ricochet, at that time I guess the shock starts to set in a bit.

'They had us laid out on the ground and they were just going through triage and treating from the most serious to the least and once the . . . worst [injured] guys were airlifted out then sort of things slowed down a bit and I got to start thinking about Sarbi and how we were going to get her back. All the boys that weren't getting airlifted out, [who] were staying there for a few more days, said they'd keep an eye out for her . . . That was a bit of a relief to know that they'd do the right thing by me and keep an eye out for the dog.'

By the time Sarbi was found fourteen months later, David was back in Australia just finishing off a promotion course. Sarbi was spotted by an American soldier who took her back to Tarin Kowt where they read her microchip and confirmed that one of their MIA had returned. 'By the time I deployed again in 2010 she was still there for about two or three months before she made her way home. So I got to see her again, back in Afghanistan. I'd like to say she remembered me. But I think dogs can be a little bit fickle and I think they'll follow whoever is feeding them at the time. By this time I had another dog and I was doing some training with him and I thought I'd give Sarbi a go as well and she was working better than the dog that I had.

'Unfortunately, I had to stick with the dog that I had. I would have loved to have taken her out but she was quite overweight at the time so she had a bit of weight to lose. Otherwise she was working perfectly. I just did a few training searches with her. Once she came home, I did an assessment on her and I recommended that she should be redeployed, preferably with myself, but they said, "No." She was to retire. That was enough for her.'

Even when David Simpson had first joined the army back in 1995 he had wanted to be an engineer, and he had wanted to be an engineer because he wanted to work with dogs. 'I have a vague recollection of the army coming around to [my] high school on one of their recruiting drives, and that's when I learned that they had dogs so from then I wanted to join the army and become an engineer and a dog handler.'

However, things didn't work out as he planned and David had many hoops to jump through to get to where he wanted to be. 'When I joined, my corps hadn't been selected before I went to Kapooka [the army recruit training centre near Wagga Wagga in NSW]. They said they thought I should go to air defence and artillery and I said, "Oh no. I'm going to be a dog handler. I'm going to be an engineer. That's what the guys recruiting told me I would be able to do." Unfortunately, they selected me to go to air defence and I spent twelve months there. Then I broke my leg so I had to spend another twelve months at air defence before I got my corps transfer.

'I've always liked dogs. I've always loved dogs. We always had dogs growing up. So it was only natural for me to want to do something with the dogs, but I had to spend another two years as a field engineer before I finally got to the dogs. All up, it took four years but I got there in the end.'

There was still one other surprise in store for David. 'I knew the dogs were explosive detection dogs. I knew they'd be out there looking for weapons and explosives. But at that time, I don't really think it crossed my mind that I'd be looking for IEDs.'

David first went to Afghanistan in 2007 with RTF 2. By this time he had been training with Sarbi for two and a half years. 'Sarbi and I were working really well together. She always worked quite well so I never had any problems or thoughts that she wasn't up to the job. We had been posted to the Incident Response Regiment but they released us to go on the Reconstruction Task Force.

'I'd had a couple of previous deployments before that as an engineer and a dog handler but that was only East Timor and the Solomon Islands. Getting to Afghanistan, there was more excitement rather than apprehension for me but as time went on and deployments went on and it started to get more to be apprehension and awareness— more aware of what was going on. But initially I think I was more excited than anything else.

'By that time I think we'd had one or two other rotations that had already gone through, so, yeah, we'd get stories back from them about minor contacts and some of the caches and things that they were finding so we had a bit of an idea but until you do it you really don't have a good idea.'

David's first patrol with Sarbi was mounted. They were driven to an area just west of Tarin Kowt (TK). 'I was in a Bushmaster so we were headed out just towards the west of TK for a patrol. The first time it really hit home what I was doing was when we came to our first creek line, a likely vulnerable point, and I had to jump out of the vehicle with Sarbi and do my first search. So I jumped out to let her exercise, put her harness on so she'd be ready to work and then it was me out in front of everybody else with the dog.

'It was quite an awakening and I felt very exposed. We were still quite a way from any buildings or compounds or anything like that so there was no immediate shoot threat that I was worried about.

There were sort of steep embankments that someone could have been hiding in but I think my main focus was potential IEDs in the roads.

'I did think about the possibility of Sarbi setting off an IED, but at that stage the pressure plates that they were using were high metal content and the metal was usually saw blades or something like that so it was going to take a fair bit of pressure to push them down. So I was pretty sort of confident that she wasn't going to set one off but there always still was that chance though.'

As it turned out, there were no IEDs there, or, it seemed, on any other of the patrols that David and Sarbi undertook on that rotation. 'Sarbi and I personally didn't find any IEDs on that rotation. But, in saying that, no vehicles went up behind us either so we were pretty confident there was nothing there to find.'

When the dogs are being trained the handlers try to get the find rate up to over 95 per cent, close to 100 per cent, all of the time. 'They were always finding what we'd put out there. When it comes to the buried IEDs it's going to drop a bit because it's going to be quite a bit harder for the dogs to find them. But, I think from all the ones that were found, I wouldn't know the exact number but it is very high. There were very few that got through.'

So how exactly do you train a dog to detect explosives? 'All of our training is reward based and our dogs are fanatical about retrieving tennis balls. So when we go out looking for IEDs, that's the only reason they are out there searching so that they can have their find and then play with a tennis ball.'

Even as a dog handler, slightly removed from the last part of 'seize, clear, hold, build', David became aware that, while the start of the rotation was more of a reconstruction phase, priorities were changing. 'We would be going out mainly doing reconstruction jobs like fixing up the schools and fixing wells and just doing infrastructure, fixing windows in buildings for the locals. But it very quickly became apparent that that wasn't working because as soon as we'd gone the Taliban would come in and destroy everything that we'd just done. So within a short period of a couple of months our role changed more to hardening the police checkpoints and their police houses and things like that and supporting the security, rather than trying to build schools.'

David's second rotation, with the SOTG in 2008, was the one in which he lost Sarbi. 'For that one I was supporting the SAS and the other dog handler that I had there with me, he was supporting the commandos. Once we got back from patrols and jobs and things like that we could train together but for much of the time we were apart.

'This one was more changing from reconstruction to the pointier end of the spear I guess, with the sort of the kill or capture sort of missions where we'd be going out looking for the Taliban rather than just trying to do reconstruction. Also, the structure of the teams changed. Previously, with RTF 2 we'd have a whole section with us and we'd patrol with our whole engineer section. Whereas with the SOTG rotations we started breaking up into smaller and smaller groups to where it was usually just maybe the EOD tech, one searcher and one dog handler, in a small group rather than the whole section there. That even broke down even further. A lot of the time it was dependent on the mission or the patrol and how many seats were available, so after a while it pretty much just became the EOD tech and the dog handler that were getting most of the jobs outside.

'I had a few finds of explosives and weapons but no IEDs again. Luckily, nothing blew up behind me that time either. In any case, our job on this rotation wasn't to go and find IEDs. Our main role as engineers was to get the special forces boys to whatever they were doing, without incident. If it was a hit on a compound our job was to get them there so we would be selecting routes that we were confident didn't have IEDs. Other times we would search the routes when there was absolutely no other way through.'

Unlike the main task force rotations, where there was a two-week leave allowed, the special ops rotations were kept to under six months so they could work straight through. 'I thought that was better, with no break in the middle. You could just work the whole way through and the whole team was there. Everybody was there and I think everything ran a bit smoother for that reason. The intensity and workload was high for the dog handlers because we were going out on pretty much every patrol. Some of the other engineers would have found it less intense but for the doggies and the EOD techs it was very high tempo.'

In his third tour in 2010, David was teamed with a new dog called Tana. 'He was a big black Labrador as well but he was quite a large dog. Very stocky, and very heavy. So he wasn't quite suited to Afghanistan. He just didn't have the stamina for it. We were doing pretty much the same work except this time I was supporting the commandos which was a bit different.' That difference, David explains, was that the SAS targets tended to be based on reports that a suspect individual or group was going to be in a certain place at a specific time. The commandos target might be an installation or group that wasn't going anywhere in the immediate future so they had more time to plan and prepare and often also conducted normal patrols as well.

At the end of that tour, David retired Tana because he wasn't performing and got another dog, Sonic. 'I went over again in 2011 with Sonic . . . with the SAS again, so more of the time sensitive and "high value" sort of targets. Sonic had already been trained so we just needed a six- to eight-week re-team period before we were assessed again.

'Sonic was a Kelpie cross. Tana was over thirty kilos, whereas Sonic, a little Kelpie, was only around twenty kilos, so two thirds of the weight of Tana. He had nice long legs. He had typical Kelpie wiry strength and endurance and was able to work for really long periods. He was a very good worker.

'In 2012, I went to the school as an instructor so I lost Sonic to another handler there—I didn't need a dog while I was instructing. That's why I received another dog for my final rotation in 2013. PJ was a little stumpy tailed cattle dog—another working breed. She was quite good, had a lot of endurance and was really keen to please. But one night we were blowing into a lot of compounds, going through the walls. The doors were booby-trapped so there were a lot of explosions and she developed a bit of PTSD [Post-traumatic Stress Disorder] after that trip. Any time there was an explosion it was quite difficult to get her to work for a little while. She didn't like it at all.'

Over the six-year period, David reckons he spent a total of two years and two months in Afghanistan. The biggest difference he noticed over that time was a simple matter of transportation. 'We'd gone from vehicle patrols to helicopter-inserted foot patrols which enabled us to get to a target and conduct an assault on it or we'd be inserted somewhere and we'd patrol for a few days. With the vehicles it was days and days of getting somewhere and then only being able to do a short foot patrol. So that was the main change that I noticed.

'Every patrol that we went on in the SOTG rotations, we'd almost always get into a contact of some sort. The contacts themselves would be a short gun-battle and that would usually be the end of it, with usually just a few enemy KIA. Whereas that one near Anaconda in 2008 was quite a large one. And then there was the Shah Wali Kot offensive in June 2010. I was on the ground for that for five days with Tana.'

In 2010, Australian forces were involved in a series of disruptive operations in the Shah Wali Kot district of northern Kandahar province, as part of a larger ISAF bid to strengthen coalition forces' hold on the region and curb the flow of arms and IEDs into Uruzgan.

They targeted an insurgent stronghold in Chenartu, and a Company Group from 2nd Commando Regiment made the initial attack, later being reinforced by an SAS troop. After five days of ferocious fighting, the surviving insurgents retreated and large numbers of weapons were captured. SAS sniper Ben Roberts-Smith later won the Victoria Cross for storming a machine-gun post that was pinning down his comrades.

'I was with the commandos for that one. We'd been inserted into Shah Wali Kot and we'd been patrolling around for the five days in constant contact and fighting. They were only about a kilometre and a half away from where we were at the time. So we'd been in contact for five days or so and the Taliban were massing in that area to come and hit us again when the SAS boys inadvertently landed right in the middle of it.

'Otherwise, there were only a few sort of small contacts. They'd only last for fifteen or twenty minutes and usually it would only be a couple of enemy each time. But you soon learn that gunfire is okay. It's not a problem. It's only when you can hear the rounds coming back the other way that you sort of start to think, *Oh, they might have a bead on me here. So I might keep my head down or change position.*'

The standard operating procedure for soldiers who come under fire is to run, seek cover, then aim and return fire. But this changes if you have a dog out there too. 'I'd instantly be recalling the dog and then running for cover as well. So, if I was in a position I'd return fire but my main focus was to get the dog back to me. There'd be enough other guys around me to put enough rounds down range for me to recover the dog and get back into cover.'

After 2013, David says he was over being shot at and would probably have declined an offer of a sixth tour, partly due to a sense that maybe his luck might be about to run out. 'During the 2010 rotation, just at the end of the Shah Wali Kot Offensive when the chopper went down with all the commandos on it, I was there for that as well. I hadn't joined another patrol but we had an engineer out on every single chopper except for the one that went down. Saint Barbara must have been looking out for us that day.'

Saint Barbara is the patron saint of explosions . . . and sappers.

Sadly, in March 2015 Sarbi died, aged twelve, from a brain tumour. 'Sarbi had a wonderful life serving Australia as an explosive detection dog and as a pet at home for the last five years,' David Simpson recalls, in a press statement. 'Sarbi will live on in everyone's hearts and minds and I hope that her story of perseverance and determination will inspire you to do whatever you can to achieve your goals and dreams.'

19

THE 'GOOD' WAR

As the northern winter approached in 2008, there was a change of focus among military planners overseeing the war in Afghanistan. Australia's new prime minister, Kevin Rudd, had announced a gradual withdrawal of Australian troops from Iraq, placating American allies with a promise to boost our involvement in the war against the Taliban. But while the war in Iraq was rapidly losing support at home, even our efforts in Afghanistan were coming under fire in the press.

'Rudd is very much persuaded of the "bad war, Iraq; good war, Afghanistan" position,' wrote Professor Richard Tanter of the Nautilus Institute, Royal Melbourne Institute of Technology, just before Rudd's election in 2007. 'Australia now has 1000 troops in Afghanistan. There will be a redeployment of combat and support forces from one theatre to the other. Australian Afghanistan operations are now taking more casualties, though still nothing like United States or Canadian levels. But they have increased sharply recently and this trend will continue.

'In April . . . the Australian Special Operations Task Group (SAS and other army special forces) was somewhat hurriedly deployed back to Uruzgan less than eight months after they were pulled out.

Pulling out of Iraq would allow them and the protective group of the Reconstruction Task Force at Tarin Kowt to be rotated more easily.'

At that time Afghanistan had been seen as being 'in danger of capsizing in a perfect storm of insurgency, terrorism, narcotics and warlords,' according to United States experts Thomas Johnson and Chris Mason, writing in *Orbis*, a US foreign policy journal.

However, wrote Scott Burchill for *The Age*, in January 2008, 'The problem for Rudd and his Western allies in Afghanistan is that the war is virtually unwinnable by any criteria that make rational sense. Defeating the Taliban seems no closer six years after the country was first attacked. This week's suicide attack on the Serena Hotel in central Kabul—a building that housed the Australian embassy—is just the most recent illustration of how little progress has been made.'

Once again, according to some observers, the lessons of history had not been learned. 'Taking on an area like we have is a bit reminiscent of our approach in Vietnam, where we took on Phuoc Tuy province,' says Clive Williams, of the Australian National University's Strategic and Defence Studies Centre. 'There's a similar sort of approach that we're doing in Uruzgan, where we think we can make a difference in a particular location. But that's not going to make a difference if the whole thing is turning into a mess around us.'

Afghanistan had been seen as a 'good war' because it offered the possibility of revenge on the Taliban and al-Qaeda for 9/11—not to mention the Bali bombings—and an opportunity to deal with a country that exported terrorism to the rest of the world. There was also the potential liberation of Afghan women and girls from the Taliban. But confidence in the idea that coalition forces could clear the Taliban out of the country and restore democracy was receding.

The two-year hiatus, while the 'coalition of the willing' went off in search of non-existent weapons of mass destruction in Iraq, had allowed the Taliban to recover and regroup. The prospect of a long war in Afghanistan and the high cost in young lives loomed large in political and military thinking. It was decided that the best, perhaps only positive outcome was represented by Afghan troops taking responsibility for their country's security. Again, the parallels with Indochina were stark. Australia had tried to teach the South Vietnamese Army to fend for themselves, and look how that turned out. But training the incumbent government's armed forces to a point where they would no longer need outside help was the only long-term exit strategy that had any support.

And so it was against that background of shifting priorities that Lieutenant Colonel, then Major, Mick Say, commanding officer of 1 CER in Darwin, prepared to play his part in the deployment of a new task force: MRTF 1 would be the first non-special forces Australian task force in Afghanistan commanded by a non-engineer, signalling a shift of focus to a plan that included more mentoring of Afghan security forces by Australian infantry.

Lieutenant Colonel Say had already tasted action before he arrived in Afghanistan to command the engineers there in November 2008: he had been part of a low-key sapper deployment in Iraq. 'There were no large force elements that deployed to Iraq but we had carpenters and joiners and plumbers who went to maintain facilities over there and we had a number of officers. I was deployed with the Brits in their multinational division in Basra but we had people in corps divisional headquarters. Our large force elements in Iraq were predominantly infantry and cavalry but there was an engineer footprint with those too.'

Mick Say's preparation for his role in Afghanistan began in February of that year, when he completed a NATO-run course for the provincial reconstruction teams along with his operations officer and one of his captains, so that they got an understanding of how they'd fit into operations in Afghanistan. 'Then we started a bunch of mission specific training and mission rehearsal exercises and we had staff from RTF 3 [the previous rotation] to come and provide oversight, which I thought was an excellent way of doing it; someone who'd been in theatre not that long ago then gave you some advice on how you were operating, noting the only difference was a change in focus from reconstruction to mentoring *and* reconstruction.'

Like most of his men, Mick Say was excited at the prospect of getting to Afghanistan. 'It's like learning to ride a horse and never getting to ride the horse. This was us getting to do our job in theatre, supporting both other nations but most importantly supporting the Afghan people. A lot of times when our guys were searching for IEDs, it's because they were going to a task site where sappers were helping Afghans rebuild a hospital or something like that. Then there was building the capacity of the Afghans so they could actually manage those sorts of things on their own.'

Mick Say's first impressions of Tarin Kowt (TK) were of extreme contrasts: the spectacular natural beauty of the mountains contrasting starkly with desolate lack of infrastructure in the town itself. 'When you are flying into TK you're surrounded by some pretty high mountains and when you come from Australia and you don't get exposed to that too often, so it catches the eye. We came in October and the snow was starting to collect on the mountain tops. We'd heard stories of the winter that RTF 3 had had the year previously, when it had dropped to [minus ten to minus 20 degrees Celsius]. For us, coming from Darwin, where September is starting to get pretty warm, and then to transition over to those freezing temperatures . . . If it hits 17 degrees Celsius in Darwin, you think it's cold. It's a little bit different over there.

'Apart from that, the township of Tarin Kowt is only a few kilometres from where the camp was. As you fly in you can see the town and you realise how little was there. And you could see the valley—how it was vegetated along the river systems—and the rest was just dusty, dusty Afghan *dasht*. Even on the patrols that we used to take into Tarin Kowt, there was no sewerage because there is a lack of running water. While there's a main river that goes through TK, it pretty much goes to essentials, which is farming—and, in a lot of cases, farming opium—so that's their priority because that's where a lot of them make their money. There were a lot of motorbikes but the only bitumen local road was very close to TK. All the rest was the dirt roads apart from Highway One, which links Kandahar and Kabul.'

Ironically, though, the lack of infrastructure offered an opportunity as well as a challenge. 'This was an effort from RTF 1 all the way through to RTF 4. Each of those organisations had a works team comprising a couple of qualified civil engineers at captain or warrant officer level: very experienced guys from plant supervisors and trade supervisors, a surveyor and, say, a draughtsman. The effect that they had in Afghanistan is a story that hasn't really been told in Australia. We are talking primary schools for both boys and girls, crossing points across rivers where people have never been able to get across. But we didn't construct those, they were constructed by local Afghan companies. Our people just project-managed them to make sure they were built to a standard that was going to last a significant period of time and the bang for buck that you got out of those six to eight people was absolutely amazing.

'They finally had a school where girls could go, which didn't happen in Afghanistan. The hospital started from RTF 1 but, because these projects took a significant period of time, you handed over the management of these projects from rotation to rotation. However, the benefit they provided, in regard to giving health, education and increas[ing] locals' ability to get around the area, was huge.

'This was where that provincial reconstruction team came into play. We had a liaison officer and he used to work with the local mayor to ensure that what we were building was linked to their development plan. The coalition [had] previously got a bad press because they've built a school in a place where no one wanted one and they just wanted to build it for the sake of building it. And, yes, there is a lot of corruption in Afghanistan. That's a given. But, while we may have built a school right near where the mayor wanted one because that's where he had a family or whatever, we engaged with the ministries and the mayor to make sure that we were delivering the facilities in line with their plans.'

The projects were built in response to a demand from the community, says Lieutenant Colonel Say, rather than orders from Kabul, and that's why they were welcomed. 'It's very difficult in Afghanistan. They don't have anything like our system of federal, state and local government. For them it is all local. It's tribal. They respond to their tribes and they don't really respond to Kabul. It's very direct and building a school was something the mayor could see as an immediate benefit. The biggest issue that occurred—not so much in Tarin Kowt but in some of the other towns and villages—was getting quality teachers in there. But even when they came some of the teachers would get threats from the Taliban to not turn up to work.'

The way the construction system worked was that the task force engineers would find out what the village wanted, then help draw up the plans and look at tenders for the work to be carried out by local builders under task force supervision. Equipment for hospitals and schools would often be supplied by AusAid. 'There would be a full tender process and if, say, four companies applied for it, the works team would review each of them to see which had the best one and then deliver the tender. Some companies were more competent than others but they would try and share it a little bit so that one company didn't have a monopoly on it all or get all the experience. So it was very transparent. You can't always build to Australian standards over there but you can find a happy medium.'

The infrastructure that was put in wasn't under too much threat from the Taliban. Previously, RTF 1 had been focused on establishing the base at Tarin Kowt, and only did what Brigadier Mick Ryan described as Backyard Blitz-type operations to try and win the hearts and minds of local people. But later RTFs had been working on that 'clear, hold, and build' principle we heard about earlier.

'By the time we got there I think we'd progressed past that. If you look at Sorkh Morghab, which is only about 10 kilometres north of Tarin Kowt, RTF 1 struggled to get into it without getting in contact. By the time we were there it was fully established. There was a health clinic that had been delivered, and markets that had been delivered. This became a thriving little metropolis and you could drive to Sorkh Morghab with no issues—until you got further north into Baluchi.'

As the coalition forces had discovered, there was no point in setting up forward patrol bases if there wasn't anyone to occupy them. But that is where there were opportunities as well as challenges offered by the mentoring aspect of Mentoring and Reconstruction Task Force 1's (MRTF 1's) mission.

'We had Afghan National Army people to put in those patrol bases to continue that security. If I'm critical, it took the coalition too long to establish that spread from TK as the first base. I think we shouldn't forget those counter-insurgency lessons from the Brits and a lot of other countries who did this in the past, of how we could push out. I think we started to develop a plan for Uruzgan linked to the whole overall Afghan plan. It wasn't just, "Okay, let's build a patrol base here," because there was a security issue in that area.'

However, explains Lieutenant Colonel Say, as you push out and increase security and have the Afghan National Army hold an area, it changes the whole social landscape: 'When we were starting to go out to Mirabad Valley it was called the Mirabadlands and we still had a lot of action out there but we were increasing that overall security.

Then [the secure area] spreads and then it starts to join up hopefully with security all over. That's why we were building patrol bases and spreading that presence of the Afghan National Army.'

Once security was established, Mick Say would conduct *shuras* with locals to find out what their priorities and main fears were, to establish what projects or assistance could be delivered. 'They just wanted to get on with their business and they weren't overly concerned. That obviously wasn't the whole population because there were a lot of threats out there. However, most of the general population there wanted to get on with business and some saw some enhancements or improvements to their quality of life as us trying to put a Western template over the top of what is a very different country.'

Lieutenant Colonel Say insists that the West can't just impose what it sees as a natural way of doing business, or crime and punishment, on people who have a very different value system. Pashtunwali is a belief system based on self-respect, justice, hospitality, love, forgiveness, tolerance, loyalty, equality, independence and, above all, honour—the last of which can't be overemphasised. A Pashtun who is considered to be without honour is pretty much cast out or ignored by the community.

'If you look at Pashtunwali, they have a long history of retribution and certain acts that they do which we don't deem as right. But you can't just try and impose our laws on them without understanding their culture because otherwise you'll just alienate them. So I made a lot of our guys read articles on Pashtunwali before we went over so they had some sort of understanding of the culture that they would be dealing with.

'As an army we got a lot better with our cultural education. It's pretty difficult to immerse yourself in that culture especially when you are seen as an invading army. You can't get an understanding of that culture even after eight and a half months.'

While the Taliban were upping the ante with increased use of IEDs, they now had a new target, the operational mentor and liaison teams (OMLT) which were basically ten to fifteen Afghan National Army members and only two Australian soldiers mentoring them. They came under direct fire more often because they were seen as a softer target. 'When we used to go out on patrol, it was the IED threat that was greater for us. We used to go out with a platoon group consisting of two ASLAVs—which are armoured vehicles with a nice cannon on the front—and a minimum platoon of 30 infantry, which consisted of a number of Bushmasters that had remote weapons systems and machine guns on them, and another ten or so engineers, and then some construction guys. We were a lot harder target so the Taliban didn't always engage. Having said that, the combat team had a number of contacts.

'The OMLTs had a very different experience. These guys would live out on the patrol bases with the Afghan National Army and in subsequent rotations a number of Australians were killed by them. That didn't occur on our rotation. But, they were stuck out in these patrol bases, which we'd built and they were left out there to start patrolling and enhancing security. The advisors were captains, lieutenants, warrant officers and sergeants—guys with high-level experience—and then they used to have an infantry section for their protection and they would go out and conduct patrols.'

Probably the most significant project the MRTF 1 sappers did, as a purely engineering project, was to drive across three provinces to Kabul province to repair one bridge but, as it turned out, fix another on the main highway between Kabul and Kandahar. 'These were concrete bridges that the Russians had built but the insurgents got quite effective at blowing them up, or parts of them, and they wanted some engineers to go and build a Mabey Johnson [prefabricated] bridge, which is just a steel modular bridge that is joined together.

So we had about an eleven-hour drive down to Kandahar to meet up with the bridge and then transfer the bridge all the way across the province and then build it. But as we were on our way to Kandahar they blew another bridge, so we had to go and build two of them. It was in winter and it was fricking cold and that was a tough gig for the guys but they did an outstanding job.'

The sappers took two platoons of infantry with them and built a camp while the infantry established an outer security cordon. The construction engineers could only start their work once the area around the site had been made safe. Once the camp was built the infantry patrolled from it while the engineers built the bridge. 'The bridges only took a couple of days each to construct [once everything was in place]. There are big panels that need cranes to move them into place so it is quite a slow operation to set up. It took us a full day to get from Tarin Kowt down to Kandahar then we spent a couple of days in Kandahar just checking all the bridge parts were there. It had been delivered by the United States and we just wanted to make sure before we rolled out the door that we had everything we needed and we didn't have to go back.

'We had to test cranes because Afghan cranes aren't very effective and so we got a couple of different crane companies in and we tested the cranes to get the best two cranes that we could. RTF 4 had done it before us and they only took one crane and had some issues with it so we thought, *Oh, we'll fix that by taking two*. We actually learned some things that they did and improved on them and as a result I think we did the bridge quicker than them even though it was in those freezing conditions. We even got some sleet and snow whilst the guys were building. All up it was about a ten-day activity that was just before Christmas so it worked pretty well for the guys to get back to Tarin Kowt so at least we could have a Christmas lunch and a couple of beers.'

Back in Tarin Kowt, there were two distinctly different aspects to mentoring. There was teaching the Afghan National Army members to be better soldiers and there was giving locals basic skills in the trade training school which was set up by RTF 1.

'The trade training school started with very basic trade skills but they continued to develop and tailor it to what sort of skills the Afghans had or required. There was some steel fixing because they were doing a lot of work linked to that, some block work, some basic plumbing. We were trying to provide a trained force that then could go and get a job with a construction company rather than become a Taliban.'

Every graduate of the trade training school was given a tool belt loaded with basic gear so they could carry on once they had gone back into their normal lives. That would give them a source of income. 'I'm pretty confident that the Australians were the first to do that under RTF 1. It was Australian-funded so they basically got a wage whilst they were on that course and then we had the contractors come in, and we'd encourage them to come along to our graduation ceremonies so they could potentially find some new work for the students.'

Otherwise the focus on the mentoring was with the Afghan National Army but it was very much infantry-based. Within each area they have *kandaks*, which is a battalion of about 600 men in the Afghan National Army (ANA).

'They had a number of infantry *kandaks* and they were only just raising the engineering one. I spoke to Colonel Gabriel, the CO, and said, "I think there's an opportunity here. I've got a spare corporal and he's an outstanding NCO. I think he can start running combat engineer courses." So I attached Corporal Mick Cole to the ANA and he worked with the Afghan major on how they could deliver combat engineer courses. This was started in deployments before ours, but it only really became official with us. We had a little bit more of a system to it when we got the M in our name for mentoring.

'So within Tarin Kowt, Cole developed a training program for basic combat engineering. The Dutch donated some detectors and we started to do some training with them. Maintenance was always an issue on that side but we had to get them to look after their kits so that they just didn't think they could get a new one straightaway.

'On the next rotations there were specific engineers to do that mentoring so it did develop that capability for Afghan engineers to support the infantry. The hardest one to crack was to try and train the EOD techs because of the high-risk nature of that role. It was very difficult with the lower education of a number of the candidates to get them up to the standard required so that they could be safe in performing their roles.'

The other part of mentoring was working with construction companies who were delivering projects and making sure that they were up to scratch. 'I had my captains tell them to tear down walls because they weren't constructed to the standards that they had to be built to, because the Afghans were trying to take short cuts. They soon learned that it wasn't worth their while to not put the reinforcement in, or whatever the case might be.

'The key to all this was establishing relationships and then maintaining them, despite the realities that the Australian troops on the ground were likely to be rotated out of country every eight months or so. The Afghans often struggled with that and it was, "Oh, here's a new face." They assumed that you were just going to promise something and not deliver. But they tried to play you sometimes as well, and say, "The last guy promised he was going to deliver this." And you go, "Oh really? Did he? He didn't cover that with me."'

But the Aussies had the ultimate incentive for getting the jobs done properly: 'Most projects were delivered in phases and we weren't going to go to the next phase until we had signed off on the last one. If they didn't get to the next phase, they didn't get their next lot of money, which was their livelihood.'

Mentoring, in its various guises, brought a whole new level of challenge to the task force, but meanwhile there was still a war going on and the Taliban were ramping up their efforts in other areas, which meant special forces sappers were required to go above and beyond anything they had done before.

20

HARD YARDS AND HESCOS

Lance Corporal Trent Goodwin was delighted when he heard he was going to Afghanistan—not least because he was going to be able to put more than a year's training into practice. 'When my mate called me—I was on my corporal's course in Sydney—and said your name's on the list, I was over the moon. We sort of had a rough idea we were going, because in training we all focused mainly on search tasks. I'd say a good eighteen months before we left, we were forever out there searching. We didn't have the same equipment as what we would have in-country—we had outdated equipment—but all the movements were the same. When we got out there we had better equipment.'

Trent had joined the army in February 2005: 'I chose the engineers mainly for the construction side—I enjoy hands-on activities. I liked the idea of learning a bit of everything, just not specifically one thing. Going to Afghanistan hit me with a bit of reality. It was all fun and games and, "Yes, I am going to Afghanistan," and then it hit me—shit! One, you've got to step up and do your job for real. Two, it's a two-way firing range, so now there are bullets coming towards you too.'

There wasn't too much time for Trent and his mates to acclimatise: 'Initially when we landed in the Middle East Area of Operations, we had two weeks of training and just general integration into the Middle East and then we flew to Tarin Kowt. For a lot of us it was our first military flight. That was my first time in a Hercules [transport plane], all geared up in our body armour and helmets. I think that brought home the reality that we were going in. The landing at Tarin Kowt was very steep.'

Trent would be part of two search teams attached to 2 Platoon of the 7th Battalion. 'My role was a Lance Jack [lance corporal], I was a No. 2, second-in-command of the team. My mate Carey was the corporal. We operated mainly as a full section but at times we'd split up into groups, so two teams of four. Carey would take one brick and I would take the other brick. Our job was pretty much "search".'

A platoon was made up of three sections of eight soldiers and each section comprised two 'bricks' of four soldiers. On some occasions, they even patrolled as only half-bricks of two men. 'I went out with infantry—we were based at Tarin Kowt. Later on, people would be stationed all around, but when we were there in MRTF 1 we were all based out of TK and we'd just shoot out from there. Sorkh Morghab might request you so you'd go out there and assist out there or Chora might request you so you'd go out there. We used Bushmasters to move between patrol bases and then from a patrol base you'd do patrols down into the green zone. We did house searches, people searches, road searches, area searches, abandoned building searches— anything that could be searched, we searched.

'We very rarely came back without at least an AK [AK-47 or Kalashnikov assault rifle]. We'd find everything from old blocks of TNT, Russian TNT, AK-47s, parts of landmines, obviously IEDs as well, IED components like battery packs, ammonia nitrate not mixed yet, sometimes we'd find it pre-mixed. Also intelligence. We'd get interpreters to read over material and they'd say, "This is something from the Taliban," and then we'd take it back with us. Also, we had a special camera that could take fingerprints and retina scans, and we had a database on there so we could see if they came up on it and if they don't, they get put in it anyway, so in six months' time, if we find a bomb with that fingerprint on it, we know it was linked to that person. There was a lot of data gathering as well.'

And by now, after four rotations, the pattern had been well established: everyone had to follow the sapper. 'There was always at least one in front, usually a minimum of two, sometimes you'd have one infantry man embedded with you. Our rifles were always on our backs because we had our mine detectors in front of us. We'd be at the front and maybe one infantry man next to us in case the shots started coming down and he could protect us while we searched. Even when we drove anywhere or walked anywhere, [there were] always engineers at the front—the only thing that would be further in front of us would be the dog. And the handler would usually be the third person back, maybe the fourth.

'The first time I came under fire was just before Christmas 2008. We were just to the west of Tarin Kowt, at this specific hill that always seemed to have IEDs on it. The Dutch certainly found a lot of IEDs there. We got our first casualty that day, not an engineer, a grunt, and he got shot in the leg. That was the first time we ever got shot at. That was interesting; all your drills kick in. If you had told me a year before that someone would be shooting at me and I'd have my rifle on my back and keep searching I'd have said. "No way, that's not happening." But we still kept searching, you heard the bullets zinging past and there were a couple of rockets in there just to mix it up a bit.'

Infantry dealt with the immediate threat but there was often a more devious reason for the Taliban shooting at the Australian searchers. 'They knew that if someone shoots at us then we would go towards them, so their tactic was to place IEDs between us and them and then shoot at us so we'd go towards them and potentially hit the IED. So we had to keep searching no matter what, otherwise we ran the risk of losing people's lives.'

By this point, MRTF 1's mentoring programs were up and running and Trent's troop was the first to train would-be ANA engineers. 'The course was run by Corporal Cole and Lance Corporal Williams. Cole ended up getting the Order of Australia medal for his efforts. They'd bring them out and we would assist. Without sounding too rude, they'd go through and search a house and we'd go in behind them and search—because they weren't the flashest. It was the first time they'd ever searched so we helped out in that way. And sometimes even when we were back in Tarin Kowt we would help with a bit of training.

'A lot of them were from the north, from Kabul and that area, and they brought them down south to us. They seemed pretty good, I never felt uncomfortable around them. But obviously towards the end all that changed when they started shooting us. I was back in Australia by that point. For me, that was odd because I felt they were on our side, maybe we let our guard down as well but I was pretty happy with them. They are not the greatest soldiers in the world, though.'

Back in Tarin Kowt, Trent and his mates got involved in less hazardous sapper tasks: filling and stacking the dreaded Hescos. These are collapsible wire mesh-reinforced sacks that are designed to be filled with rocks and soil, and then stacked into defensive walls or even basic buildings like guard posts. They are dreaded because the work of filling them is tedious and physically demanding.

'We extended the outer wall of the base—it felt like by about 4 kilometres—with Hescos. That's a lot of dirt. We didn't do it by hand, thank God.'

The Hesco bags arrived folded flat and the sappers would extend them out to full size and a front-end loader would be used to fill them with dirt and rocks. 'Not so much construction as shovelling stones—that was the biggest thing, the base extension,' recalls Trent, noting ruefully that physical work is so much harder when you are wearing body armour.

Among their other tasks around Tarin Kowt was taking turns with the section camera. 'They told us that, down the track, [the data we captured] would all be put on a massive database somewhere in the world and if Terry Taliban flies from Kabul to Sydney for his Christmas holidays, once they get the technology up they would be able to scan everyone's eyes and, "Hold on, you were in Afghanistan, and we found your fingerprints on a bomb ten years ago."'

But this impressive technology, and the massive Hesco-reinforced walls surrounding them, ultimately provided Trent with very little reassurance and the ever-present possibility of serious injury and death became a heavier and heavier burden to bear. The threat to your own and your comrades' lives, the deaths and serious injuries of friends, and the expectation that you might have to kill another human being took its toll on some more than others. But that is the lot of the modern sapper, especially when strategy demands that your troop must go looking for trouble.

21

LIFE AND DEATH WITH SPECIAL FORCES

The major task forces and the Special Operation Task Groups operated on different rotations, so it was in January 2009, halfway through MRTF 1's time in Afghanistan, that Corporal Shane Potter, whom we met in Chapter 8, found himself back in Afghanistan, again attached to a Special Operations Task Group. His extensive and detailed account of his second tour of Afghanistan provides a unique insight into life for an Incident Response Regiment sapper attached to special forces.

'Since my last deployment in 2007 the initial role as a sapper, which was primarily Reconstruction Task Force, was starting to change,' he writes. 'It was now 2009 and Australian troops were starting to be injured and killed. The threat to Australian and ISAF troops was increasing daily. It was the middle of a cold winter and we were told it would be a quiet period. How wrong this assumption was. It was only one month into the deployed task force rotation and Lieutenant Michael Fussell had already been killed by an IED and the body of Gregory Sher from 1st Commando Regiment was being repatriated back to Australia after a fatal incident only days before we arrived.'

Lieutenant Michael Fussell, an artillery officer, was a member of the 4th Battalion (Commando), operating in central Uruzgan. He was killed when he stepped on the pressure plate of an IED during a trek through rugged terrain to a suspected Taliban compound. An inquiry following his death reported that before the explosion, the soldiers did not follow 'track discipline', by keeping to a path that had been cleared of IEDs or previously walked over.

Private Gregory Michael Sher, a member of the Sydney-based 1st Commando Regiment, was killed in a rocket attack on a patrol base in Baluchi Valley. 'We had been sent into country earlier than the rest of our troop to support 1st Commando Regiment, the reserve commando unit, and we had no idea what we were getting into for this deployment. Winter operations are a different mindset and often the work involved requires good planning.'

Shane and his team arrived in early January and immediately trained with the reservists of 1st Commando Regiment, many of whom were police officers in civilian life. 'We didn't have much time to settle in and before too long we were out leading the patrols from the front. One night, we were conducting a search on a suspected insurgent's mud house near Sorkh Morghab. It was dirty work. Sappers had to crawl through goat pens and haystacks and get covered in a lot of dust and do it with an aggressive dog nearby. Our mine detectors' tones somehow had a way of annoying the dog with high squelching sound. After not finding any caches we were all told to prepare for extraction off the target.

'As we rallied into one building waiting for the vehicles, one of the teams noticed a light on in a compound 20 metres away. The commander of the task group gave the okay for a commando section to go investigate the building but all hell broke out when the startled occupant of the building opened fire with an AK-47.'

Five children and an adult civilian died, and another two children and two adults were injured, as the Special Operations Task Group undertook the compound clearance. This sparked an investigation back in Australia that ultimately led to three soldiers facing charges, including manslaughter and failing to comply with a lawful general order. Following several inquiries and a subsequent review, two years after the event, the charges were not pursued. 'After the incident, we sappers had to act very fast that night, firstly by clearing a safe landing zone for a medical extraction helicopter to arrive, providing safe passage to the wounded and conducting a thorough building clearance straight afterwards.'

On his deployment with 1st Commando Regiment, often involving long foot patrols, Shane's unit found some of the biggest caches of weapons and drugs he had ever seen. 'With one mission we needed to get two escorted trucks to come from the forward operating base into Tarin Kowt township to remove a large cache for destruction. Nobody had previously found such a huge cache of weapons and drugs so close to our base.

'The task group was then given the nickname of "TK Swat" as a lot of the reserve commandos were police officers in civvy street and our missions involved in and out raids. They were a very different group of soldiers to work with than the regular army counterparts as they were predominantly not full-time soldiers. Working with this task force gave us a greater appreciation of the diverse skills that set the part-time soldiers apart from the full time. The reservists' civilian police background, including their ability to estimate the true value of our cache finds and drugs street value, helped immensely.'

Out on patrol, to avoid announcing their presence in the area, the team had to park their vehicles a long way from the villages, which meant long foot patrols. As the IEDs became more common, and bearing in mind what had happened with Lieutenant Fussell, sappers had to take the lead and clear a safe path into and out of these villages. This entailed constant searching while carrying heavy loads of equipment which, on one occasion, had unexpected consequences. 'One sapper was leading the patrol into a target house at night to find that it was surrounded by large aqueducts. Looking for a crossing point, the section found a small log and decided this would be used as a bridge. The lead sapper was told to go over first to ensure that it was safe and free from any booby traps.

'Using night vision and laden down with weapons, a mine detector and a backpack, he slipped off the branch and fell head first into the water. Being the middle of winter the instant shock of the cold overwhelmed him and the section nearby had to jump in to pull him out. He had been completely saturated and was shaking uncontrollably. After the building was cleared, he disappeared. When we did find him, he was busy making a fire to get his body temperature up, saying, "So cold, so cold." It was decided if we ever went on a mission again with wide aqueducts we were going to bring a small foot bridge. On the next rotation a few months later with 2nd Commando Regiment, we returned to the same mud house, this time with a foot bridge.' However somebody had miscalculated the measurements and it was too short. 'The poor guys who carried it on the patrol weren't happy. At least it was summer this time.'

When 1st Commando Regiment went back home to Australia, the regular soldiers from 2nd Commando Regiment and the SAS began to arrive into the country with the rest of Shane's troop and with two other sections of sappers to support them.

'Being the experienced sapper team in the country, it was now our job to train our fellow sappers on how the war was beginning to change. Our role was developing from a support role mission to more of an active sapper's war.

'The Taliban could not defeat us with conventional tactics as we were so much better trained and with superior assets and weapon capabilities. So they increasingly used IEDs. Freedom of movement was becoming very restricted and the battle space had changed dangerously. Sappers were now the eyes and ears of each vehicle and foot patrol. Patrols could not happen unless an engineer support was assigned to each mission plan.'

This took a major change of mindset by some SAS and commandos, having to work with 'non-beret' soldiers who were not hardened by their intense training. The SAS and commandos had to help train the sappers, EOD techs and dog handlers to be able to work with them.

'This meant lowering their often arrogant attitudes towards other non-beret troops and accepting them into their small teams,' Shane recalls, remembering when he was relegated to the Afghan police vehicle. 'But they would still only accept good fitness and professional, diligent, soldierly conduct. We needed to become one force. Sappers needed to raise their standards in order to work with them, often on very long endurance missions.

'Our vehicle would check the unknown ground first. If we were not thorough, we were the first to be affected, as our Bushmaster would be the first to feel the full force of any IED. So our unit had to become better. It was from here on that many of the members of the unit took a more professional view of our own individual skills and capabilities to meet the mission requirements—a very different approach from the conventional army sappers.

'We were often asked to demonstrate higher physical endurance, undertake night-time operations, work reverse cycle sleeping patterns and mentoring roles, while still being level-headed enough to work in difficult working environments with the really high threat of knowing the next step could be your last. As sappers we would be dealing with unseen and unknown threats daily in the most adverse conditions, always way out in front in harm's way, so we needed to evolve to become smarter and fitter.'

The very real dangers involved in clearing pathways for the patrols was brought home devastatingly on 19 March 2009 on the longest vehicle patrol to ever be conducted by an Australian task group. Shane and his special forces group were on their way to north Kajaki, in the northern Helmand province, to be part of Operation Aabi Toorah. This major assault was intended to disrupt Taliban activity there and divert Taliban forces away from an area further south where British commandos were pinned down in patrol bases by intense insurgent activity. To some extent they would be bait in a massive coalition effort, also involving troops from the United Kingdom, United States and Holland, supporting Afghan National Army forces in attacks on Taliban strongholds.

They were heading towards the Chambarak Valley—which runs almost due north from Deh Rawud, a forward operating base to the west of Tarin Kowt—when Sergeant Brett Till spotted a roadside IED. Sergeant Till fired a controlled blast to destroy the bomb and was inspecting the result when its main 20-kilogram charge suddenly detonated and he became the tenth digger and the first sapper to be killed in action in Afghanistan.

'Our team of nine sappers [had just] witnessed the most horrific of scenes—seeing one of your team commanders being blown up in front of you. To then get out and look for secondary devices so we could safely repatriate his remains brought home the reality of how dangerous our job really was. We cleared a safe helicopter landing area and gave him an honourable send-off with his team of sappers, which he once led, escorting his body to the helicopter for a final farewell, while our section walked in front of our fellow sappers and cleared a safe passage for them.

'Experiencing an event like that can really change people. After that day a bond like no other was formed between all of the team-members. Even the commandos noticed this sapper camaraderie.

But we then immediately refocused back on our work, with no time to mourn the loss of the team leader.'

Shane's team needed to stay alert. They were getting closer to the infamous Chambarak Pass and beyond that lay Helmand province, their objective, which was known to be one of the most dangerous places in Afghanistan, especially for a sapper.

'As we walked up the hill towards the pass, we could see blown up vehicle skeletons littering the hill. Metal from previous IED blasts was scattered everywhere. The mine detectors that we use to clear the safe passage were now made redundant and it's in times like this the sappers' sixth sense shows its value. The threat triad indicators of loose soil, rocks, markers, as well as the observation of what doesn't look normal, comes into play.

'As we moved forward to find a clear route, I noticed a 50-calibre machine gun on the dividing road on the hill, along with a body armour chest plate sitting on the ground and two large craters opposite each other. The only safe and quick way through the pass was through the metal-littered cliff face. Even though it's easier to search the road with the abandoned 50-calibre machine gun and body armour, it was not worth the risk of the threat of a lethal booby-trapped IED, especially when we only just lost a sapper team leader a few hours ago.'

The mortar platoons fired onto the pass ahead, to clear the hillsides of any lurking insurgents. This would prove very fortunate for the sappers. As the mortars rained down on the hill, pockets of Taliban were digging in new IEDs. No doubt thinking they had been spotted and were being targeted, they abandoned their efforts and retreated without placing the main charges and battery packs.

'The search team discovered a battery pack, sitting on rocks wrapped in plastic, near a pre-dug hole the size of a palm oil container. We then continued up the pass and as we neared the top, a sapper within our team had a positive indication on his mine detector. After notifying his team leader he investigated with his trusty prodder and discovered a large vehicle pressure plate buried deep within the vehicle track. The vehicle was reversed back carefully into a safe area on the pass and we blew up the device. The blast was very big and made a huge hole in the road.

'We had to repair the road so that we could get to the top of the pass, to our luck, and there we saw the palm-oil container sitting on the side of the track. The mortar attack had prevented the insurgents from placing a second live IED. On the way up to the pass we had fourteen overall possible IED indications, which we mostly marked with GPS map grid positions and bypassed. The officer commanding the task force was impressed with our performance: through hours of careful checking, we had cleared the pass.'

After 15 hours of walking along 10 kilometres of road, through both day and night, rotating nine sappers and one explosive detection dog named Jeb, they had cleared the pass. The task group found an area off the track and formed up for all-round protection and rest. It didn't last long. 'The Taliban fired a 107-millimetre rocket at our position. The radio chatter was getting frantic, saying, "The Americans are here," not knowing who we were until later. After their welcoming rocket, the situation went quiet.

'That night we rested up and got a parachute resupply of fuel and food. After dividing it up equally amongst the teams, we noticed we had too much fuel to carry. With everything already maxed out on our vehicles, we had to decide what to do with the fuel. The order was given to use explosives and blow up the fuel rather than letting it fall into the insurgents' hands. The explosion was incredible. If the insurgents didn't know we were in the area after that night of mushroom cloud fireball explosions, they never would.

'Later during that night many of the task force soldiers dropped their egos and offered our two sapper teams sincere condolences. Some said everything bad they'd said about us they took back, admiring our ability to get on with the dangerous job nobody envied. To keep up the morale, our team sadistically played the Bee Gees song "Staying Alive" over the headsets in the Bushmaster. When a job came up we would play rock/paper/scissors for who would get the job. It was from here on the barriers between us started to come down and we started to learn new tactical skills from each other and when it came to the IEDs, our word was never questioned.'

22

MOVING TARGETS

Having picked their way through the dangerous Chambarak mountain pass, the special forces unit was now facing another problem—their vehicles weren't designed to carry heavy loads over rough terrain for long distances.

'The next day the task group moved into a defensive harbour position [basically a guarded camp] as it was becoming apparent that the heavy load of supplies, equipment, people and terrain was affecting the axles on the long-range vehicles and they were starting to break down,' recalls Shane. 'It was suggested that we stay longer in the defensive position. The drivers started to repair their vehicles. Despite hours of bush mechanic work by the drivers, we had to fly mechanics from the forward operating base into the field with spare parts for serious repairs.'

As much as they were enjoying the respite, it wasn't wise to stay in the same place too long. Only the day before the Taliban had fired a random rocket in their direction and it was only luck that it dropped short. Every hour they stayed put, the Taliban had time to observe from a distance.

'We were told to prepare for a foot patrol into the local village and they sent us on the patrol with three sections,' recalls Shane. 'As we walked through the Afghan agricultural crops and small aqueducts, the place seemed like a ghost town. The only people we could see in the village were one or two farmers, one of whom we found out later was a spotter for the local Taliban. We found in Afghanistan that if there were no women or children present, despite a place having a lot of mud houses, it was a sign something was about to happen or we were being watched. As we came up to our first large mud house the place was locked by a padlock and chain and nobody was present.

'It was decided by a section team leader that the locks needed to be cut and that we needed to search the compound. This was our first compound search with this task force and all that experience from working with 1st Commando paid off. We found a large cache of rockets, weapons, mortars and ammunition hidden in cavities in walls and the floor. We split up the cache amongst the platoon and carried off the find for destruction.

'As we were searching in the village the Taliban fired a machine gun on the platoon. After returning gunfire, we arrived back at camp and our team commander was impressed with our performance, but pissed with himself for not going. Once again, the commandos acknowledged our efforts.'

Vehicle mechanics with spare parts had by this time been flown into the position and the repairs were under way. But the insurgents were watching from a distance, so the next day they were sent on another foot patrol, deeper into the village, to see how the convoy could get through it safely.

'This time we were ambushed with shots fired upon us from the top of the steep ridgeline. It was the first time I had been shot at directly. The task force returned fire and after about an hour the skirmish was over and the insurgents had fled. That night after dark we were told that all vehicles had been repaired and it was time to move. As our search team was in the forward position we took the lead and the other search team stayed and followed up with the vehicles.

'We were about 30 minutes into the route search when we came to a choke point—a part of the road that channels you into one area. The sapper search team got a high metal signature in the wheel tracks of the road. As we were doing the search at night we did not want to alert the locals, so we had to mark the grid position of the IED and bypass. The areas near the track were not easily passable as they had steep embankments so our team leader decided we had to walk across agricultural fields to find a better way round. After about 15 minutes we found a crossing place and continued the search. We then made our way back onto the road and walked through the village as silently as we could, marking the road for the vehicles who were waiting at the start point to follow. They were only going to move once we had made our way through the village.'

The platoon then went up to the high ground and waited for the vehicles to move through. After half an hour, Shane and his team saw the convoy coming through, and climbed back down the hill. But then they saw something very strange.

'As the front vehicle passed through the last known roadside marker, we noticed somebody starting to clear the road frantically, with an Afghan soldier. As we approached, we noticed it was our troop commander who had flown out with the vehicle mechanics and was the only person mine-detecting the road.

'He was definitely happy to see us. He was exhausted from trying to tell the Afghan soldier to walk behind him, not beside him on the uncleared part of road. He then explained that due to our platoon having walked through the village, they had put the remaining sapper search team in our vehicles manning the guns in the rear of the convoy. So he was the only engineer left to clear the way at the front of the convoy.

'The platoon commander then came over the radio and started barking orders to hurry up, as he thought the search was going too slow. As this could be heard by all, it made us sappers angry, as we had been working hard all night and were now being told to work harder. The entire platoon could see we were angry and an angry section of sappers is not a good thing when your life depends on them.

'So we once again picked up our mine detectors and started the route search. One hundred metres into the search I spotted a pile of rocks across the road near another choke point and went to investigate. As I moved forward I noticed some loose soil and two exposed wires coming from the ground. So I cleared a good place to lie on the ground for a closer inspection.

'As I brushed away the soil I noticed a cable running off the road along a linear feature. As I looked ahead through my blurring-up night vision I could see some large rocks across the road, channelling vehicles to that direction. So I marked the suspicious-looking area, moved back to the rear of the vehicle, and spoke with my team commander. The search team commander, an EOD tech, then moved forward to verify that I had found an IED. The order was given to move the convoy vehicles back to a safe distance. The road dipped into a creek—there was no way to bypass.'

Shane's team commander had found a couple of mortars daisy-chained up to a pressure plate. As this was the first live IED since the death of Sergeant Till and it was being cleared at night, everybody was cautious. They didn't want to lose another EOD tech. Apart from everything else, he was the only EOD tech on the patrol and, until his replacement technician arrived, he had to manage two sections of sappers supporting two platoons.

'After a successful explosion and clearance we moved through and drove for about an hour using the cover of darkness to get into a safe area to rest up. The platoon commander, who had been urging us to hurry up, was very silent after we had found and cleared the IED.

'As morning broke, in the far distance the beautiful high mountains could be seen. We were enjoying a hot brew and some food when our troop commander came over and praised us for the good work we did that night. He said everybody back home in our unit was thinking of us and were hoping for our safe return. We then had a good laugh with him over the Afghan soldier incident last night and watching him trying to clear the road by himself quickly. He told us we would be moving to a safe area for a resupply and he would be leaving us to go back to Tarin Kowt. The sapper section that had lost their team commander had bonded real well over the tragic incident and would finally have another experienced operational sapper as their leader arriving soon.

'That day as we moved towards Helmand province, we lost another sapper, this time to a back injury. He was pushing hard, searching and doing his best, but the pain was becoming unbearable and he needed to be replaced. Even so, as we had to get to the next destination and we were already overworked, he kept going. We drove through the valley and the order was to rest up overnight near an isolated village. However, as we drove into position the platoon commander became complacent after all our search successes and decided to drive the Bushmasters onto an overwatch position on higher ground.'

Shane and the other sappers had warned the others that overwatch positions needed searching before driving onto them. The Taliban knew these tactics well and they could spot a good overwatch position as well as anyone, so they knew exactly where to place their IEDs.

'In fact, the OC of the task force had parked his Bushmaster only a metre from a pressure plate IED but everyone was oblivious to it, as there was no search done,' says Shane. 'Meanwhile, one of the team-members on another overwatch position saw a hole and a strange piece of plastic and called for sapper assistance. So we moved to their position to investigate, to find out if the plastic was the outer case shell of an exploded mine.

'As we searched the area we didn't find anything else and then all of a sudden there was a huge, loud explosion. The OC's Bushmaster had been moved just a few metres forward to get a better view of the valley and had driven directly over the pressure plate IED. Unfortunately, four soldiers who were nearby were knocked over by the explosion and two were seriously hurt. We watched from the hill opposite thinking it might be mortar incoming on to our position, and then it came over the radio the OC vehicle had hit an IED and we were needed at the site.

'We immediately found out that one of the seriously hurt was the sapper who was due to go home soon as he had injured his back. It looked like he would be going back even sooner as debris from the blast had hit his arm and he had a possible broken bone. An Afghan National Army soldier had borne the brunt of the explosion with debris in his back. The other soldiers were shaken up but not injured.

'We then scurried over to the site where we went into engineer search mode and began marking the site and looking at the blast effects. It was getting dark quickly so we were racing the sunlight and needed to work fast and there were only three of us sappers to do this job. Everybody then in the task force became paranoid and asked us to search around all their vehicles, so we began working endlessly until darkness came and the helicopter arrived.'

Shane and his teammates then had to load up the two injured guys' backpacks and weapons onto their backs and walk ahead of them as guides as they could not see the ground in front of them. 'We had to get them to put a hand on our shoulder and we guided them down the hill to the helicopter. Then the weather turned and it started to pour down with rain. We were absolutely saturated and must have looked like drowned rats. We were miserable, not least because our section was now down to three.

'That was one of the longest nights for us sappers. In pouring rain and pitch darkness we cleared safe areas, as the others looked on. As we sat in the Bushmaster vehicle later in complete silence, sharing a brew of hot coffee, drying out our soaked uniforms, in deep thought, all we could think of was what was planned for us tomorrow. When we woke up we looked around and saw mud, debris and safe markings from all our hard work the previous night . . . and one less sapper. Everybody was curious and they were like tourists to the incident site. We had to remind them that they should be more cautious until we'd done another search around the damaged Bushmaster, so that no secondary devices were present in the area to prevent any further incidents.'

The damaged Bushmaster was then inspected and, while it was still in good condition overall, the front left tyre bracket was unrepairable in the field and the mission still had to continue, so the decision was made to destroy it. All sensitive equipment and stores were then off-loaded into different vehicles already crammed for space.

'Everybody was reshuffled and once again we drew the short straw and took on the Afghan National Army soldiers, who were quite good actually, but this meant very cramped working conditions. The Bushmaster was too close to the village. If we were going to destroy it, it had to be dragged to a safe area, especially as it had been decided the best way to do that was to use an air strike. So the joint tactical air controller (JTAC) got on his radio and called in two 500-pound bombs onto the target. To everybody's dismay the first two missed and only created two large holes and a burning vehicle. The JTAC then radioed the pilots again. This time a woman responded. Everybody was shocked: it was a female United States fighter pilot. We all listened into the radio as she did her pass over the damaged Bushmaster, released her payload and destroyed the vehicle. Everybody was impressed and laughed how it took three bombs to destroy the Bushmaster.

'It was now time to move again and we entered a large valley full of mud houses. We had to make up for time so we had to keep off the roads and the decision was to take the high ground where we could. This really took the local Taliban off-guard. We passed that village unscathed really quickly by clinging onto the Bushmaster as it passed by on the hillside. One of the sappers went down to the road looking for a crossing point and found a sunken piece of ground in the road. When he placed his mine detector over the area a high metal signature was given, so we marked the area and bypassed it and continued hugging the high ground. Once we passed the village we made our way back to the road. We were only hours now from our mission objective, north Kajaki, and we were about to start a night search that would be full of surprises. We were getting very conditioned now and were learning to dread the night, for as soon as darkness came we all knew we would be out working again.'

23

INTO HELMAND

The special forces group, complete with Shane and his sappers, were now in Helmand province and only four hours away from north Kajaki, one of the most dangerous places in Afghanistan. The British normally operated in Helmand province and Australian troops had very limited exposure there. The stories of what had been inflicted upon the British over the years were relentless and horrific. The IEDs found there had been recorded as some of the most dangerous and sophisticated. However, sappers often had great success in removing the dangers of the battlefield to make others safe. The insurgents understood this and in Helmand they had a different strategy: stop the sappers. According to Shane, they targeted sappers and EOD techs because removing them would make the task group more vulnerable, less mobile and therefore easier to hit.

'We were told by our team commander we were going to be in for a big night of route searching, and so to rest up and get a good feed into us. When it turned dark we were destined for a nonstop route search until we got to a safe area through the mountainous road,' says Shane. 'As soon as the mortar team finished firing on all the high-ground positions overlooking the mountain track, our search began. As the

Bushmaster was positioned for another route search the entire hillside where the mortars had just fired upon looked like a bushfire scene and the hillside truly glowed red. The "Go" order was radioed over and the route search began and ran all through the night, rotating between sappers, until we came to a clearing and could see large aqueducts and power lines in the distance, all over the valley. It was difficult to choose a reliable safe route now so we had to search everything.

'The group found the open area they needed for another resupply and to pick up their replacement EOD technician and sapper. Both the new sappers, who had only just arrived from Australia to go straight into this patrol, had been on an operational deployment five months ago so both were experienced, and needed to be.

'We woke in the morning to a roaring sound and looked up to see two Chinook helicopters in-bound under the escort of an Apache attack helicopter. Our resupply was finally here, along with our much-needed new sappers. The task force stood to in case we were attacked. It was great to see the new faces come into our search teams, as it gave us some time for a brief reflection, hear what was happening back in Australia, and tell them what we had been through. We had been working very hard with very minimal rest and to have that lull on the battlefield was always a welcome experience.'

The next day it rained and to avoid vehicles getting stuck on an exposed road and becoming vulnerable the task group stayed where they were while the task force team leaders started mission planning for the final push into Kajaki. As the soldiers rested in their defensive position, their morning was abruptly interrupted by automatic machine-gun fire from an AK-47.

'Everyone in our position was caught off guard, soldiers were running everywhere and it was chaos. Our guys returned fire in the direction of where the burst of machine-gun fire came from but orders came over the radio [to] cease fire unless positive identification was seen. The rest of the day we conducted vehicle-mounted security watch and we had no more incidents. But we were learning that every time we got closer to our objective, the locals were not happy and would "shoot and scoot". It was now becoming evident that the word was being spread among the local insurgents that a large force had arrived and the Americans were here, still not knowing who we really were.

'We prepared the vehicles and manoeuvred the convoy towards north Kajaki. We travelled quietly through the night and did very limited searches. As we arrived into north Kajaki the place was very lush and green, very quiet and deserted. Mud houses could be seen in the distance and all around us were high mountains. We sat in a defensive position and were starting to eat breakfast when an RPG came straight over the top of us. It was surreal, like a moment caught in time; despite the danger, it looked really cool. It was our first morning and our welcome to Helmand had begun. What happened the next day was like someone prodding a wasp nest.'

That night the word went out that there was intelligence that had located a high-profile Taliban target, and the order was given that the group was to conduct a night mission. However, the mission was over before it had begun.

'We were less than 20 minutes into it when it came over the radio that there had been an IED strike, involving one serious priority-one casualty with life-threatening injuries.'

The two platoons had decided to split and one group, moving up into a hillside overwatch position, had hit an IED. The platoon commander had, once again, decided not to search the overwatch.

'Many infantry and combat units have a tendency to be very mission focused and when you think like this you seriously open yourself up to danger,' says Shane. 'The lessons of only a week ago had already been forgotten. The platoon commander was the same one who also made us hurry up during the search once we cleared the Chambarak Pass.

The decision he made this night—to move a vehicle without searching for IEDs—had cost Private Damien Thomlinson both his legs, and nearly his life. When asked [before] why we were not searching, he said, "What's your fascination with sweeping hills?"'

Within minutes, sappers were on top of the hill trying to clear the site, while medics tried to save his life. One of those medics was Scott Palmer, a commando who later died in a helicopter crash in Afghanistan. Damien met with Scott Palmer's father later on, and honoured Scott by walking the Kokoda Track in his memory once he recovered from his injuries. In the book, *Without Warning*, Damien gives his account of what happened and how he felt about that decision not to search the overwatch position. He is also unstinting in his praise of the sapper searchers, who worked for hours on end, for days at a time.

The insurgents continued to pressure the team and over the next few days the serious engagements intensified. The insurgents in Helmand province were very battle-hardened and seemed prepared to fight anyone—not something that was usual in Uruzgan province. The team's radio operators, with translators at their sides, were able to tune into Taliban radio communications using scanners.

'All this time they had been trying to test us by small engagements on our journey to north Kajaki and thought that we were Americans. The insurgents only realised their foolish mistake when they realised we weren't clean shaven. It came frantically over the radio, "It's not the Americans . . . it's the men with the beards." We were not from the normal army, and they knew they needed to get out of town or be prepared to fight, as we meant business and the firepower that we had was way too strong for them. But it was only after they'd committed themselves that they realised who we were and what they had got themselves into and in realising this started to retreat fast out of the area.'

Realising they were being assaulted by a much superior force meant the insurgents had to call for reinforcements from north Kajaki. This gave the British soldiers in Kajaki some battlefield relief and they were able to withdraw from their small outposts. The battle that went on in Kajaki made the Al Jazeera news and the insurgency took a heavy loss along with a very major morale defeat.

In an official communiqué, Major General Mark Kelly, then commander of Australian forces in the Middle East, said: 'The SOTG were in the field, deep inside a Taliban stronghold for 26 days. They were involved in eleven major contacts with Taliban insurgents that resulted in significant disruptions to Taliban activities.'

Major General Kelly added that the SOTG force element faced the daily threat of small-arms fire and rocket attack, as well as IEDs. In one day alone, fourteen IEDs were identified. On one occasion insurgents that were spotted laying a device were directly targeted using close-air support. 'On the first of April, Australian troops entered an area that was considered an insurgent stronghold and came under heavy and sustained contact with the Taliban. It was a day-long series of attacks through twelve compounds. Australian forces responded aggressively against the attackers and while the Taliban were determined in their actions, they were seriously routed.'

But Major General Kelly noted that the operation 'was not without its downside', with the tragic death of Sergeant Brett Till on 19 March, and the wounding of four others, one seriously. 'Success is not without its risks and the special forces soldiers continued to prosecute their objectives. The success of this operation is evidenced by the fact that the Taliban have been denied their freedom of movement while Afghan locals, the Afghan national security forces and coalition forces are now able to operate more freely in the region. The Taliban insurgent network has been seriously disrupted while its resources have been significantly degraded,' Major General Kelly said.

'As the objective of our mission was now complete we started planning our exit back to Tarin Kowt. The next few nights and days for us sappers was spent clearing roads. We now had a sense of pride and enthusiasm come over us. After spending a hard three weeks in the field our team morale—knowing we were finally going back to Tarin Kowt—skyrocketed. Knowing fresh food, a comfortable bed and a warm shower awaited us was pretty enticing.'

As the group rolled into Deh Rawud province, they came upon an Afghan police checkpoint. Their route searches were becoming very time consuming, so the platoon commander negotiated a deal with the Afghan police. The police offered to escort the group safely to the Dutch and United States FOB in Deh Rawud in exchange for food, fuel and some money.

'By doing this we gained two days and at the FOB we rested up and serviced our vehicles for the last push home to Tarin Kowt. It was also during this time the soldiers made some swap and supply trades with the United States soldiers. Some of the task force soldiers swapped T-shirts and coins, while I went for more treasured items and negotiated a deal with a United States army ranger for highly sought-after Rhino night-vision helmet mounts in exchange for a jacket. Once the news came out that I had negotiated a trade of Rhino mounts, soldiers started to approach me and were trying to trade whatever they had.

'After a farewell barbecue with our United States friends, it was now time to leave on the final convoy move to Tarin Kowt. We were now out of the dangerous IED-known areas and were now going into the more populated areas, which meant more suicide bomber or shoot threats. This next push home we were told we would not be stopping and it would be at least five hours of solid driving. After four hours of manoeuvring the convoy we came through the valley. We could now see the communications tower, often known as the navigational marker to soldiers, for as soon as you could see that tower in the distance, wherever you were in Uruzgan, you automatically knew the safety of the base was very near. After five hours of driving with no serious incidents we had made it back to our forward operating base in Tarin Kowt. We had endured a lot over the last three weeks and were relieved to be home.'

After that mission, says Shane, it was decided that it was too logistically demanding to maintain the task force within the field. The amount of vehicle repairs, fuel and, food resupplies by helicopters and the loss of two soldiers, one killed in action and the other seriously injured, was considered unsustainable. The next few months they were kept to the confines of missions within the province of Uruzgan.

'However, the respect that we had earned as sappers after that mission would never be forgotten. Our unit had its place in the command from that day on. We had lost one of our own—the first sapper of the campaign. Even though I didn't really know Sergeant Brett Till personally, he was well respected and his loss was not just felt from our unit but throughout Australia in units where he had once served.

'While other soldiers of the special ops command had to endure lengthy selection periods that developed very close-knit teams, we showed, through working in adverse conditions, we sappers could also become close-knit too. Commandos didn't like working with outsiders and would often keep to their own until you gained their trust and showed competence. So every patrol you went on, the sappers had to earn their respect.

'A week after we arrived back in Tarin Kowt we had some time to honour our fallen and injured comrades with a small ceremony. After the high tempo of the operation we now had time to grieve. The old mess on the forward operating base within Camp Russell became a recreation hut named JT Tavern, in Sergeant "JT" Till's honour.

Many fun sapper nights were later held there until we built our own private sapper entertainment area called the JT Saloon. It was the hidden sappers den, built near our accommodation, where all the mischievous sapper planning [happened] and games were played.

'Having been taught to speak the local language, I organised through my Afghan friends and interpreters for a free pay television to be connected into the JT Saloon right next to our sleeping accommodation. This made a lot of sappers happy, to watch the latest documentaries and films and have a good laugh at all the Bollywood channels as well.

'One member of our troop used his talent as a sign-writer in his previous life to make up a remembrance board for our first ever unit loss. As the deployments rotated between the different troops so did the work on the JT Saloon. It was like each sapper was a custodian . . . and added their own unique troop style to the JT Saloon. Tilly would be so proud of all the sappers' efforts to honour his ultimate sacrifice.'

At the end of their rotation, Shane's troop was farewelled at Tarin Kowt airstrip by the Middle East Commander Major General Mark Kelly, who had heard of their efforts during a briefing with ISAF. The unit had been acknowledged at a very senior level for doing very dangerous and difficult work. The OC commanding the task force in the field had stated at an ISAF briefing that the hardest working people in the task group were the sappers. Shane's team commander, an EOD tech, was recognised with the award of Medal of Gallantry for his tireless efforts during the rotation.

'The troop commander of our rotation received a gold commendation for our efforts, to acknowledge our bravery doing a high-risk job for long periods under dangerous conditions,' says Shane. 'He acknowledged all of us and said if he had the opportunity he would cut up the award and give it to everyone who served under his command.'

The sappers from the troop's seven-month deployment were never the same after that tour, according to Shane. Many of them were posted out of the unit or discharged out of the army. From that patrol mission only four sappers are still serving in the army at time of writing; two went on to become EOD techs and two, including Shane, became instructors. Only a handful later redeployed back to Afghanistan.

This was a turning point for the sappers, as part of the army as a whole. It had now been proven beyond doubt—acknowledged and accepted—that sappers could function as a very effective fighting unit alongside the army's elite.

If sappers are a breed apart, the special ops sappers are something else again.

24

BUILDING RELATIONSHIPS

If the short-term aim was to defeat the Taliban, the long-term plan was to leave enough skills, and a culture of reconstruction, behind so that Afghanistan wouldn't slide back to the kind of society that would allow the Taliban and al-Qaeda to flourish again. So, while the special ops sappers were off chasing Taliban, the MRTFs were rolling in and out of Tarin Kowt. Captain Josh Porter arrived in the spring of 2009 with MRTF 2, deployed as the construction troop commander in the engineer squadron but was promoted halfway through his deployment, taking on the role of an engagement officer.

'I know there's a lot of interest about the search guys and deservedly so, but there were many sappers who were tradesmen and who were deployed in those roles but were under fire there as well,' he says. 'I had a troop of guys, tradesmen and plant operators, all sappers of course. We went to each patrol base up Baluchi Valley and Mirabad. We did repair work and minor upgrades and we were continually outside the wire. We also, during the course of my deployment, designed and built a new patrol base in Mirabad.

'The construction troop primary function was to do the infra-structure support outside of Tarin Kowt base so we were supporting all the patrol bases. They held a company group—so no more than a hundred, depending on the size of the patrol base—and they were not all infantry, it was mixed.'

Josh didn't come into MRTF 2 completely unprepared: 'When I finished my basic course at the school of military engineering, I was told that I was deploying with the troop to go to Afghanistan. I was excited, I worked really hard to get in, there was only one trip available and I got it so I was happy. I did the full pre-deployment package as the troop commander with the battle group that I was deploying with. It was the full administrative mission rehearsal exercises, out bush a lot . . . almost like deploying before deploying. We built a patrol base at high range at Townsville. We did other construction tasks. We did all the tactics, convoy rehearsals, a fairly robust package. It wasn't perfect but . . .

'I think most guys who went through the pretty common process in that early deployment in southern Afghanistan would agree that it was very much combat focused. Particularly the infantry soldiers, and the guys that didn't have a lot of life experience, went into Afghanistan thinking they were going to fight. So I think we were under-prepared for the softer parts of the deployment.'

And despite nearly six years of education and training as both a soldier and an engineer, Josh wasn't completely prepared for what confronted him when he first arrived in Tarin Kowt. 'It was hot, and I was nervous. I had 30 guys under me. It's a very distant memory now but it was very exciting. Helicopters coming in and out. It was exciting for a young bloke . . . for us all.

'I was also in charge of the trade training school, which was set up within Kamp Holland. It was run by sappers, and in my opinion was the most successful activity that the coalition forces did in that whole province. It was extended for a time and in five or six years we pumped through probably close to a thousand local boys. We gave them a trade, gave them a tool bag and then, combined with a lot of the other high-level contracts that we were managing for construction in the community, they were then employed by those contractors. So it was long-term employment. That was highly successful; a lot of hard work from the guys, so it was basically like a TAFE.'

Five or six times a year there would be a graduation ceremony where a senior officer would hand out a certificate and a tool bag to each of the trainees who had completed the course. Outside the wire, it was a different challenge altogether.

'The way it would work was, the convoy commander was an infantry platoon commander but he would have a section of sappers under his command. The engineer OC would say, "We need to go to this FOB to do a repair task." They would then attach me to a platoon team commander whose job over his whole tour was to do convoy escorts—he was expert at it. Personally I didn't really get involved. I would assist with the planning and tell him how many vehicles we had.

'I would order stores [such as building materials] from Dubai or anywhere I could get my hands on them, I would get them delivered and load them onto our trucks and would have an infantry platoon attached and we would drive out of the base through Tarin Kowt. The truck would then visit bases and sometimes we encountered IEDs en route.

'If the shit hit the fan it would be the troop commander who would control the situation. It happened almost every time [they left the FOB]: they would find an IED and get out and dispose of it and clear it.

'A lot of our work was repairing existing places. We would be repairing everything until they were fully functional . . . we fixed all the electrical wiring, waste-water systems. We expanded bases. We fixed up a lot of overhead protection. We installed kitchens and bunkers. While we were working we got contacted a lot. They were basically castles on the top of a hill, put in dominant positions for a reason. They were hit a lot of the time.

'We were lucky enough that they were inaccurate, at least in my time, but we had a lot of close calls. There was one time I was out the back with my plant section commander and we [were filling] up some Hescos. We both had to hit the deck [as] we had a fuel rocket coming over the top of us. Hescos were the bane of our existence [but they provided] blast protection. They were as good as digging in, essentially, without actually having to dig.

'Often the nature of the work the guys were doing meant they were exposed to potential attacks. [While] filling up sand bags on top of the outpost . . . anyone who was a good shot could take you. The soldiers were forced to wear body armour even when they were working.'

One of Josh's jobs was to identify a spot for a new patrol base, then build a road to it, then build the base. 'They'd done an air-mobile insertion [delivered ground troops by helicopter] into Mirabad valley, which was traditionally a Taliban stronghold. The special forces had done a lot of operations through there over the last couple of years. Then the conventional forces went in air mobiles, a new style of operation for us in Afghanistan. I remember one of the commanders saying it was the biggest air mobile operation since Vietnam. They went in and occupied platoon houses inside the green zone.

'My job was to come in from the *dasht* and work with the CO of the battle group, advising on a good tactical position for an FOB and then build it as quickly as I could. Over the space of a few hours we walked a couple of spots, I recommended this particular spot and we had to build a road through it. I had Afghan army engineers attached so we used them basically as labourers for their development.

'Once we were on a task that I had spent ages planning, we were going to drop a bore hole for water, a quite typical task and then the boss came over and said, "No, we need to cancel this job. Recover everything you can because we are going to close this patrol base and we are going to build a new one." Within a week I had to pack up the guys, convoy back to Tarin Kowt, work out what supplies I'd got. We didn't even know where we were going to build it and what the ground conditions were going to be like so I had to come up with a template design that we could build. And then I would deal with reconnaissance and then call my plant selection forward for them to start tunnelling the road to the site. I then went back picked up all the stores, gave the convoy orders and deployed back out and started building and that was all in two weeks—so it wasn't perfect.

'It was an engineering construction site essentially on the edge of the green zone. We set up a defensive harbour just in about 400 metres from the green zone so we'd be outside of RPG range. We didn't get engaged for some reason . . . I think mobile operations had already saturated the green zone so we had some security. We built a patrol base over time. We put in septic tanks, all the creature comforts that we could. We dropped the bore. This was done by a local contractor. He had a diesel engine—he was on there all day, engaging the clutch and disengaging the clutch to drive the drill, [for] about nine weeks, just doing this all day. Incredible. I paid him well and looked after him, made sure he was fed.'

Building patrol bases—which are basically forts, usually on the tops of hills—happens in stages. The first part is getting the basic defensive walls up and then you add the facilities.

'It's usually very quick, as you've only got limited resources, but then the sappers that come on other rotations make it better. You've got to realise you couldn't do it all and it's only going to get better and better.

'We built about twenty Hesco-based accommodation bunkers. These cost about 20,000 dollars together—expensive but a lot quicker than digging in. The Afghan National Army members were living in the same camp so we got them on the tools and then they built their own wood-fired oven using mud bricks [made from] local mud from down the river. We got involved in that process as well; they were showing us—not that we really cared for mud bricks but it was a bit of rapport. We developed a good relationship with the Afghan sappers. I would encourage one of my partners to come in and have dinner with the Afghans. I would grab a few sappers and say, "You're coming in." A lot of them would just want to do their job and not engage with the locals.'

Later, the issue of green on blue killings—Afghan National Army soldiers turning their guns on coalition soldiers—would surface, and, in fact, three Australians were killed at this particular patrol base. But that was long after MRTF 2 and Josh's time in Afghanistan.

'It's really important to be seen to be engaging and be trying to humanise your relationship with these guys, because it's part of your job, it makes things more secure. But you always have your weapon in the correct place—you want to know where he is, keep your peripheral vision going. You've got to be smart about it. It does get hard because you get tired and you get complacent—that happens with everyone. That was definitely the message that most commanders would pass on to their soldiers.

'When we built this patrol base you had the Afghan National Army living inside too. So when you were walking in and around you were protected from the green zone. You had a level of mistrust with the Afghan soldiers but you would be in a fairly relaxed state. However, when you went into your hardened accommodation bunker, I think most guys were just happy to be there. I think you were playing probabilities by that stage.'

One of the biggest changes in the way they operated was started by Captain Rodney Davies, who suggested that, instead of sappers doing all the major infrastructure projects in and around Tarin

Kowt [TK] city and building patrol bases, that they hire locals. 'He thought we would get more involved with the community. We could pay them and get them to do some work. I followed from his initial ground-work and used the Afghan National Army to get into the community and do some work around, very small scale. I got the PsyOps [Psychological Operations] guys to do some flyers, showing how the Afghan National Army was coming to help and how they were building things for the community. I was told that the commander of the ISAF got this and said it was the first time he'd seen this in all of Afghanistan: an actual Afghan uniformed soldier formally doing infrastructure support for the community. Usually it's always just been us doing it. We tried to continue that throughout my tour, anyway.'

About halfway through his deployment, Josh was promoted to captain and given the task of engagement officer. 'The role wasn't formalised. I think it was created for the purpose of our operations and I'm sure it wasn't formally on the Order of Battle and it probably didn't last after I left. I got some direction from the commander back in TK about what sort of effects he wanted. It wasn't specific tasks, but I was supposed to create opportunities for local infrastructure development, build rapport and liaise.'

Josh and an infantry platoon occupied an existing *qala* once owned by a senior Taliban commander who now lives in Pakistan. It was a small, fortified base on the fringe of Sorkh Lez village in the Mirabad valley. 'We had two sentries—one on the roof and one at the front edge of the building—all the time, night and day. So when our guys did their air mobile research into Mirabad Valley . . . they went in and occupied existing *qalas* as a firm base, and then they patrolled out of it, because they didn't have patrol bases built for them at this stage. Concurrently we built them a large patrol base out of Hescos and the like.

'What they ended up doing was to use the patrol base as the command centre. They did have quite a substantial force there. They would patrol because the valley was quite hostile and we had the patrol base on the hill. If you try to do all your patrols out of one spot you end up walking the same ground, which is dangerous, so what was done was to set up platoon houses [in existing *qalas*]. In my time we only had one or two, one at each side. They had an infantry platoon, an engineering section, and me, in this particular platoon house.

'So I wasn't in command of the engineers, even though I was an engineering officer. I did help—I was the ranking officer—but the infantry platoon commander was the technical security commander and I was there as an engagement officer and adviser about the patrol program. I went on every patrol—two patrols a day—and I spoke with locals. One particular guy—an elder—was a bit dubious, but we paid him to pay locals to build a new mosque for this part of the village. We set up a little contract for him; it was one way to get local employment going.

'We were using quadbikes on patrol from time to time and it helped to re-supply the platoon houses as well, because they were in tricky areas at times. But we couldn't actually get across the river with the 4WD motorbikes, as it was a bit doubtful whether the bridges would take the load. So I sourced some materials from Tarin Kowt, did a quick design and one of the [combat] engineer troops got together as a troop task, which was very rare—this was like an engineer troop task—and we built a river crossing.

'I had my own interpreters—I had three over time. I briefed them every night, they slept next to me; I made a real concerted effort for them to feel part of the team. To me, they were the most important help we had, not just because I was in the engagement role. I think most sappers would agree that when you are searching and trying to do a preliminary engagement before you search a house, you've got to be really clear to the elder or the homeowner about what he needs to do. It's important that the interpreter can communicate that. You can say all you like in English but the interpreter can get it across.

'Every night I would sit down and we would talk about what discussions we had had. I would give them my opinions and ask their advice. It got to a point where we were so close that they knew my approach and they were anticipating. But they would never talk for me because I didn't want to let the locals think I was not completely in control.

'It wasn't just engineering related—I don't need to talk about that much—I spent a lot of time working on the elders, trying to get info on the Taliban, intelligence gathering. This was a Taliban village—a lot of Taliban fighters and leaders came from this area, this is what I'd been told—so they had a lot of disunity in the community. One of the ways we hoped to eliminate that was to create employment that the community could work on together like an infrastructure project. That was the idea, anyway, but we couldn't really get it up and running. But it gave us something to talk about anyway.

'My thoughts at the time were that the process was more important than the outcome. So all this talking about something was better than talking about nothing. So we were talking to the elders and accepting their hospitality, and getting a feel for the hierarchy and the different sub-tribes. Say the intelligence came through from high up and we got tasked to search a building—I could go and see who the homeowner was, and I could go and engage with him, have tea with him for half an hour, and say, "Okay, we need to do a search. Can I ask you to put all your women in one room." All these courtesies you would afford any homeowner.'

Josh tried to understand the community as best he could, if only to ensure his men weren't being shot at for no good reason.

'I grew a beard, partly because I didn't have to shave—if you didn't have running water you didn't have to shave. But it actually really helped me—they called me Red Beard. Even though I wasn't a total commander they looked to me as [though] I was the one in charge, which really helped, because elders only want to talk with the blokes that are in charge—they didn't want to be stuck around soldiers.'

As good as the relations were that Josh developed with the locals, they would come under considerable strain if villagers were arrested for being suspected Taliban.

'This was always a heartbreaking process for me, because there was always a story. I could be having a good relationship with an elder and he would say, "No, you can't, this is my son, and he's a good boy. He was just sleeping nearby, he didn't know about all this!" Then I'm caught in between because I've got the boss on the radio saying, "Take him, PUC [person under capture] 'em," and I had to deal with that issue with the locals.

'We searched this guy—he had a lot of very violent Taliban propaganda on his phone, beheadings and all that sort of stuff, so we took him back for questioning. The elders came in straightaway and they came to me and they were saying, "No, all the kids have all this on their phones." It was quite hard to manage because only a few days prior you would have been sitting in their home having chai tea with them.'

But Josh knew the elders were also caught in the middle—between the coalition forces and the Taliban. 'These elders were in the middle in their whole lives—a very complex web. And we are not there anymore, are we. I was in this village for four months, and now I'm back in Australia. Those guys are still living there, sowing seeds for their crops. These guys just have to do what they have to do to survive. I had no illusions that any of these guys would protect me, or that any of them wouldn't flip.

'At times I felt like we were our own worst enemy. I think we were clumsy. For instance, you've got all these fields and they were very well irrigated so the soil was quite soft. And this is the livelihood of the farmers. In between all the fields you had dirt tracks . . . which the locals would walk on. They would never walk across fields because you'd be stepping on your crops and your livelihood. Those footpaths were effectively channels, which were easy for the Taliban to target with pressure-pad IEDs and eventually one of us was going to walk on that footpath. Therefore we would walk on the fields, but that would damage the crops. I had a feeling that a lot of the time we were shot at just by farmers who were pissed off at us for damaging their crops.

'So, it's very hard because if you go one way you're probably putting the soldiers lives' at risk by walking on the paths in order to build the community support, and the other way you're making your soldiers safer but you're building anger in the community which might lead to more engagements. It's a catch-22.'

25

THE DAY OF THE WELL

WO2 W, who was first on the scene after his mate Michael Lyddiard was badly injured by a booby-trapped IED in 2008, returned to Afghanistan in 2010 and again in 2013, after stepping up to EOD tech. And while he found that the Taliban's use of IEDs was definitely on the increase, it's the searches that he remembers best—particularly the day that he and his team found one of the largest caches ever discovered by Australian forces: two buildings with hidden rooms and secret walls, lined with ammunition, explosives, RPGs, and even rare surface-to-air missiles.

Around this time WO2 W, while out with the SAS, found the sappers had a lot of independence to search for weapon caches themselves—and inevitably they would find a lot. On the day they found the record haul they were south towards Kandahar, deep into the badlands that the conventional forces didn't venture into often. 'This thing was massive,' he recalls. 'Not only did we find a big cache that we were after, we got the guy who was the big distributor. We were after this particular guy who was the quartermaster for that area. He was dishing out weapons and ammunition left, right and centre. The intelligence guys knew that and we went into this area to kick up a bit of dust I guess.'

WO2 W had split his team up to do the building searches. He sent some to one part of the valley, himself and his mate Tom to another part, and the dog handler to a third. 'My dog handler searched with his dog, obviously, but if the dog needed a rest or wasn't needed at all the handler would pull out his Minelab and use it like the others in his section.

'So Tom and I were patrolling up this one side, just doing our thing, just searching buildings as we go, any areas of concern, not really finding much more than a few old rounds and stuff. But then I could hear over the radio that the other part of my team had found a cache in a building, starting with a couple of RPGs and I'm like, "Yeah, that's fine, they can deal with that stuff—they've got enough explosives on them to get rid of it."

'So, as the day progressed, it started out with ten RPGs and then it grew to twenty. And over the space of an hour or two, by the time it got to 60, I was thinking those guys probably didn't have enough explosives to get rid of that amount of RPGs. So I got on the radio and said, "Look, these guys probably don't have enough bang. We're probably going to move to their location to give them a hand." Obviously, I'm carrying explosives and Tom was carrying some gear as well, but I just wanted to get a handle on what was happening.'

When WO2 W finally caught up with his men, his No. 2 took him to a hay shed type of building inside the main compound where they had found a floor that was basically a layer of RPGs with dirt and hay piled over the top.

'He then led me down to another area that he was working in and there was a wall that he'd put his metal detector up on and got an indication so he started chipping away and soon he uncovered this whole room and inside were some AKs and a couple of RPG launchers and stuff.

'And then he took me down to one of the other boys, Joe, who was down the bottom end and he was dealing with a wall that was a bunch of ammunition boxes, all stacked up and plastered over with mud to create a wall. So I'm thinking this is fairly impressive and I started stocktaking what we had.'

WO2 W then went into an adjacent building and noticed right away that there was something amiss. 'There was this wall that didn't add up given the way the building was built. The room just seemed to have the wrong angles on it. I thought, *Yeah, righto, I'll just check this out.* So I got my detector out and ran that up and down the wall. And, sure as shit, I got an indication. So I started chipping away. I'd probably thrown a couple of swings at this wall, not too heavy, and this massive chunk of mud fell off the wall and revealed this doorway. It was probably at about chest to shoulder height from the ground and it's like, *Ah huh, oh yeah, we're on here.*

'It had this dirty great big padlock on it, but everything had been mudded over, so someone just quickly sticking their head in would have seen a nice, normal mud-brick wall. By the time I'd dusted the lock off, I opened it up, got a grip of the situation and it was like, *Holy shit!* I got back on the radio and gave the boss a heads-up. I said, "I probably need more sappers and I probably need more bang. I will give you the figures soon."'

WO2 W carried on searching and soon had SAS members carrying boxes of arms and ammo out to a central disposal point. There were about 140,000 rounds of small-arms ammunition and these were all in tins. There were 432 RPGs of varying types. There were two wire-guided anti-tank missiles, that you put on a tripod, aim at a tank and control with a joystick. And then there were two Blowpipe surface-to-air missiles that the British had given to the Mujaheddin to fight the Russians. 'I put in the request that said I need about five more sappers and I gave them a big run-down of bang. Because by this point it was getting late in the arvo and I knew we were getting to the end of what we were finding.

'There were also probably 50-odd AKs of varying descriptions. There were boxes that used to contain the AKs and in the boxes there were all the ammunition pouches, still brand new, although degraded. It was like they'd hit a convoy, taken the load, stored it in this room and then sealed off the room. There's probably stuff that we missed in there. There were small caches of the old RPG rounds and in other parts of other rooms there were rocket launchers and grenades.'

Meanwhile, the dog handler had found something that was potentially even more damaging to the Taliban than losing all that weaponry. 'He found this pillow and inside this pillow it had a pair of ladies underwear, a little pistol and this really little notepad. This notepad turned out to be the little black book of where all this ammunition and explosives was going to. He had found gold. It was all in code: "Person A receives this many rounds per month; Person B . . .", and so on. We had no idea who Person A or Person B were but that was some good intel that we were able to feed back.'

As if that wasn't enough good fortune for one tour, WO2 W then nailed the Taliban quartermaster. 'We tracked down the dude that owned the notebook and all the gear and we locked him down in a specific area. The SAS had gone into this compound on a tiny little hill. Gone in, done their bit, then come out and said, "Yeah, you're good to go in there and start searching."

'There was a bunch of women in there and we usually didn't have too much to do with women because of the whole respect thing over there, and trying to do the courteous thing. So we searched around this building and these women were just sitting around this well. And the well hole was flush with the ground but it had like a frame over the top. And I thought, *These women sometimes stash mobile phones up their dresses and stuff,* so all I wanted to do was separate them individually and wave my Minelab around them to see if there was any metal indication. If you get a big strong hit, you know that, well, it's probably not jewellery.

'So I did that to all these women and then there was this last old duck. She was being a pain in the arse, to put it bluntly. I would tell her to stand over there and she was carrying on—I have no idea what she was saying. And I finally got her away from the well and I ran the Minelab over her and nothing. I wasn't going to check the well but I thought I'd better. For whatever reason I decided to walk around the well and come in from the other side. But behind me I had my partnering force guy, who was on one side of the well, and I was on the other.

'I had to crouch right down to bend and then I kicked the lid off this thing. And all that I saw—well, I saw lights flash before my eyes—this AK barrel was pointing up towards me. And there's obviously a dude on the other end of it. He let off this burst about half a metre away from my face. If I'd been standing on the other side I'd be dead right now. I would have copped that burst from the balls to the face. The dude who was following behind me copped a round in his chest plate, but it was right on the bottom edge. If it had been a centimetre lower, it would have gone through his guts. However, it just clipped the bottom edge of his body armour and he ended up with this massive welt around his gut.

'The SAS weren't in the compound at this time. It was me, Tom, a couple of the partnering force and these women. The women immediately pissed off out the back door and we all just started shooting into the well and as we were shooting we were moving backwards in order to get behind some sort of cover . . . One of the SAS patrol commanders said to me after he thought we were burning ammunition or something, cos that's sort of like [what it sounds like] when you hear rounds shoot with a suppressor on and then you burn rounds—it's just like a light pop, it's not like a normal gunshot.

'Anyway, we shot a lot of rounds in there and I got on the radio— I thought [I sounded] casual and controlled—and said, "We've got some guys down the well and we need assistance." The SAS guys reckon I sounded more like a girl screaming over the radio. I'm not sure who's telling the truth. But anyway, the SAS came in and at that point they took the lead and they were moving up shooting in the well and dropping grenades down.

'We used up our grenades. There was no return fire but we were all concerned that maybe inside the well there were tunnels leading off. We threw grenades down to concuss, and when we ran out of grenades we started throwing smoke grenades down, then ran out of [them]. I used to carry a couple of thermite grenades—which get really hot—to burn caches and what have you. I made a charge out of some my explosives in my bag, lowered that down, blew that up. As if that wasn't enough, they called in the helicopters then sent two Hellfire missiles down the well.'

A few days later WO2 W received an intelligence report to confirm it was the Taliban quartermaster and two bodyguards that they'd killed in that well.

'So not only did we find his major supplies and his little black book, but I was directly involved in eradicating him. I call it The Day of the Well. I know my buddy Tom does too. It was certainly a close shave.

'One of the saddest moments for our rotation came on our last job. Most of the guys had stripped down their gear, but we got this call to go out on a job. And we landed in this area and did this job, but unfortunately an SAS sergeant by the name of Blaine Diddams was killed on that. I think about his poor kids that were expecting him

home within a week or two and that being the very last job we were
doing that he was killed on.

'All my trips I regard as memorable, whether they are sad memories
or happy memories. I see the first trip as being very productive and
great exposure. That's a great privilege I've had, and many others have
had: I've been in direct command of soldiers in wartime operations.'

26

21ST-CENTURY TUNNEL RATS

By the time 2010 came around, many things were changing dramatically in Afghanistan—and many were staying exactly the same. The Dutch rolled out of Tarin Kowt in August 2010, at the end of their four-year commitment to the NATO-led coalition. They were replaced by Americans as part of the much trumpeted 'surge' of an additional 30,000 United States troops into the country. For the Australian forces who had made it clear at a political level that they were NOT interested in taking over command from the Dutch, it was, 'Meet the new boss, same as the old boss'.

MRTF 2 had been replaced by MTF 1. The word 'reconstruction' had been dropped from the task force's assignation, signalling yet another adjustment in focus: this time presaging a major shift towards preparing Afghan troops for the day that they would be on their own against the insurgents.

Meanwhile, engineers were no longer commanding the task forces, as they had been with the first four rotations and whether or not the combat engineers were allowed to do their jobs swung like a pendulum, depending on the infantry troops recognising the need for their paths forward to be cleared of IEDs. Typically, on a mounted patrol, the cavalry vehicles would deliver the troops to a muster point and then drive up to higher ground to provide overwatch. Coalition troops had been doing this for years and the Taliban knew this, so they would plant IEDs on the higher ground. But the decision to check for IEDs before laying up was down to the platoon commanders. If they chose not to, whether or not they were hit by IEDs was more a matter of luck.

Needless to say, however, when sappers are involved, someone is going to take the piss. One group of sappers were out in the field when they got a call from their cavalry overwatch group. The cavalry boys had belatedly done a sweep around their vehicles and got a positive reading. The sappers down below promptly mounted their metal detectors like hobbyhorses and 'rode' them up the hill to where the ASLAVs and Bushmasters were parked. The cavalry boys thought the sappers were mad but it was they who were left red-faced when the engineers revealed the reading was from a can ring-pull and the cavalry had their mine detector sensitivity turned up way too high.

The same sappers were resting up in a forward operating base on the night of Eid ul-Fitr, the festival that marks the end of the Muslim holy month of Ramadan and its related fast. They were perched on the Hesco wall of their fort, watching fireworks going off all down Baluchi Valley and enjoying what appeared to be a laser light show. They could hear gunshots but that is not unusual during celebrations in this part of the world. They took cover after realising that the lasers were in fact tracer bullets and they were getting ever closer to their perch. Discretion was the better part of valour on that occasion.

The flip side of the coin in regards to sappers not being properly utilised was that it became apparent when there just weren't enough of them. Senior officers were having to intervene to stop sapper burnout. They had to explain to infantry troop commanders that sappers work to a different rhythm—they have all the same stresses and challenges as infantrymen, but when a convoy or patrol stopped for route clearance, the infantry could rest up while the sappers were involved in the most stressful part of their jobs.

This reached its nadir in one rotation where the sappers were embedded so deeply with their infantry platoons that their own officers couldn't get in touch with them, even when they were in camp. However, a little sappernuity soon fixed that. Some construction and transport engineers had decided that camp life was just a little too dull so they constructed a little club in the corner of the camp that looked from the outside no more inviting than a couple of shipping containers but inside was a haven where movies could be watched, the internet could be accessed, computer or card games could be played. The sappers' officer soon worked out where he could meet his men.

Meanwhile, Major Mark Willetts, who, you may recall, was in Afghanistan long before al-Qaeda was a byword for evil, was in Kandahar at regional command south where he was NATO's deputy chief engineer for the region. His job, basically, was to keep the main highway through Afghanistan open, for both strategic and political reasons.

'The NATO budget was about six hundred thousand dollars for road maintenance across the entire theatre. One pothole in regional command south, because of the threat to the contractors, could cost eighty thousand dollars [to fix] so it was a big problem,' he recalls. 'Highway One was basically the ring road around Afghanistan, which went right through regional command south and was our main east–west route. For national reasons they wanted it sealed and they wanted it flat.'

Before Major Willetts' time, a contract for creating culverts (where drains cross underneath roads) along Highway One had been tendered. 'But it was a cost plus profit contract, which means the contractor is motivated to do as much work as possible, whether it's needed or not, because each bit of work gets him a bit of profit. So, we found we had hundreds of culverts across this stretch of road.' There were plenty of useless culverts at the top of hills, as well as useful ones at the bottom. All of them provided an opportunity for the Taliban.

'There were bloody hundreds of the things that were pointless—unless you wanted to plant an IED in them, in which case they were perfect. We wanted to dig out unnecessary culverts and replace some road but of course, you know, it's eighty thousand dollars for a pothole. Removing a culvert and rebuilding it was going to be expensive. So we had all sorts of wild schemes, [involving] concrete blocks and huge pieces of metal, to try and stop the bad guys from getting explosive devices into the culverts. But it's spy versus spy—everything we'd attempt, they'd get around. And so we'd do something else, and they'd get around it again. It's the nature of conflict—that was our daily existence.'

Such is the circle of life, even in the army, that three years later, when Mark returned to Afghanistan in 2013, he was doing a very similar job to that which had taken him there twenty years previously: clearing mines. 'This was a United States Army unit called the Mine Action Co-ordination Centre. Up until that time it had been focused purely on clearing the minefields inside the wire at Bagram Airfield and they'd been hot to trot and working with contractors for years. These were almost entirely Russian government or Afghan government minefields intended to protect the airbase.

'Initially the Mine Action Co-ordination Centre, which Australians ran on behalf of the Americans, only dealt with mines inside the wire at Bagram. Then, on an Australian initiative, it became the Theatre Mine Action Centre. So when I took over I was responsible for all of Afghanistan.'

There were two types of work envisaged. Firstly to clear the minefields inside Bagram and the other coalition bases, and then there was a separate plan to clear areas that were to be used as Afghan bases before anyone could start building on them. But Mark is adamant there is a third strand that is being ignored.

Mark points out that Australia is a signatory to the Convention on Certain Conventional Weapons, which includes a protocol called Explosive Remnants of War. This requires all combatants to clear up their unexploded ordnance after the conflict is over. However, he points out, while NATO is making great headway in clearing up Russian ordnance, they haven't even begun to think about their own leftovers. That's another battle for another day.

While Mark Willetts has gone full circle, Shane Potter's career took a wildly different route, which nevertheless makes sense given that the special forces had inadvertently been partnered with the Afghan police. Add in the fact that Shane had acquired Pashtu language skills and an affinity for dealing with Afghans, and the logical ducks line up. One of the problems they were facing in Afghanistan was that they were arresting suspected insurgents and gathering evidence but the cases were falling apart in court. Part of the mentoring process had to be finding a way of making legal cases stick.

'I was embedded with the Australian Federal Police for four months to learn about crime-scene investigation processes,' says Shane. 'I was trained up in forensics and stuff like that and then had to find a way that we could pass this on to the Afghan police. But the problem is that you are trying to pass on Western methodology to a pretty primitive culture. So what they did was to place me with the Attorney General's office and the prosecutors in Afghanistan. It was all about the evidence the sappers found in the field from IEDs, then what we got in the lab, and then what we could present in court, all interlinking with each other.

'Part of the problem was that we were conducting these operations and catching the bad guys but then letting them go because we didn't have enough evidence to convict. But then the locals who'd had their lives disrupted by the raids in the first place would see the bad guys coming back into the community and they'd wonder why they would ever help us. When you are trying to train police who have, like, grade one literacy, it's just not going to happen. But when you identify the leaders, the smart ones, they end up educating you.'

And that's how Shane—the man who lost two police cars in his first tour, and then who crossed the notorious Chambarak Pass to kick some serious Taliban arse in his second tour—ended up playing the leading man in *CSI Kabul* in his last tour in 2011. At one point he was lecturing senior members of the Afghan legal system, from judges and prosecutors to clerks and cops, in Pashtun, about the importance of uncontaminated forensics and the chain of evidence. A senior officer walking past stopped in his tracks, looked in and said: 'What rank are you, soldier?' 'Lance Corporal, sir,' Shane replied blithely, revealing he was the second-lowest rank in the army. The officer looked at the assembled heavy hitters, shook his head and marched on.

Also around this time, over the winter of 2010–11, Warrant Officer, then Sergeant, Benjamin King discovered something in the Dorafshan Valley, just north of Tarin Kowt, that made his day. In fact, he says it was the highlight of his tour. Benjamin was supporting an infantry patrol whose commander was so gung-ho in his determination to engage with Taliban fighters that, according to Benjamin, he failed to notice vehicles full of fighting-age men heading out of the area they were heading into.

'At one point we found these tunnels and I got very excited, knowing all about the Tunnel Rats and all that. I basically stopped the patrol and said, "We've got to go down these tunnels. We've got to go down these tunnels." The infantry commander was not keen on it, he had his own mission. But I made him promise me we could go back and check this tunnel after we'd finished. So we ended up finishing off the patrol and coming back and putting up a defence all around it.

'I wasn't convinced the entry we found was the main entrance they were using. It looked like a bit of a slump hole and due to the weather had ended up collapsing in at that point. At first we threw smoke grenades to see if it came out anywhere else, and it did come out of a couple of places. One was in a *qala*—one of the houses—and also further on down the track. So we waited for that to settle down, then decided to rope into the tunnel.

'It was probably a metre and a half high and 700 centimetres wide. For a combat engineer it's pretty juicy. We thought there could be something down there. We went down—myself and my searcher, Sapper Luck—and, sure enough, it was a man-made tunnel. They weren't caves—they were leading into *qalas* and out to the creek in a rat-run.

'We searched around the entrance, then roped down and searched the bottom of the tunnel and from there took the EOD team with us and basically cleared the whole tunnel.

'Where we started the main group protecting us was probably 100 metres out from the tunnel entrance. By the time we finished searching, we were probably 150 metres beyond where they were. We found RPGs, rifles, bullets, bandoliers, a number of grenades, and stuff like that . . . It would open up into larger areas, and you'd see on the sides they'd dug out a bit of a shelf, put the stuff there and then put rocks up against it to hide it.

'We weren't able to blow the whole tunnel. It went forever. But the problem was, we were finding so many RPGs, mortars, other rounds and explosives, that we couldn't carry them all when patrolling. So we moved all the explosives into a central location in the tunnel, then we moved out, blew them up and collapsed it. If we'd had to blow them up outside, we [would've] had to worry about other places and buildings and people. Easier to blow up in the tunnel as then it's controlled.'

If the sappers were in Tunnel Rat heaven, the one person not impressed was the infantry commander. 'All he wanted to do was find the enemy all the time and get himself a VC,' says Benjamin. 'But after a few days, we knew there was no enemy. He'd been stuck in Tarin Kowt so he'd seen no action. This was his first time outside the wire and he saw nothing. But afterwards I was sitting there with my sappers and we talked about the history of the Tunnel Rats. I told them, "Today's a day you can be proud of." Others had significant contacts, but getting down the tunnel and staying down there and finding stuff was important. It was a big deal for us.'

A big deal, indeed, although not a matter of life and death . . . unless there had been a carefully concealed IED down there. This was the almost bipolar life that our soldiers had to lead in the war zone: excitement at being able to do their jobs and half an eye on the reality that their jobs meant someone was trying to kill them.

27

FATAL ATTRACTION

Call it thrill-seeking, adrenalin addiction or testosterone-fuelled machismo, but some people, young men especially, can't resist putting themselves in dangerous situations. It's that need to test your own mettle combined with a feeling of invincibility (which tends to recede as grey hairs arrive). In June 2010, that feeling, if it existed in any Australian soldiers in Afghanistan, may have been enhanced by the fact that it had been almost a year since any of their number had died.

Certainly then Corporal Tyson Murray had a sense of excitement rather than dread when the bullets started flying. 'People find this strange but I don't think anything compares to the thrill of combat. That's what it is. It's a thrill, is all I can say. It's almost surreal. I remember the very first time I was shot at we were down at Sorkh Lez Bridge and it was almost surreal. You'd just hear the little crack and the thump and you'd think, *Oh shit. We're being shot at!* But instead of everybody taking cover you've got all these boys sticking their heads up trying to see where the shots are coming from. We were making bigger targets of ourselves because we were just that excited and wanted to get rounds off so much.

'I'm always thankful we were thrown in right from day dot. So we had to adapt then and there. There was no build-up to it for us . . . It was day one: fucken boom! On the money. So we didn't have a choice.'

But there was a downside: the sappers were needed on every patrol that went out so they were operating to the point of exhaustion, literally.

'We were as ripped as cheetahs because we were carrying a huge weight, fighting and moving through the green zone. We were just lean muscle and we just kept going and going and going. The average patrol route would be 10 to 12 kilometres and you needed the adrenalin from the contact just to break it up.

'Soldiers thrive on that. You fucken love it. And that's what I miss so much now. Nothing compared to the thrill I got from being there and the next thing you're putting rounds down and you think, *That one was close*. It's exciting. It's an adrenalin rush . . . that I haven't found anything compares to. That's why, when things are working in your favour—we had been in that many contacts and found that many IEDs—we almost felt invincible. Whatever the insurgents threw at us, we found it. Up until 7 June we'd never missed a device, that we were aware of, and when it came to firepower we always came out on top. That's a good feeling, knowing that you are always the winner. And then it becomes something you grow to need . . . I was so desperate to get back overseas to experience the combat—to experience that rush—because it was something that I'll never forget.'

That sense of immortality evaporated when the fates proved, in the cruellest possible way, that members of Tyson's team were very mortal indeed. And he concedes that a combination of exhaustion, complacency and over-confidence may have contributed to the deaths of Sappers Jacob Moerland and Darren Smith. 'Once you do something for long enough and you're proficient enough at it, regardless of what that is, eventually complacency is going to creep in. We'd been at it for six months and we were absolutely exhausted. We were shattered.

We'd patrol every day and then of a night we had picket duty and so we weren't eating properly. We didn't have showers at the platoon house. We just had to wash ourselves with a bottle. We didn't have fresh clothes. We didn't have fresh food. We had nothing, so we were really pushing ourselves to the limit and it's possible that complacency crept in through sheer exhaustion. But you can't stop doing your job. The reason we get out and we find this shit is for our mates: if we don't get out and find the devices then someone's going to die. As simple as that. The grunts can't do their job if we don't go out and find the stuff first. But it's exhausting.'

On 7 June, Tyson's team had enjoyed a successful morning in a target operation in Sorkh Lez in the Mirabad Valley. They had recently moved out of a platoon house which was getting shot at every day, even with RPGs, so they'd withdrawn to Patrol Base Wali and were operating from there.

'It had been about a 3 or 4 am start. We got into the area, the infantry set a cordon and then gave us free rein so we searched the entire area to look for whatever we deemed to be suspect and we recovered an immense amount of caches, to the point where we couldn't carry any more. We were returning to the patrol base about 11 am when Darren and Jake identified a suspect item. They were standing right on the device when it was found. I was sort of to the east of them, about 15 or 20 metres away when it's come over the radio that they found something . . . We called the patrol to a halt, and just as I was looking up, and thinking they were standing a bit close to each other, the device detonated and it killed them both.'

Darren Smith's explosives detection dog Herbie was also killed in the blast. There are different opinions about what triggered the device. Some say it was remote-controlled, others that it was booby-trapped.

'Unfortunately, it was set up right on the edge of an aqueduct and so when the device has gone off [it] made a ten-metre crater that filled with water and so we couldn't recover any remnants from it. So there was no way of really telling [what had happened].

'MTF 1 was a rough trip. We got back to the patrol base and the company sergeant major [CSM] made a speech to us, and he says, "Look, lads, grieve if you need to but tomorrow we're back on the job." And he got us out the door and that was hard. Like it was backing up the next day after going from the position where you thought, *Well, nothing is going to get past us*, to having lost two mates. The CSM came out on patrol with us and we needed that. And a couple of days later we went into Tarin Kowt for the boys' Ramp Ceremony [funeral].

'That was one of the hardest things I've ever done. I was still only a young fellow and it was hard lining the runway and then seeing the boys off. It rocked us. But, yeah, I can remember that half the section was on leave at the time because it was in the middle of our deployment and we had two weeks leave to go and see our families. I remember coming back to Tarin Kowt and the boys had just come back from their leave and seeing them for the first time and just like—I was speechless. I was absolutely speechless. I was a wreck.'

Nothing can easily explain the sense of loss and possibly even survivor guilt that affects those left behind when their mates lose their lives. Some of the men Tyson mentioned who were on leave admitted feeling guilty that they hadn't been there, even though they could have done nothing to prevent it. The death toll was mounting in Afghanistan. Three commandos would die in a helicopter crash within a fortnight after Jacob Moerland and Darren Smith's demise.

Almost exactly a year after Moerland and Smith died, Jeff Newman also lost a comrade and a good friend. Jeff's team were on an operation with the American Drug Enforcement Agency (DEA). It's not widely known that the DEA had their own troops and helicopters in Afghanistan, and would partner up with ISAF for specific missions.

It worked for both parties. The Aussies used DEA choppers to get into areas they wanted to patrol and the DEA used Australian troops to bolster their fighting troops on the ground so they could safely get in and out of places that held the drug-making facilities and supplies. It was a trade that paid off for both sides. The DEA was reducing the flow of drugs globally, and at the same time that reduced the profits funnelling back to the Taliban to spend on arms and equipment.

'If we walked into someone's compound and they had bags of raw opium, we would confiscate it and the DEA agents would take care of it. We'd do the search and hand it over to them to look after—they would generally burn it,' recalls Jeff. 'We'd go out in Russian Mi-17 helicopters that the DEA agents were using. I enjoyed those. They were roomy, you had the door open at the back seat so you could shoot out.

'These Afghans weren't necessarily Taliban—just local people trying to make some money. They grew the poppies to get the resin and then bag up the resin and take it to the next person to sell. The Afghan government would go through and destroy the opium or the poppy fields. Then they would give them seeds to grow corn or whatever, to try to get them out of growing poppies to growing fruit or veg. But the farmers can't make a lot of money growing veg and they make a bit of money off the opium. They would put the resin through drug presses and those were the things we blow up. It would be the same story if we came across any 44-gallon drums of chemicals used in the manufacture of the drug. This is where my guys would need a good understanding of demolitions so they could do the most damage with the least amount of explosives for the simple reason that we were not carrying a lot.'

On 6 June 2011, Jeff and his team were part of a commando raid into northern Helmand province with the intention of disrupting Taliban supply lines into Uruzgan. The team was supported by DEA troops who were piggy-backing onto the raids to conduct village searches for opium and drug-making equipment.

'When we got to a village our platoon moved into overwatch positions and then we sent in a search element which was another team with the DEA agents. Their partnering force would move in, search the bazaar and then they would leave and then, when they were safe, we would leave too.

'Each team had been allocated an area that they would go to to provide overwatch and outer security for the searchers to come in and search the bazaar. Originally I was going to the spot where Rowan 'Robbo' Robinson was going but then I was allowed to get another engineer on the helicopter so Robbo went with Sergeant Todd Langley. I always had Rowan paired up with Todd, who was a team leader within the commando platoon.

'We all got into our spots, no drama. The area I went to with the platoon headquarters and the area that Robbo went to were old Russian trench lines on the hillside. We needed to have engineers go with the teams to clear any former Russian emplacements. The Russians liked to lay minefields around their fortifications and a lot of times they didn't recover them. There had been evidence that IEDs had been placed in these positions previously before we arrived; [things like] scattered plastic oil containers with evidence of blast damage and batteries.'

The main role of Jeff's team for this first phase of the operation was to clear the area of IEDs and landmines to make sure the commandos would get into their positions safely. Robbo Robinson cleared the whole trench line for them, and then the unit sat down and waited.

'It was always good when we had helicopters flying over, it was generally pretty quiet then. [There were a] couple of pot shots here and there. And then the gunships had to leave to refuel and that's when the firing picked up. Robbo was off one of the flanks as part of the security for the team he was supporting. Then he started receiving intense fire. Rounds were falling all around him. I remember the conversation over the platoon radio net between him and Sergeant Langley. Todd's going, "Robbo, are you okay out there?" and Robbo's going, "No, it's starting to get a bit hairy out here. Can I move in?" So they threw some smoke and he made his way in to where the rest of the team was. The fighting intensified. Robbo was helping the guys in the gunfight and he just popped his head up at the wrong time and a sniper got him.

'I was about 300 metres away with platoon headquarters on a hill watching it all unfold, and we were copping rounds in and amongst us up there. I just remember over the radio: "We've got a man down."'

The commandos provided first aid but Robbo had pretty much died straightaway from the sniper round. Even so the commandos didn't stop working on him until the medivac helicopter arrived and the handover was conducted.

'I also remember seeing the commandos firing on the enemy while dragging Rowan out along the trench line towards the helicopter landing zone. By this time the search team had already been through the bazaar. A couple of the engineers in that team had to run up and blow the power lines so the helicopter could come in and land.

'It was probably about three or four hours later when we got extracted. We found out when we got back that Robbo had died. The team was upset and so were the commandos because we'd worked together for so long in that platoon. When we landed, the commandos were all huddled together and their platoon commander was talking to them about what was going on. The other engineers from my troop picked up me and the remainder of my team to take us to where Robbo's body was, so we got to go in and say goodbye.'

Robbo Robinson was only 23 years old when he died on that hill-side in Afghanistan. It's a measure of the closeness of the special ops sappers and the commandos that Robbo's parents asked that, rather than flowers at his funeral, donations be made to the Commando Welfare Trust. Two weeks before Robbo was killed, highly decorated Sergeant Brett Wood, aged 32, of 2nd Commando Regiment, died when an IED was detonated as he and two comrades were lured into a trap in Keshmesh Khan in Helmand province. Sergeant Wood was the first commando ever to receive the Medal for Gallantry, awarded for his heroics in a battle near Chora in 2006.

Exactly four weeks after Robbo died, another member of the commando platoon, Sergeant Todd Langley, aged 35 and on his fifth rotation in Afghanistan, was also killed in a firefight.

'I think about those blokes every day,' says Jeff.

In all, 41 Diggers died in Afghanistan, among them nine sappers:

- Brett Till, aged 31, a sergeant and explosive ordnance disposal (EOD) technician from the Incident Response Regiment, was killed on 19 March 2009 while trying to defuse an IED (see Chapter 21).
- Jacob Moerland, aged 21, a sapper in 2 CER serving with MTF 1, was killed on 7 June 2010 by an IED in the Mirabad Valley region of Uruzgan province.
- Darren Smith, aged 26, a sapper in 2 CER, was fatally injured in the same incident as Sapper Moerland. Also killed was his explosives detection dog Herbie.
- Richard Atkinson, aged 22, a corporal in 1 CER serving with MTF 2, was killed by an IED on 2 February 2011.
- Sapper Jamie Larcombe, aged 21, of 1 CER serving with MTF 2, and an Afghan man employed as an interpreter, were shot in the Mirabad region on 19 February 2011.
- Ashley Birt, aged 22, a corporal serving as a geospatial technician in the 6 Engineer Support Regiment, was shot and killed in an 'insider attack' on 29 October 2011.

- James Martin, aged 21, a sapper from 2 CER, was shot and killed in another 'insider attack' by a member of the Afghan National Army on 29 August 2012.
- Scott Smith, aged 24, a corporal in the newly formed Special Operations Engineer Regiment, was killed by an IED on 21 October 2012.

The funerals of all the soldiers who died in Afghanistan were painful and poignant affairs. Their deaths had a profound effect on their families and loved ones, of course, but also on their mates in the forces. It was possibly all best summed up by Lieutenant Colonel Paul Foura of the 2nd Combat Engineer Regiment at Sapper Martin's funeral in Brisbane, when he said his fellow soldiers wanted Sapper Martin's mother, younger siblings and grandparents to know they shared in his loss.

'You are more than a team-member, you are a mate and a brother,' Lieutenant Colonel Foura said on behalf of Sapper Martin's unit. 'Marto, the regiment, the army, the world, won't be the same without you.' He held his hand on Martin's coffin for several moments before stepping back and saluting 'the sapper, the son, the brother, the grandson, the friend'.

Every soldier at every rank who goes into a war zone knows there is a chance, however slim, that they won't come home but the deaths from insider attacks were perhaps the hardest to swallow. Australian soldiers knew that IEDs and the Taliban were the enemy—Afghan National Army soldiers were supposed to be on their side.

28

TRAINERS AND TURNCOATS

The history of Australia's mentoring of the Afghan National Army (ANA) ranges from the comic to the truly tragic but it had a very serious intent. These were the people expected to fight the Taliban once the coalition forces had gone home. We have seen how various rotations implemented different training programs but they were all dealing with very raw recruits. At the very basic level, Afghan soldiers were far from home, underpaid, often poorly educated and seldom highly motivated. And then, of course, there was the language barrier. So how did our guys at the coalface cope? After all, they were soldiers, not teachers or social workers.

Warrant Officer Andrew Pitt had a lot to do with ANA soldiers in the winter of 2010–11. Based in Kandahar, it was his job to train them up in explosive hazard reduction, which was basically getting them to the level where they could partner coalition personnel when they were dealing with known explosive threats. 'If an IED had been found by a farmer, say, they had to be able to assess whether or not they were able to deal with it and, if appropriate, BIP it,' explains Warrant Officer Pitt. 'We did a lot of work with the corps advisory team. The Afghan troops were very receptive but like with anything else, if it got too hard, they'd stop for a cup of chai.

'The first week I was there I was told by the bloke I replaced, "You are [like] the favourite great uncle on Christmas Day. You are the one who always smiles and tells jokes and is nice to the nephews and nieces." So that was the attitude I took—I was not the master or the boss. So every day I gave them a big smile, a shake . . . a hug.

'There was a lot of smart ones who did take notes and did take a lot in but honestly, the IQ of the very basic Afghan soldier isn't that high. Their concentration span was very poor, but the ones who really wanted to pass concentrated and tried their hardest. We'd show them drawings on whiteboard exactly how we'd do it then go out and demonstrate, then they'd practise. We'd have about six practice runs on things before their final assessments. That's when you could see all of a sudden one soldier would go off and miss big areas when sweeping. But I had a policeman on the second course who was so good in the first practical test he did we said he's not going to do an assessment, it was perfect. A week later he nailed it.'

Andrew had a high failure rate—about 50 per cent across three courses—and was eventually pulled up for that. 'The high-ups asked me why I was failing so many and I said I needed to know that they could do that job to a standard. I had to ask myself if I could partner this person with one of my mob. Can we have him standing right next to you?

'The Afghans often didn't take it that well. One or two of the Afghan soldiers I failed said they were going to go back to their unit and get beaten up because they look at failure as something shameful. They would get beaten up and ostracised by their sergeants.

'Two of [the guys I failed] I was worried about, and one I was very wary of, and had my 9 mm [pistol] in my pocket when he was around. The day that I failed him, I didn't like the look of him at all, so I called his unit and said, "I am just about to fail this guy and I don't want him here." Half an hour later a car came and took him away.'

Warrant Officer Benjamin King had a different kind of experience with the Afghan troops—for a start, he was out in the field with them, performing live searches and patrols. 'I felt we had a pretty good relationship with them, considering we were working with them every day. As long as you understand our cultural differences and understand they're not going to have the same levels of skills as the Australian sappers and don't work the same number of hours as we do, and are not as driven as Australian soldiers, you'll be okay. That's probably why we got on so well and got more out of them than perhaps others did. We took it for what it was, understood it and didn't try to make it something it was never going to be.

'It was hard sometimes, though. If they didn't want to patrol any more, they'd just stop and take their boots off and wash their feet. I had my guys backing me up so I started going out with them on patrol, and if all turned to poo, I'd know I could resort back to my guys, patrol and get the hell out of there. But I had to be careful because as soon as [the Afghan soldiers] stopped, they would put their mine detectors over their shoulders and . . . walk back to base in the shortest, quickest and most direct route possible, which was pretty dangerous.

'But you can't tell them off, you have to let them save face. You can't yell at them, as then they won't walk out the next day, or do what you want them to do. It's like dealing with children, to some degree . . . You have to negotiate, you have to save face with them all the time as they're very proud and if they don't want to do something, they won't. But overall, they still came out on patrol every day. Okay, timings were varied, we just knew that when they got tired, that we couldn't stick around any longer. We had to manage that and not become a target on the ground.'

At a totally different level SGT T, with special forces, also did his share of mentoring. 'They would always be on patrol with us, even back in 2009. It's just that the numbers increased in 2013. They increased quite a lot. We would dedicate a training member to, say, mentor the Afghan engineer component that was similar to us and commandos would provide a mentoring team for their infantry company, so we mirrored each other's set-up.

'They have in a lot of instances an uncanny ability to sense out caches. They just know where shit is. Sometimes they can just tell where an IED is. We've got our methods as well but they can just sniff them out sometimes. I found that they're quite a valuable asset with securing caches and what not, but they could be a liability with their conduct. Their infantry tactics weren't quite up to par with us. The same with the standard of shooting and assaulting. Their culture is very different to ours, obviously, and I don't think that they reflect the same work ethic.'

In 2013, when political decisions were being made to withdraw from Afghanistan, there was a clear need to make sure there were enough trained troops on the ground to replace the coalition forces when they left. That meant a surge, not of NATO forces, but of Afghan soldiers who could be trained and who could then go on to train others.

'Late in our pre-deployment training they told us they were sending over a second combat team and were also sending in additional mentors. They went under the [my] command . . . and under Gordon Wing—who is a very sharp guy—as well . . . He made sure that they were able to manage that tempo but they did a lot of training just on the base and then sort of built up the capacity to have the Afghans do their own level of support to their own patrols and that kind of thing.

'When we built Patrol Base Wali in Mirabad, we had an Afghan engineer troop working with us to build the patrol base. Our tradesmen would provide some advice to them on how to do the specs and so they built some of the bunkers and strong points and Hesco containers and walls and that kind of stuff.

'And then they worked up to doing a job for the community, putting a foot bridge across an area where there was a pole and rope crossing. It was all about getting the engineers out doing stuff too so it wasn't just an Australian show. And you could see the Afghans out working as well which was good. I would talk to the Afghan platoon commander who spoke English, which was very helpful and I always had the Australian mentor on the side if there were any issues but the Afghan engineers were pretty good. Actually, they worked up to the point where they provided the search for a re-supply mission from Tarin Kowt down to Kandahar and back, which was no small deal. That was actually pretty impressive.

'The Afghan sappers did searches too. We provided a section to support them but we didn't want to have the Afghan guys search and then have our guys searching behind it because it completely undermines them. So the Aussies were there, just in case really, but they weren't required. The Afghan guys went through and did the forward search but, admittedly the road on that route was sealed and it's harder to bury stuff in a sealed road. However, you've got to check the culverts and that kind of thing and they did all of that. The trainers and mentors did a great job getting them to that standard in a couple of months.'

Corporal Jonathon Marshall witnessed a very clear example of how far the ANA had to come when he was posted to Kabul to help with mine clearance: 'There was an incident when they found a bomb and I said we've got an EOD specialist to come up. And this Afghan bloke came up and booted the thing. They've got no fear. They don't mind if they die, it's *inshallah*—what's meant to be will be. That's their religion.'

IED kickers aside, the growing relationships between the Afghans and their mentors were proving too fruitful for the Taliban's comfort. The worst thing imaginable for them would have been if the coalition forces left but the level of security wasn't diminished. They had to drive a wedge between the ISAF troops and ANA members and, according to a BBC report, in 2010, the Taliban decided to increase the number of their supporters who were infiltrating the security services.

Whether that was true or not, the number of insider attacks increased steadily. The same report revealed that a disproportionate number of the insider attackers came from Taliban supporting areas near the Pakistan border. It also claimed that many of the attackers had provided highly suspect paperwork for their enrolment applications. However, there was also the possibility that the attacks occurred when Western troops inadvertently insulted Afghan soldiers whose Pashtunwali culture has pride and honour at its very core.

At the time of writing more than 140 people had died in insider attacks by Afghan soldiers, seven of them Australian soldiers. The Taliban routinely claim credit for the attacks, although, since the gunmen are usually either killed or escape, it's hard to verify.

Jonathon Marshall actually witnessed one such attack when he was stationed with the 101 Force Protection Platoon in Kabul: 'We were based right next door to an ANA training grounds and then just further over was the Army National Officer Academy so we had all their officers and bigwigs around. There was an insider attack just outside our base. I saw it myself. There were ANA soldiers and a New Zealand guy. Fortunately he only got shot through the foot but the ANA soldier put eleven rounds down to the backs of the soldiers that were only about 10 metres away. Only one person got hit but a round ricocheted off one of the weapons and that's how the

New Zealander got shot in the foot. Then obviously we returned fire and ended the situation.

'After that, there was definitely a lot of tension, and it went from us being very sociable to two weeks of us being very cautious. That cohesion wasn't there anymore. Everyone gets comfortable in the situation that you're in and then something like that occurs and you've got to take that step back and realise, *Oh, wait a second. Although we are there to assist these guys, these guys can turn around and shoot me at any time!*'

That reaction of increased caution, if not downright suspicion, was repeated across Afghanistan. It would take another entire book to examine the incidents and speculate about what was really behind them. But dog handler Sergeant David Simpson's response was fairly typical: 'There were a couple of instances there where I was aware of it and I actually positioned myself before patrolling so that I wasn't directly in front of an Afghan soldier. I'd actually push them in front of me. Especially some instances if one of them was being a bit stupid or a bit weird, you'd take more notice of them and you'd think, *Oh, what could happen here?* It did actually start to cross my mind a bit. Especially towards the later years.'

One other less-than-savoury aspect that was allegedly part of Afghan army culture was 'chai boys'—kids who made tea and ran errands for Afghan soldiers—being raped by the men at night. We were told about senior Afghan officers having very obvious 'toy boy' adjutants trailing them around like love-struck teenagers. And we heard just as many claims that none of this was true and, if it was, it was done so discreetly that no one ever witnessed it. One sapper, however, told us he still can't sleep at night because he remembers the screams of the chai boys.

29

WOUNDED WARRIORS

There's a suspicion—or maybe it's a myth—that the toughest men take the loss of their mates hardest. But there's more to it than one too many ramp ceremonies. Sooner or later the physical wear and tear of long, demanding patrols, the mental stress of wondering if the next IED has your name on it, the gnawing concern that the Afghan soldier coming towards you might raise the barrel of his gun and become, in that instant, your enemy rather than your friend—all of these elements can add up to something that not only tears you apart emotionally, but undermines your whole sense of self and worth. Recent figures from the United States show that more American soldiers died from suicide last year than in combat.

Jeff Newman, now back in civvy street, was one of the most highly regarded team leaders in the Special Forces Task Group. He now has to take daily medication to deal with what being in Afghanistan did to him, including the death of a good friend right before his eyes.

At time of writing Lance Corporal Trent Goodwin was on medication, pending medical discharge after having been diagnosed with depression and PTSD: 'I put it more down to the stress,' he explains. 'We were getting shot at and forever searching for bombs but

I think the stress was the main thing that threw me around. I'm a lot steadier now than I was; I wouldn't have been able to do this interview two years ago, no way!

'I'm a medic now. Towards the end of this trip I put my transfer in. I'm not going to search again. As much as I loved it, I just knew I wouldn't do it again. We always had a bit of a giggle that you wouldn't know if you hit an IED because it would get you before you knew it, that sort of dark humour. Once I got towards the end and I knew the home front was nearly there, I thought, *Is it really the be all and end all?* But I loved it and if I could do it again without the mental damage I would do it again in a heartbeat. But I've lost four mates from Afghanistan, four sappers. They all died [there] after I got back.'

The army is more aware of the effects of PTSD than ever and is making serious efforts to get their men and women back to full mental health. The problem is that the soldiers have to ask for help—but many won't do it because it could mean they will not be allowed to do what they love, the very thing that's destroying them. It's the flipside of the original catch-22: the guys who needed help most were the ones least likely to ask for it.

Corporal Tyson Murray was offered counselling after he watched two of his friends and team-members killed by an IED right before his eyes. 'You spoke to the psych and to be honest you just sort of told them what they want to hear because you didn't want to be sent back whilst your boys were out still doing the job. So providing you weren't going to kill yourself you pretty much got on with it. While you still have some sort of goal to work towards it's easier to suppress what's really happening.'

Tyson can't remember thinking about the boys and what happened over the next three months, or at least dwelling on it, not least because of the relentless demands to keep going out on patrol.

'It wasn't until I came home, where I lost that momentum. I'd been operating on this roller-coaster for so long, performing at this tempo. When I came back to Australia, this tempo has gone from up here to down there. And that's when it all caught up with me.

'My first night on the piss, I can remember staying at South Bank, Brisbane, in a motel. I'd been on the cans all day and I walked out onto the balcony and it was pissing down rain and I just stood there and threw my arms out and I cried and that was the first time I can remember crying since the incident. That's when it all started and from there, it just got worse and worse. But you'd keep a lid on it because there was talk of another deployment and another operation and I'd keep suppressing these emotions and keep working through it. And, the longer you suppress something that needs to be released, the more violent and destructive that is when it finally comes out.

'Eventually I got to the point where I'd suppressed so much for so long, it got to the point where I had an emotional breakdown pretty much and I ended up having to go and see the psychs and say, "Well, this is where I'm at." And, you know, that was pretty hard for me to do.'

But despite approaching the army psychologists and medical teams, Tyson was still reluctant to reveal the extent of his mental troubles, and it's possible that even after treatment the army could not have known that he wasn't fit. 'I knew I needed help but I wasn't letting on how much I was actually struggling. So I went to see the psychs and got their opinion and all that sort of stuff. But when it was locked in that there was another deployment coming up, I 'miraculously' started to get better. I was telling the psychs what they needed to hear so I would get the ticks in the boxes so I could go back overseas. That all worked and everything was progressing well until our engineer certification exercise that you need to do before you can be signed off as a high-risk search team commander.

'We were doing a scenario of simulated IED blasts and then they had explosives in the ground . . . I was controlling the search and when the device detonated, I sort of blacked out a little bit and just lost it . . . That was when I had to come clean to the OC and the squadron sergeant major. They knew something wasn't right. I said I had been struggling for the last twelve months and I've still rocked up to work every day and I've still done my job. I was still the senior corporal there. I was doing a brilliant job until this one scenario sort of set me off.

'So unfortunately, I wasn't able to be deployed as the search commander again. They said, "We don't want you . . . you're a risk." That was my lowest point, I think. My heart was broken because this was my dream job and I was told I wasn't allowed to do it. It was a huge blow for me, especially because I'd run all the training for all the boys but my OC, having faith in me, said he still wanted me to deploy with the unit, so they sent me as the operations sergeant instead.'

Tyson's new job was more of an administration role working out of Tarin Kowt, looking for trends and patterns in the enemy's tactics and procedures and gathering intelligence from other organisations like the Americans and the Dutch, then interpreting that and relaying it to the boys on the ground. It was valuable work but it was not what Tyson wanted to do.

'I was fucken miserable. I didn't want to be sitting behind a desk. My boys were out there getting shot at and blown up and I'm sitting behind a desk drinking caramel lattes. Like, I'd rather slam my cock in a door ten times than sit through that again. I wanted to be on the ground with the boys but I figured at least I can be there and I could help as best I could. It wasn't ideal but it was the best I could do at the time.'

After three months Tyson had to go to America on a course for a couple of weeks and then returned to Australia rather than

Afghanistan. 'So I came home earlier than the boys and when I returned to Australia once again I'd lost that goal to work towards. While I was in the desert I had no dramas. I was good. I was still living the dream. But when I came back to Australia, the boys were still deployed without me. My support network and my closest mates are still being shot at and blown up and I wasn't there and so the fact that they were there constantly ate away at me and just drove me into an emotional breakdown. I became a pisshead and was just on the cans all the time. I was just on a pretty bad path of destruction. And, so I ended up seeing the psychs again and was eventually diagnosed with PTSD. From there the army pretty much said they didn't have any use for me anymore.

'I was more disappointed in myself, I think. I don't know if I was let down by the army but there was a bit of pain there. This is something I'd given my life to but, that being said, 2 CER was very good. The CO was absolutely brilliant and the same as the OC and the squadron sergeant major and they really went out of their way to sort of help me out and make sure I was doing okay. But once the army has no use for you then that's it, really. So that was hard to bear.'

That was when Tyson turned to the Queensland RSL–backed organisation called Mates4Mates. It had been recently formed, knowing there was a need to offer support to former soldiers like Tyson, but not knowing exactly how they were going to provide it. Their smart and clean office is as much a gym as a meeting place. It's certainly a place where men can feel at home.

'Initially I came here for help because I couldn't relate to your traditional rehabilitation methods like sitting there with a psychologist and getting all touchy feely. It didn't work for me. And so I came here and got involved with the organisation. They took me on Kokoda and got me interacting with other veterans and got me to do the kayak paddle from Sydney to Brisbane. They basically helped me find myself again. Through determination and hard work and surrounding yourself with good people you can really achieve amazing things and this organisation reminded me of that.

'Thankfully, I got back on my feet and I got through the bad place I was in and when I left the army in December they asked me if I wanted a job and I said "Why not?" and now I can dedicate my time to helping blokes that are in the position I was in.'

Tyson was for a while the liaison officer for Mates4Mates, which has about 450 ex-servicemen on its books, including a few Vietnam vets. 'It goes up and down. So some days we might have twenty people come through in one day and other days we might have two or three. We have regulars that come every day and just come for a workout and some people just come and get a massage or some come and see the psychs. It's for any generation but generally we don't see many of them older than Vietnam, sadly, because they're so old. But they're certainly welcome to use the facility.'

Originally, a combination of word of mouth and professional referrals from doctors and the Department of Veterans Affairs, the RSL and the army had led veterans to the cottage in Higgs Street, Albion, where Mates4Mates was formed.

'I was the first success story for Mates and so I was literally here from almost the start,' says Tyson, who now does voluntary work for 'Mates'. 'It was very, very new. It had probably only been open a few weeks and I was one of the first ones through. It was originally started just for the contemporary veterans of Somalia and then we sort of opened it up to all veterans. But it's very hard to cater for all veterans really, simply because of the different generations. Vietnam veterans aren't interested so much in doing what Afghanistan veterans are interested in. There's not a lot of Vietnam vets that want to get out and kayak from Sydney to Brisbane. They're all getting on a little bit.'

Coverage in the media helps get the word out but it doesn't necessarily lead to a flood of new members banging down the door. 'It can be very random. Obviously whatever publicity we can get helps get the word out and gets people in, but the hardest thing, even for me, is the stigma attached with mental health. Fellas, especially soldiers, don't want to put their hand up and say, "Yeah, I'm struggling. I've got a problem and I need help." We've got fathers and husbands here who don't want to bring shame to their family by admitting they have a problem. And so, it's very hard to entice people to come in here.'

One of the most common manifestations of PTSD is problem drinking, which can both mask and exacerbate the condition.

'Alcohol is definitely probably the number one coping mechanism for soldiers. When you're going through PTSD or you're struggling, you feel like you are completely alone and there's no one else out there that's going through what you are and so you don't feel like you can talk to anyone and so you cope with the only mechanism you know and that is to get drunk.

'I'm in a lot better position than I was. There was a point where when I first came here I was that emotionally high strung I couldn't even speak. But people ask, "Are you cured of PTSD?" and I don't think you can ever be cured. You just get to a position where it becomes manageable and like anyone I have good days and I have bad days and I still have days when I don't feel like I can get out of bed and I feel shit. Even now, when on a special occasion the boys might get on the cans and have a bit of a cry and that sort of stuff, that's just the way it is.

'I'm in a position now where I can manage it. That's a hell of a lot further ahead than a lot of the people with PTSD. And for a lot of fellows that are suffering alone, it takes over their lives.'

Mates4Mates can be contacted via their website, mates4mates.org, where you will also find details of all their services, including their

Family Recovery Centres in Brisbane, Townsville and Hobart. Another organisation, Soldier On, has offices in Sydney, Canberra and Adelaide. They have contact numbers for all states and territories on their website, soldieron.org.au.

For Michael Lyddiard, who was injured while trying to defuse an IED, the struggle wasn't just mental and emotional but physical too. He lost his right arm below the elbow, his thumb and index finger on his left hand. His small finger is fused so he still has three fingers but only two really work. He's lost his right eye, his left eye's vision is impaired where he's had a buckle put around the eye to help it stay in. He's also had a cornea transplant and has to wear glasses. On top of that he has scarring, obviously, and there's still shrapnel in his face.

'When I got back to Australia I just kept trying to fight through things, got through all my rehabilitation and I thought the best way to help me and to show my gratitude for the people that had saved my life and helped me in other ways was to try to make the most of my life and I ended up getting back into swimming.'

Many people were surprised that he could swim at all so he did the Magnetic Island swim in Queensland, which is 8 kilometres, and later did the Rottnest Island swim in Western Australia, which is about 20 kilometres. Meanwhile, he was sending videos of himself doing one-arm push-ups to his mates still in Afghanistan. All of this was, in part at least, to prove to the army that he could still function as a soldier. His problem was even though he was super-fit, the army didn't have a role for him and eventually told him he would have to move on, all of which took its toll emotionally.

'I was putting up with a lot of stuff. I got admitted into hospital with PTSD. I went through a bit of a rough trot, I hit alcohol, I had the police and that called around.'

Now, with the army's assistance, and more recently the Department of Veteran Affairs', he has completed a degree in business management and is competing in triathlons with the hope of qualifying for the Paralympics in Rio next year. At time of writing, he was making plans for an event where his able-bodied off-sider was going to be WO2 W, his No. 2 the day that a booby-trapped IED changed his life forever.

30

WAS IT WORTH IT?

On 13 March 2013, then Prime Minister Julia Gillard announced that most Australian troops would be out of Afghanistan by Christmas that year. At that time there were about 1600 Australian Army personnel in the country. On 16 December 2013, Tony Abbott, her successor as prime minister, announced that the last Australians had left Uruzgan, although 400 would remain in Kabul and Kandahar in advisory and training roles. Those troops are expected to leave by 2016, in line with the United States' withdrawal program. As usual, sappers would be among the very last to leave, just as they were among the first to arrive. Someone has to turn off the lights.

Almost exactly two years after Julia Gillard's announcement, on 21 March 2015, a 'welcome home' march was held in Sydney. Operation Slipper, the longest overseas deployment of Australian combat troops, was over. Across the entire campaign, 41 Australian soldiers had died. Many more had been injured—some seriously. And countless others had been traumatised. Many more Afghan civilians also died. The cost to the Australian taxpayer was about 8.5 billion dollars but the war had always had bipartisan support politically.

On the other hand, the Taliban had been kept at bay, there had been democratic elections and lasting improvements had been made to the country's infrastructure, education, sustainability and security.

But was it worth it? We asked people who had actually been there, and contributed to the changes in the country, what they thought. Their responses are reproduced as they came to us, without favour or comment.

Brigadier Mick Ryan

The first thing we showed was that we could develop a relationship with the Afghan people and work with them to introduce infrastructure and train people. The second thing was that we could build momentum for a mission, which was essentially rebuilding a society that had had thirty years of hard knocks through the Russians, the Taliban, and through their own predations. The third thing we proved is that the Australian soldiers of the twenty-first century are the equal of any that have gone before them. They really are. They are magnificent.

I have no regrets. I came home very satisfied. I think we achieved everything. We had a limited mission. We went beyond that in a lot of things. Training the Afghan army engineers was part of it. We did more reconstruction missions than we anticipated and we trained more people in the trade training school. We trained people in a broader range of skills than we anticipated so I came back very satisfied. Not losing any of my soldiers was obviously fantastic. It's hard to describe the feeling of satisfaction to be the last person to walk off the plane and know that every single one of your soldiers walked off in front of you.

Was it was a good idea for Australians or any of the Allied troops to be there? Yes, it was. I was in the United States with a bunch of marines at Quantico on September 11. I saw firsthand what it did and we were there to ensure that Afghanistan did not again become a sanctuary for terrorists and murderers who wanted to do things like they did in Bali, in London, and in Washington and New York. That's why we were there. Was it executed perfectly? Well, history will be the judge of that. It's too soon to tell whether we've been fully successful in Afghanistan but we certainly removed al-Qaeda from Afghanistan, there's no doubt about that. The Taliban is a totally separate issue. The Taliban have never been an organisation that's looked beyond the borders of Afghanistan, notwithstanding the fact that they are a troubling presence, but I'm confident that we were there to deny sanctuary to terrorists and I'm confident that we played our albeit small part, that we played a role in that.

Major Rachel Brennan

Was the Australian involvement in Afghanistan productive? Certainly for the Tarin Kowt area but that's only a tiny aspect of Afghanistan. So as regards the overall impact on Afghanistan, I don't know how much we, the Australians, achieved. But for that tiny township, Sorkh Morghab, yes, sure, we had a pretty big impact.

Lieutenant Colonel Mick Say

I definitely think it was worth it. When there's a girl with a smiling face and she's now going to school, to me that's success. Otherwise she would never have had an opportunity. We're donating books and the kids, they just want information. They want to be able to read. Even if it's just pictures, these kids'll pick things up very quickly. Those sorts of things. Now when you'd go to the hospital and you'll actually see people getting care.

There are health clinics in Sorkh Morghab, some of the locals wouldn't be able to get to Tarin Kowt before the Aussies got there. There wasn't really a hospital there before. The cholera ward before was an old white tent, the kind that you see in a lot of Arab countries, a Bedouin camp type tent. Now it's a proper building where there are facilities there to actually deal with people who have a significant disease. Those sorts of things, they definitely make it worth it.

As to whether or not it's sustainable, I think the Afghan National Army have the ability to sustain, but the police still aren't at that level. The police force was extremely corrupt and it was very difficult for them to establish a sustainable presence. That would undercut a lot of good work and development of where it needed to go. Too much is done on the basis of 'He's my cousin'. Those sorts of simple things don't make systems robust.

WO2 W

This is what I saw. I could feel in RTF 3 the changes for good that were happening—we were building these patrol bases, there was some money coming into the community. We could see smiles on the faces of the kids and for the most part locals were supporting us being there, to a degree. Yes, there were elements in there that would shoot us. But I could see these bad individuals slowly disappearing. So I see that as progress as well, where we were doing the bad things that nobody else wants to do, in eliminating these individuals.

At the same time, we're not just all about shooting people, it has to also be about hearts and minds elements. In RTF 3 we did work on a medical centre, and work on schools and community outlets. What we appreciate back in this society, I could see that working over there. Will it work forever? I can't answer that question—I don't think anyone can. I could see changes for good, but I could also see changes for bad.

Captain Leigh Potter

I think we made a significant difference in the area we operated in and the way that we mentored our Afghan partners. I believe we were quite far ahead of our American counterparts in different areas. Maybe that was because Uruzgan wasn't quite as dangerous or Taliban-heavy as other areas, but I think our contribution in that area was quite significant and the influence the Taliban had in our area after we left was still quite low. There wasn't a lot coming out from that area that the police and army couldn't deal with themselves. Whereas back down into Kandahar, where the Americans were operating, they were still having significant difficulties dealing with the Taliban in the area, noting that both areas are quite different. I believe the small issue force we had there were able to provide quite a strong contribution in that the Afghan National Army are now operating by themselves without issue.

Corporal Dennis Delaris

To be honest with you, you can look at lots of negative aspects the whole day long, but one way I look at it is, in the outermost areas we pushed out enemies that were really active. Also, in the beginning, you'd see the kids—they'd just throw rocks all day in the fields and chase their goats. They'd get to go to the *madrassa* once a week where the *mullah* would just tell them everything that they should believe and it's either the Good Mullah or the Bad Mullah who teaches them. There's so much chatter it's very, very easy to fill their head with crap. You can tell them pretty much everything.

At least since we've been there, I've seen, even in the main area of Tarin Kowt, kids going to school. Girls going to school for the ten years we've been in there—and you can't take that education away from them. So I reckon, at least in that time, we've maybe enlightened certain generations and that might help in the future whether the Taliban has a resurgence or not. Once you educate people in thinking, you can't really sort of take it away from them. So hopefully, at the very least there's now a bit of a groundswell of people that know better now that there are different ways that they can live and they don't have to be oppressed like they are in certain areas. I mean, they'll never want to live like us. They don't want to live like us but they're still better off.

Also in Kabul, there are a lot of interpreters that come from there. They're pretty progressive and under the Taliban there was almost no way they could be like how they are. For example, they enjoy going to parties, I know a few of them like to drink. I'm sure that if the Taliban took control of that they'd go back to square one but at the moment they must be a huge population there that think otherwise.

Captain Andrew Unis

I think it helped the army, in the fact that we are no longer a peacetime army. I don't think it was as intense as Vietnam was, nowhere near, but it provided a combat experience that the army had been lacking since the end of Vietnam. Whether the loss of life is worth the army being better postured to go forward again . . . But having seen some form of combat—the guys having seen what happens on operations— was a good outcome of the operations.

But I think because Australia chose to put us into a backwater province and was risk-adverse about us conducting large-scale operations to go and kill or capture—like we did in Vietnam—that a lot of the potential value was lost. It's also created a generation of soldiers [where] all they know is sitting behind a wall where you have TV, internet and phone reception all the time. I would say that the soldiers are no longer as robust as they were prior to Afghanistan. The lack of communications that the guys had with their families was harder on them in Shoalwater Bay in Australia, in a benign environment, than it was in Afghan—at Shoalwater Bay they couldn't call home and they lived in the field, they didn't have a bed at night, they slept on the ground for three months on stretchers, and stuff like that. I think Afghanistan bred a loss of robustness. If you look at what the army is trying to do now, they are going back to those large-scale exercises where people spend a lot of time away in harsh conditions in order to try to rebuild that robustness.

Former Sergeant Michael Lyddiard

There's not one ounce of me that regrets the choice that I made. In a way I deserved what I copped because I chose to join the army. I chose to be a combat engineer, I elected to be a bomb disposalist and I went about it with pride and honour, as an engineer, as we all do. I'm not disgruntled with us being over there. I had a lot of comments thrown at me, like, 'You're just over there for the money. It's all about money with you.' I don't think any soldier is over there for money. Every soldier wants to protect Australia's interests and follow the Australian Anzac spirit. I believe that we were over there to defend and protect Australia's interests but I personally do not see how you can personally not be against terrorism. You can't win against terrorism. It is such a broad sword and you don't know who they are, what they are capable of and you don't even know when and where. We were never going to win it . . . but I do not regret going over there. It was the right decision for Australian troops to go over there and I'd like to think that we did our job and we all did our job well.

Former Warrant Officer Jeff Newman

Personally, the country will never change because the people that live there just want their simple life. The people that live there don't care whether it's the Taliban running their country. A lot of them just want to be left alone to grow their poppies, farm their fields, look after their livestock. That's all they want to do.

Lance Corporal James Lederhose

To be perfectly honest, I just want my mates back, and nothing will change that. [Lance Corporal Lederhose was in the same unit as Sappers Larcombe and Atkinson.] But were we doing the right thing? Yes, absolutely. Every person is entitled to feel free in their own country, and not be persecuted or oppressed. Having grown up in the country that I have, I feel empowered to pass on the gigantic benefits that I've enjoyed my entire life. It's a bittersweet 'yes'.

The country can only go whichever way they choose to make it go. I'm hopeful. The foundation of a good, successful country is a well-educated population of women. Not men. Who gives a crap about men? It's all about well-educated women. People learn the majority of stuff they're ever going to know from their mothers and if you have mothers who don't take crap from anyone, and don't just believe whatever they're told, because they're well educated, then, boom! You're going to have a successful country. Done and dusted. It's going to be a couple of years before we see the benefits of that, but I'm hopeful, very hopeful.

AFTERWORD

BEATING THE RETREAT

As the focus shifts to Iraq and the role of Australian troops in training Iraqis to fight the terror tactics of extreme Islamists IS, it's worth looking again at the Tunnel Rats, what they did, and the thread that runs through every sapper from Vietnam to Tarin Kowt and beyond.

In Vietnam, rigid military structures were blown away by the need to adapt and evolve when presented with a different kind of military opponent. Sappers found themselves at the front of patrols rather than bringing up the rear and those Tunnel Rats probably did much more, tactically, than those whose exploits in the underground city at Cu Chi are still legendary.

The lessons of Cu Chi, forgotten in the intervening half-century, were quickly re-learned in Afghanistan where those who ignored the importance of combat engineer searchers did so at their very real peril. A cunning and resourceful enemy had to be matched with sappernuity, as much as brute force and technical superiority.

IEDs are the weapon of choice in guerrilla wars these days. But now we have sophisticated equipment like the Huskys that can detect even buried devices with low metal content, making the search for these bombs faster and safer.

No doubt the traders in terror will come up with another way of bringing death and destruction to their theatres of war. And would you bet against the spiritual descendants of the Tunnel Rats being the men and women who are given the job of countering them?

Never again should we forget that battle cry: Follow the sapper.

GLOSSARY

AK-47—Kalashnikov assault rifle, very popular with guerrilla forces from Vietnam to Northern Ireland

bang—colloquial term used by sappers for explosives

brick—half a section (usually four soldiers)

cavalry—mounted troops, usually in light armoured vehicles (ASLAVs), used primarily to get men and equipment to where they needed to be

dasht—desert

defensive harbour—a temporary set-up in the field, usually around a camp, which can be guarded and if necessary defended in case of attack

fighting-age men—prime suspects, as they are potential Taliban insurgents

green zone—the area along the bank of a river where trees and plants grow

Hesco—a wire-reinforced bag intended to be filled with earth and rocks and used as a basic building block for fortifications; much bigger and more substantial than a sandbag

kandak—battalion in the Afghan National Army

madrassa—Islamic religious school

malik—village chief

man pack—portable device that could block radio and microwave signals in the immediate vicinity to prevent remote triggering of IEDs

Minelab—portable metal detector that clipped on to sappers' belts

Mujaheddin—Muslim guerrilla fighters, especially in Afghanistan and Iran

mullah—Muslim religious leader

Order of Battle—the command structure, strength, disposition of personnel, and equipment of units of an armed force

Pashtunwali—Pashtun code of honour

picket (also picquet or piquet)—sentry or guard duty

plant—heavy equipment such as diggers, cranes, bulldozers, graders and front-end loaders

platoon—two sections

PsyOps—psychological operations, such as information and even propaganda for distribution to civilians

qala—a local's house, usually with a compound

quartermaster—in charge of storing and distributing supplies and equipment

rotation—tour of duty

sapper—generic term for an army engineer, but also a rank, equivalent to private in the infantry

section—for combat engineers, this is usually eight men, comprised of two 'bricks' or mini-teams

sharia law—legal system based on Islamic beliefs

shura—meeting

Special Forces and Operations—SAS, commandos and engineers using stealth and speed to mount surprise attacks

vehicle pack—a much larger version of the man pack that can block signals into a larger area

ACKNOWLEDGEMENTS

The authors would like to thank the current and former sappers from the three Combat Engineer Regiments whom we talked to in Darwin, Brisbane and Adelaide, and at the School of Military Engineering and Special Operations Engineer Regiment in Holsworthy, Sydney, who gave of their time so freely to help us with this book. Not all of you are named but your contributions to helping us build a full picture of life in Afghanistan were invaluable. Specifically, we are indebted to Jeff Newman, Shane Potter, Josh Porter, Michael Lyddiard, David Simpson, Mark Willetts, Tyson Murray and others, like WO2 W and SGT T, whom we are not allowed to name for security reasons. You know who you are.

We'd also like to thank the Australian Defence Force, and specifically Kate Kovacevic, for help in getting access to the soldiers, pictures, maps and other materials, and Brigadiers Mick Ryan, Wayne Budd and David Wainwright, and Lieutenant Colonels Mick Say and 'S' for their time and assistance.

We acknowledge the hard work, wise counsel and patience of Rebecca Kaiser, Angela Handley and Aziza Kuypers at Allen & Unwin.

And we thank Sandra MacGregor and Edna Williams for their typing skills and Sue Williams for her encouragement.

Finally, we acknowledge the men and women of the Australian Defence Force—and their families—who risk so much to ensure that we have the freedom to tell stories like this as truthfully as we can.

FURTHER READING

You will find more interviews with Australian sappers who were in Afghanistan, and more photos, at **www.tunnelratsvtaliban.com**.

Tunnel Rats vs the Taliban is Jimmy Thomson and Sandy MacGregor's third book about Australian sappers. *Tunnel Rats* (2011) was the story of 3 Field Troop, who were commanded by Sandy in 1965–66 when they discovered the tunnels of Cu Chi, Vietnam, and were the first Allied troops to explore and investigate them. *A Sappers' War* (2013) followed the exploits of Australian sappers from before the official involvement in the Vietnam War, all the way through to Australia's withdrawal from the country in 1975.

Both of these books were published by Allen & Unwin and there is more information about them at **www.sapperswar.com**. All three books are available as ebooks (including Kindle) and as audio books from Bolinda.

No Need for Heroes, an earlier, self-published biography of Sandy (also co-written with Jimmy), covered Sandy's life story, including, of course, the original Tunnel Rats. It is available through Sandy's website **www.calm.com.au**.